Praise for *Llewellyn's Complete Book of Meditation*

"Celebrating the meditative experience in all its forms, this book is the perfect place to begin if you seek guidance on meditation. This comprehensive exploration invites into your own practice the one that most suits the needs of your heart and soul."

—Elena Brower, bestselling author of *Practice You*

"Meditation saved my life. Literally. When I learned it in 1968 at the age of eighteen (Transcendental Meditation, in my case) I had dropped out of two high schools, been arrested for drugs twice, and had started dabbling in hard drugs. One fateful evening, reading *Zen Flesh, Zen Bones* while high on some psychedelic, I realized that by comparison with those who had seriously striven for enlightenment, I was just fooling around and would live a short, miserable life unless I changed course. I resolved to stop taking drugs and learn meditation. Two weeks later, I learned. My initial experience was profound, and my life was soon transformed. I haven't missed a meditation since that first day of instruction. This book offers an overview of many forms of meditation and their underlying mechanics. Shai does not recommend that you learn and practice them all. His aim is to help you find one that suits you. I hope you do, and that you benefit from its practice as much as I have from mine."

—Rick Archer, creator and host of *Buddha at the Gas Pump* podcast

"Shai Tubali is a very advanced soul here to guide us to the truths within ourselves. In reading this outstanding masterpiece, you will learn about yourself on the deepest level."

—Echo Bodine, author of *How to Live a Happily Ever Afterlife*

"Shai has written a real magnum opus on meditation, which shows how indeed it is a subject that is vast and extremely powerful and effective. There are multitudes of books on meditation, but few are like this book, which demystifies meditation without simplifying or diluting it. The book addresses, with some tenderness and care, meditation as the meeting with the existential ground of our being, rather than another self-improvement skill. It wisely relates to meditation as an invitation to a more unlimited view of ourselves, and as an open door to the sublime. There is wonderful precision and an insightful summary of many of the main meditation methods commonly available, but it does not lose sight of the way 'the mind, by its very nature, is made of infinite space,' in Shai's words. I recommend this book as a companion to those who would like to become familiar with meditation in all its great richness."

—Dr. Stephen Fulder, author of *What's Beyond Mindfulness* and *The Five Powers*

"I felt excitement as I read through the incredible list of meditations in this book. Think of it as your personal meditation bible, filled with practice options that would fit any mood, any situation, any moment in your life."

—Dr. Itai Ivtzan, author of *Awareness Is Freedom*

LLEWELLYN'S

COMPLETE BOOK OF

MEDITATION

© Carolin Saage

About the Author

Shai Tubali is an international speaker, author, and spiritual teacher. He is one of Europe's leading authorities in the field of chakras and the subtle body and has published twelve books. Shai also serves as an academic researcher at the University of Leeds and has developed several meditation-based therapeutic methods. Visit him online at ShaiTubali.com.

LLEWELLYN'S

COMPLETE BOOK OF

MEDITATION

A Comprehensive Guide to Effective Techniques
for Calming Your Mind and Spirit

SHAI TUBALI

LLEWELLYN PUBLICATIONS
Woodbury, Minnesota

FIRST EDITION
First Printing, 2023

Cover design by Cassie Willett
Interior art by Llewellyn Art Department
Figures on pages xix and 246 by Mary Ann Zapalac

Llewellyn Publishing is a registered trademark of Llewellyn Worldwide Ltd.

Library of Congress Cataloging-in-Publication Data (Pending)
ISBN: 978-0-7387-7206-6

Llewellyn Worldwide Ltd. does not participate in, endorse, or have any authority or responsibility concerning private business transactions between our authors and the public.

All mail addressed to the author is forwarded, but the publisher cannot, unless specifically instructed by the author, give out an address or phone number.

Any internet references contained in this work are current at publication time, but the publisher cannot guarantee that a specific location will continue to be maintained. Please refer to the publisher's website for links to authors' websites and other sources.

Llewellyn Publications
A Division of Llewellyn Worldwide Ltd.
2143 Wooddale Drive
Woodbury, MN 55125-2989
www.llewellyn.com

Printed in the United States of America

Other Books by Shai Tubali

7 Day Chakras

A Guide to Bliss

Indestructible You

The Journey to Inner Power

The Seven Chakra Personality Types

The Seven Wisdoms of Life

Unlocking the 7 Secret Powers of the Heart

Forthcoming Books by Shai Tubali

Philosophical Dialogue as Spiritual Exercise

Contents

Contents

• • • • • • • •

· · · · · · · ·

Contents

Meditations

· · · · · · ·

Disclaimer

The information in this book is not intended to diagnose or treat any medical or emotional condition. The techniques in this book are simplified versions of complex systems of meditation. As such, if you wish to pursue these practices more thoroughly, seek the guidance of meditation experts.

Some postures and techniques are not advised for adults who are pregnant or have just given birth. If you are experiencing any medical conditions or are unsure if a pose or exercise is safe for you, consult your doctor. The author and publisher encourage you to consult a professional if you have any questions about the use or efficacy of the techniques or insights in this book.

Acknowledgments

My spiritual journey was inaugurated by reading a meditation book: Osho's *Meditation: The First and Last Freedom*. I will never forget the night in which my heart, mind, and spirit began to sing in response to the ecstatic words that guided one of the practices. Having this intense impression still alive in me, I know that a meditation book, like the one you are holding in your hands, can change lives. I am filled with gratitude toward Osho and the rest of the meditation masters who appear in this book for designing these gateways through which we can reach unknown regions within our being.

This book is loosely based on an eight-month meditation teacher training that I guided in 2019–2020. Although the book contains much new content, I was greatly aided by the training's transcripts, which had been lovingly prepared by Ines Jaeger and Lizelot de Stigter. Another source of generous support was Ralf Müller-Amenitsch, whose devotion to the spiritual life and great research skills have made him an expert in meditation. Thank you, Ralf, for leading me to some meditation techniques I have never known before! One last form of support came from Harry Eagles, a copyeditor who enthusiastically helped me to improve the manuscript's readability.

Above all, I am thankful for the Llewellyn family for embracing this book with care and joyful dedication. I especially wish to acknowledge the unending nurturing presence of my editors, Amy Glaser and Nicole Borneman.

Chakra Basics

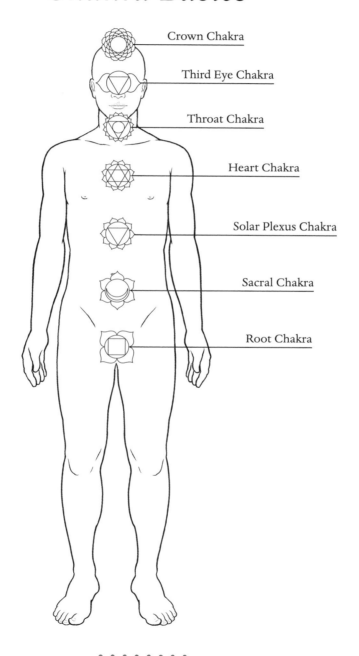

Crown Chakra

Third Eye Chakra

Throat Chakra

Heart Chakra

Solar Plexus Chakra

Sacral Chakra

Root Chakra

Chakra	Sanskrit Name and Meaning	Location	Element	Associated Color	Seed Mantra	Psychological Aspects	Meditative State
Root chakra	Mooladhara ("root" or "foundation")	Inside the perineum; corresponds to the legs and the skeletal and muscular systems	Earth	Red	Lam	Instinct, earthly and biological existence, security, groundedness, physical foundation and health, fear of instability and change, trauma	Inner stability
Sacral chakra	Swadhisthana ("one's dwelling place")	Lowest point of the spinal cord, at the level of the pubic bone; corresponds to the sex organs and the sacral plexus of nerves	Water	Orange/red	Vam	Feeling and impulse, vitality, adventure, totality, enjoyment, sensuality, pursuit of pleasure, sexuality, shame, the unconscious	Unconditional joy
Solar plexus chakra	Manipura ("city of jewels")	Behind the navel; corresponds to the digestive system and the solar plexus	Fire	Bright yellow	Ram	Willpower, individuality, independence, ambition, intensity, dynamism, courage, control, anger	True inner power; self-presence

CHAKRA	SANSKRIT NAME AND MEANING	LOCATION	ELEMENT	ASSOCIATED COLOR	SEED MANTRA	PSYCHOLOGICAL ASPECTS	MEDITATIVE STATE
Heart chakra	Anahata ("unstruck" or "unbeaten")	Behind the base of the heart, at the level of the depression in the sternum; corresponds to the cardiac plexus of nerves	Air	Blue	Yam	Emotions, relationships, love, attachment and dependency, betrayal and disappointment, forgiveness, letting go	Unconditional love; unity consciousness
Throat chakra	Vishuddhi ("purity")	Behind the throat pit; corresponds to the cervical plexus of nerves	Ether	Violet	Ham	Communication, self-expression, leadership, manifestation, vision, authenticity, transparency	Boundless space
Brow chakra, also known as the third eye chakra or the guru chakra	Ajna ("command")	In the brain, behind the center of the eyebrows; corresponds to the pineal gland	Light	Silver/gray	Aum	Intuition, intellect, clarity, insight, mental order, discrimination, attention, curiosity	Nondual perception
Crown chakra	Sahasrara ("one thousand")	Center of the top of the head, in the brain; corresponds to the pituitary gland	Cosmos; pure light and source of creation	Multicolored	Ah	Spirit, meditation, transcendence, timelessness, nonattachment, divine nature, universality	Unlimited consciousness

• • • • • • •

INTRODUCTION

Some time ago I met two high school students. They came to talk with me because they were enthusiastic about their newfound discovery of the world of meditation. As two excited young boys, they were filled with a sense of promise. We had an hour-long conversation, during which I asked them questions and vice versa. Near the end of our meeting I suggested, "Let's just close our eyes for one moment now. Let's tune in to the frequency of meditation itself, because we have been talking so much."

One of them became alarmed. "But I have never meditated, really—I don't know what to do."

I replied, "There is no need for instructions. Let's just be together for a moment."

As we closed our eyes, a sense of presence permeated the room. It was just one moment, perhaps two minutes in time, and I quickly stopped it because I didn't want to scare them or make things too intense. After we opened our eyes, both of them said that it felt as if everything had changed, as if nothing were as it was before.

This is the magic of meditation. It shifts you to a perspective that changes everything, and it does so extremely quickly. It adds something to your life, to your presence, to your sense of self-existence, to such a degree that as soon as you begin to get in touch with it, you don't understand how you have lived your whole life without it—how you could manage at all without having this indispensable perspective.

In this sense, it is very important to understand that meditation—both the practice and the experience of the meditative state (we will explore the differences in chapter 1)—is not a luxury. Meditation is a deep human need, almost like the need for water, food, and good sleep. Of course, for as long as you don't integrate it into your life, you will not be able to recognize that it is a need. Until then, you will imagine that you can do without it, that everything is fine, and that you are coping. But as soon as you imbibe the meditative fragrance into your lungs, mind, and being, you realize that your whole being has been thirsty for it, just as your body is thirsty for water.

· · · · · · · ·

Even though meditation is a human need, and even though one minute of meditation can change everything and instantly make everything feel profound, meaningful, and full of presence, many people still don't integrate it into their lives.

There are countless reasons for this. I think one of the reasons is that most people don't fully understand what meditation is and why it is so important—what it can do for us. There is now plenty of research on the benefits of meditation. We know that, among other things, meditation can reduce stress and anxiety; it can help control pain, lengthen attention span, and reduce age-related memory loss; it can improve sleep and decrease blood pressure.[1] But still we don't understand what it is, why we need it, and how to do it. The latter point—how to do it—is, I believe, truly important: How can meditation be more than just a short-lived experience that disappears as soon as you open your eyes? How should we cope with the challenges of meditation? How can we love it rather than fight it? How can we *enjoy* it?

Throughout this introduction, I will partially answer some of these questions. But to fully answer them, a very comprehensive book is required! These are, after all, big questions; I hope you will have the patience for them.

In so many ways, meditation is like entering a committed relationship in your life. It is, first of all, a relationship with yourself. Second, it is a relationship between you and the universe, you and the invisible reality—but also between you and your thoughts and feelings, and between you and your true other half, the other part of yourself that you are usually unaware of. This relationship can be cultivated and grown. But, naturally, relationships have moments of fighting and disharmony. Instead of just running away, packing up our things, exclaiming, "I'm not doing this anymore!" and slamming the door behind us, we need to know how to navigate challenging moments.

The Fifteen Purposes of Meditation

There is evidence of the existence of meditation as a position and practice dating back seven thousand years. Some archaeologists date meditation back to as early as 5000 BCE. This means that meditation has been with humans since the dawn of culture.[2] The earliest evidence comes from ancient India, where there are wall-art paintings of people sitting in a certain posture with half-closed eyes, obviously meditating. There it all started, with the tradition of sitting in caves and sending young students to forests, where there were schools of meditation.[3]

We don't know the exact nature of the earliest meditation techniques, but I can imagine the way they came into being. A meditation technique is something that is created quite acci-

1. Thorpe and Link, "12 Science-Based Benefits of Meditation."
2. Ross, "How Meditation Went Mainstream."
3. Easwaran, *The Upanishads*, 19.

. . . .

dentally: someone finds themselves in an unexpected meditative state as a result of some kind of position, movement, action, or thought in their mind, and they become deeply relaxed and immersed in this beautiful state. Soon after, people approach them and ask, "How did you do it? I also want to be in that state!" So the meditator thinks, *How exactly* did *I do it?* Then they return to the specific thing they did and make a sort of metaphor out of it. Thus, the technique is imitating some internal or external gesture because it has succeeded for others, and it is gradually made into a system.

Another way meditation techniques may have come into being is simply by thinking of the meditative state metaphorically. If one of meditation's attributes is that it is unchanging—a discovery of the unchanging in us—then why not create a physical metaphor for this unchanging nature? "Let's remain perfectly motionless for one long hour—let's be mountainlike!"

Not only do these techniques explain how meditation came into being, but they also explain the way preparatory techniques such as the yoga asanas (postures) were probably developed: people discovered for themselves that doing something could lead to the state of meditation, then made it into a structure, a form, something that other people could repeat. Did this repetition work for everyone? Not at all, because what worked for one person wouldn't necessarily work for others. That is why we have plenty of meditations.

This can be considered the first purpose of meditation: imitating the meditative state, creating a repeated structure, in order to do the opposite. At first people reached a state as a result of doing something, then did that something in the hopes that it would lead them back to the state.

There are many other purposes of meditation. When I say "purposes," I don't mean benefits; benefits and purposes are two very different things. *Purpose* is what meditation can do, why it has been created, and what it can show or teach you. *Benefit*, on the other hand, is what you can get as a result of this teaching, as the outcome of achieving these goals. The Western world focuses greatly on benefits; meditation is mostly talked about in terms of what it can do for us. But here, I want to discuss purposes, since the benefits are just by-products. Yes, unintentionally, you sleep better, your concentration is far better, your decision-making is clearer, your joy in life is regained—but these are benefits, not purposes.

Let's briefly explore the different purposes of meditation practice. Although I will present fifteen purposes here, I could come up with twenty or thirty, but I've chosen these fifteen because they are the major ones. These fifteen purposes may be enough to convince someone to start meditating, and they help us understand how many aspects the principle of meditation includes.

1. **Meditation brings us back to our original nature.** This is perhaps the most important purpose, and that is why it is listed first. Our original nature is what

humans were at the beginning, as natural beings. Before we started to think in such complicated ways, we were simply a part of the cosmos, a part of life, like animals, plants, and stars. With the aid of meditation, we move back from the thinking self to this state of original, natural being.

2. **Meditation makes us complete.** When we enter meditation, we meet our other half. Sometimes we look for our other half in romantic relationships, but actually, our search for romantic partners in this psychological sense only happens because we don't have a sufficient acquaintance with our other half. Our other half is our "negative self": not in the sense of a shadow-self, but more like the invisible self that is actually the opposite of what we are. It is connected to timelessness, being, and nonaction. It is our passive side or passive aspect, our nonpersonality. As soon as we begin to meditate, we feel a sense of wholeness, as if our two halves are meeting and we are finally one unified being. This is because we need this other half. Without this other half we only know action, time, and personality. Living without knowing ourselves in this complete sense is a very limiting type of existence.

3. **Meditation frees our awareness.** Another interesting aspect of being human: we innately believe that we are just our thoughts and feelings. But through meditation, we are able to retrain our attention and bring it back to a pure, free state.

4. **Meditation develops concentration and other qualities.** This has traditionally been considered a lower purpose of meditation, but it is actually highly important. Do you really know how to concentrate? Do you really know how to gather all your being and to pay attention to such a degree that you become one with what you do? This is concentration. In this, I include the ability to play with our attention, to keep it flexible. But there are also other qualities that can be developed through meditation, like self-discipline, inner knowing, and the ability to not react. Meditation helps us develop certain capacities and abilities even while we struggle with it: through our difficulties, we achieve precious qualities.

5. **Meditation is nourishment.** Meditation is like plugging our being into the cosmic socket, plugging into a divine reservoir of energy. Meditation awakens dormant nourishing energies inside our being. This form of nourishment is not essentially different from oxygen or food: cosmic energy feeds and sustains us all the time anyway, but meditation allows us to do this consciously, and thus enhances the flow within our body and mind.

. . . .

6. **Meditation heals physical and emotional conditions.** Meditation has the power of healing, and it can heal both physically and emotionally. Whenever I go through some kind of serious treatment, like a dental operation, instead of taking painkillers I simply go to my room, close the windows, darken the room, and sit for meditation for a few hours. In this way, I evoke all the healing powers of the body. And why is that? It is because I immediately connect with an ideal of health. Meditation is a state of wholeness, a state that has never been affected by anything. By connecting with it, my body begins to align with this state of perfection and so begins to return to a state of health, which is the condition I was in before. If you're curious, try meditating next time you are in pain and see if it accelerates the healing process. Meditation may also be a potent healer of trauma, since it brings us back to a state before time and before memory, where nothing has ever happened to us. Can anything be more healing than that?

7. **Meditation creates intimacy with ourselves.** Meditation is our chance to spend time with ourselves. Not just time with ourselves in the sense of reading books, painting, or listening to music, but as a form of the deepest intimacy with oneself that is possible. You rest inside yourself and experience being at peace with yourself. Thus, meditation is the ultimate form of self-acceptance: when you are in this state, you cannot resist liking yourself, because you get to know yourself in the purest, most beautiful condition.

8. **Meditation prepares us for action.** This is also essential: meditation prepares us for action in the world. It not only takes us away and provides us with an inner haven, it also teaches us a certain inner posture. Think of the Buddha posture, which is the ultimate meditation posture. Eventually this becomes a sort of inner position in us: an erect, proud, fearless, all-accepting, completely open and available way of being. This makes us powerful beings who can come out of the sitting position with lucid minds, free of the need to react and contract, and capable of quietly responding to the challenges of life.

9. **Meditation provides the relief of limitlessness.** We spend our lives feeling as if we are stuck in a physical form, as if we are inside a box, unable to come out. This is also the reality of our mind, which can feel like a box of stifling thoughts; all we can do is powerlessly press up against the walls, floor, and ceiling while feeling that there is no way out. One of our greatest unconscious needs is to be able to return to our original state of limitlessness from time to time. We come

· · · · · · · ·

from limitlessness—we were not always this small—so we need these reminders, this feeling that it is possible to experience a state of no limit. This includes not only physical limits, but the internal sense that we can spread and expand our being and feel ourselves become far bigger. Ultimately, these states enable us to make peace with the limitations inherent in our human existence.

10. **Meditation helps us achieve true existence.** As we are, we don't fully exist, because we are just a bundle of conditioning—familial, religious, national, and social forms of conditioning. If we removed the contents of our environmental conditioning, and also the past and present relationships that have shaped our beings, would we still exist? Would we still have some kind of presence, even if all of that was taken away from us? In the New Testament, Jesus is quoted as saying that we are ultimately meant to be born twice: in the body and in the spirit.[4] In meditation, we begin to be born for the second time, and until we are born in the spirit, we are spiritually "unborn," existing only in the physical sense. Even through the process of resistance during meditation—refusing to pay attention to certain thoughts and feelings that are obsessed with matters of the outer world—we begin to become fully independent beings that don't rely on the stimuli of the external world for validation. Instead, we become self-empowering, self-sustaining, and self-confirming beings. You may have noticed that there is a paradox here: in meditation we return to our original state, but we also create ourselves for the first time, because we don't really exist as independent beings. This is because connecting to your deeper nature actually makes you natural for the first time. You start to become a part of the real world, since you previously belonged to the unnatural world of thoughts—like plastic flowers as opposed to the vibrant flowers that grow in gardens.

11. **Meditation balances the chakras.** This is the first of four purposes that are related to our subtle or energy body. Chakras are the centerpiece of this energy body, which consists of a network of tens of thousands of subtle tubes or channels called *nadis*. The chakras, which are commonly viewed as seven major confluences within this network, are situated deep within the central channel (*sushumna nadi*) that runs parallel to the spine. Chakras not only play a major role as a part of our energy body, they function as mediators between the different realms of spirit, psyche, and body, and thus the way that they function—whether they are balanced or unbalanced—dramatically affects, and is affected

4. John 3:3–7 (New International Version).

by, all the other systems. The ancient Indian meditators who became conscious of the existence of this hidden system more than 2,500 years ago (according to the oldest extant texts of the *Upanishads*) came to realize, that among other things, chakras function as gateways to broader states of consciousness and immediately respond to relaxation and meditation. As soon as we enter the state of calm, our seven energy centers are quickly brought to a state of balance. Much of the turbulence we feel in our body and mind is the result of our unbalanced energy centers, such as turmoil in the heart chakra or the brow chakra. In meditation, we supply the chakras with what they need most, harmony and peace, and as a result they instantly align. When our seven chakras are aligned, they become superconductors of energy that flows into our body and nourishes our physical being, as well as our mental and emotional levels, and clears the pathways of our energy system.

12. **Meditation awakens the root chakra.** The root chakra represents our earthly identity and all our attachments—everything that connects us to the earth. It physically obeys the law of gravity and thus won't let us transcend or soar high. In other words, it won't let us be spiritual. One of the most important subtle functions of meditation is to convince the root chakra that it can trust the spiritual state enough to allow us to move beyond gravity, in the other direction. Awakening the root chakra is therefore our permission to leave the world behind. As long as the root chakra remains unawakened, we will fear meditation. This fear is a projection or an extension of the instinctual fear of non-existence. The conscious mind asks, *If you let go of the known and the familiar, who would you be? Where would you be? This shift represents death.* This is, however, a complete lie, because meditation is life, not death. Once the root chakra becomes convinced and trusts the meditative process sufficiently, it manages to overcome the instinctual habit to cling to the known. This is why an individual's entire spiritual journey depends on the awakening of the first chakra. The root chakra is like the gatekeeper: if it doesn't open the door, you can't have full experiences, and you will never really embark on the journey of transformation.

13. **Meditation awakens the kundalini.** At the base of the spine, where the root chakra and the sacral chakra exist, there is a tremendous force, a highly potent life force energy that is traditionally called *kundalini*. As soon as you begin to

meditate, you may feel an energy stream flowing upward through your spine. This is usually followed by excitation or chilling of the nerves and the feeling of heightened awareness. As we shall discover throughout this book, it is vital to awaken the kundalini, and meditation is the supreme catalyst for achieving this purpose.

14. **Meditation awakens the third eye.** Usually the third eye, which is meant to govern the world of our thoughts and functions as the supreme and all-commanding element of our being, is in a state of scatteredness and lacks concentration. When we begin to meditate, we awaken the third eye (or sixth chakra), and in this way we bring the master back home. This inner guru dominates all our disoriented feelings and confused thoughts and tells us what is real and what is false. When your sixth chakra is awake, you can actually decide what you do and don't want to identify with. This is probably the greatest power that one can ever have.

15. **Meditation allows us to come into direct contact with the universe and with the divine.** I have kept this one at the bottom of the list because most meditators don't have this kind of aspiration. Nevertheless, this may be why meditation was invented seven thousand years ago. While religion has provided us with many pathways, like worship, prayer, and moral action and conduct, there is only one way we can directly experience divinity. As long as you pray, you still feel that there is something *out there* in which you believe and trust. Meditation is the only way we have of directly knowing what we can call God or the divine—directly knowing it within our hearts and through our bodies. How do we do this? By turning ourselves into empty channels that can be filled with this presence. For that, we need to reach a complete state of nonaction that makes us completely available. I believe that this is how meditation started. There is a statement by Padre Pio, one of the greatest twentieth-century leaders of the Christian world, which perfectly conveys this purpose: "Through study of books one seeks God. By meditation one finds Him."[5]

When you understand that all these purposes can be fulfilled by simply engaging in the act of meditation, you may feel greatly inspired. So, out of this list of fifteen, which are your purposes? What meditation will be like for you and how transformative your practice can be depends on what your purposes are and on the depth of intention with which you enter the meditation.

5. Kelly, *The Rosary*, 79, 86.

The Four Major Goals of Our Journey

Note: Although I have four major goals, you may have some other goals of your own. Feel free to add your own goals to this list.

1. **Acquiring the art of meditation.** Meditation is, after all, a form of art. When we practice it, we are like artists approaching a process of creation—in this context, the process of self-creation. What we create is ourselves, our own state of mind, and our own way of being. But it is an art, which means that it is very delicate and requires precision and deep mastery of the tools that you have at your disposal. To make meditation effortless, beautiful, harmonious, and ever-deepening, we need to actually become masters.

2. **Making the meditative experience transformative and profound.** You may have found a meditation technique that feels good, but the question is, how can we come out of meditation in a way that changes us? How can we go through it in a way that becomes a transformation? This also requires great learning, and we will examine it throughout the book.

3. **Learning the range of techniques and understanding their guiding principles.** There are plenty of meditation techniques out there. There is no one school, one religion, or one system that is the source of meditation. Meditation is a universal principle around which so many types of techniques have come into being, among them Hindu, Buddhist, Sufi, Taoist, Jewish, Christian, Muslim, and New Age meditations, and a great many more come from various independent teachers. Even I have contributed to the overwhelming variety of the world of meditation by adding dozens of meditation techniques! First of all, we need to become familiar with the existing range of techniques, particularly the leading and most established ones. This requires walking a thin line somehow, since we are going to study the religious or traditional contexts in which these techniques emerged while remembering that at our point in time, these meditations have been separated from their contexts. When these techniques were used traditionally, they were practiced within a certain context: each was just one practice among many others, with a clear set of rules, regulations, and ways of action. Nowadays we isolate the meditative techniques themselves. Of course, we will unavoidably be

exposed to these traditional contexts, but much more importantly, we will have the chance to study the guiding principles of these techniques: why they were designed in certain ways, what the mechanism is behind them, etc. You are welcome to choose which techniques are your favorites, but I encourage you to also pay attention to which techniques challenge you. Some people will feel more inclined toward the closed-eyes meditations, which can be considered the classical form of meditation: sitting with eyes closed in a certain posture, focusing on something or not focusing on anything. Others will prefer more dynamic types of meditation. Whatever the case, it's important to master and understand all of them. Then we can choose techniques that are especially relevant to each point of our evolution, wherever we are on our journey.

4. **Inspiring you to guide others with confidence.** After sufficient learning and practice, perhaps you will feel confident enough to sit with your patients, partners, friends, or children and bring them into the state of meditation. By the time you finish reading this book, you will understand the mechanisms of meditation, the difficulties and hindrances, and how to remove them; how to create a certain energy field in the room that makes it possible for people to enter meditation; how to respond to any questions about the process; and how to guide others to come out of the meditation and reenter their daily lives. You will have a range of meditation techniques at your disposal, and if you wish to guide an ongoing process, you will feel able to select the appropriate techniques for each stage along the way. If you know how to meditate, if you are confident about meditation, and if you have gone through all the difficulties in the meditative process and have been transformed through meditation, you have already done much of the work required to become a meditation teacher. If you understand yourself, you understand everyone else. Once you understand the principles of meditation, you may even be inspired to create your own. You can meditate however you want, as long as the technique manages to give rise to the state of meditation.

This Book's Journey

Our journey into the world of meditation is divided into seven layers or dimensions, based on a meaningful concept that I will briefly explain here.

In part I, we explore the fundamentals of meditation. This is not yet the time to approach specific meditation techniques. We must first take a step back and ask "What is meditation?" and explore the basics that are often forgotten when we rush into the actual practice: differences between technique and state, the nature of the meditative perspective as opposed to our ordinary perception, and the ways that meditation can be improved and deepened.

The second part of this book consists of seven extensive chapters, which are loosely based on and inspired by the principle of the chakras. This does not mean that we are simply going to meditate on our chakras! Chakra meditations are just a small part of the world of meditations. However, the map of seven chakras is an elegant way of classifying all the meditation techniques in the world into seven distinct categories or seven gateways—seven ways to enter and reach the meditative state. These can also be thought of as seven different types of awakening enabled by the world of meditation. So, although I will discuss chakras as the seven energy centers that we awaken using certain meditations, they will certainly not be our focus of attention. Think of the chapters as building on one another. With each chapter we are going to enhance our meditative capacity, since the chakra ladder also makes it possible for us to build our being from the root upward.

In part II, chapter 4 explores techniques that deal with unifying and aligning body and mind. This subject is deeply related to the root chakra, whose process of balancing and awakening has a lot to do with bodily awareness. The root chakra–related techniques help us leave our thoughts behind and attain bodily awareness and presence. They make use of the liberating potential of true physical presence. At the same time, they free our being from attachment to our material existence, as they awaken the root chakra's dormant spiritual potential. Here we are going to study very well-known techniques, such as the Buddhist mindfulness of breathing and walking meditation, the Qigong standing meditation, Jon Kabat-Zinn's Body Scan, and Zazen (the classical Zen meditation).

Chapter 5 contains sacral chakra–related techniques, and it is concerned with meditations whose main purpose is to lead us to total experience. This type of meditation is focused on physical release, life force enhancement, unconditional joy, and freeing our being from the observer that separates us from life and experience—therein lies the unique challenge of these meditations, since in many ways they invite us to become one with our meditation. Here we are going to study the Taoist inner smile, Osho's Mystic Rose, my own expansion of positive feelings method, Japanese forest bathing, and the Taoist testicle/ovarian breathing. This is a wild chapter!

Chapter 6 is all about building our pure and powerful presence. These are the techniques related to the solar plexus chakra. These techniques challenge our bodily attachments and help us find in ourselves an indestructible self, a fully independent "I am" awareness. In this way, they help us create unconditional inner power and centeredness. This chapter has techniques such as Jon Kabat-Zinn's mountain meditation, Gurdjieff's "I Am" meditation, Sufi Whirling, the tantric Buddhist vase breathing, and the Hindu kumbhaka. This is a rather serious chapter. (As you make your way through this book, you will feel that each chapter has a very different fragrance, quality, and direction.)

We will then shift to the heart chakra–related techniques, which are all about recognizing oneness: recognizing the self in the other, and even in all that is. These techniques help us connect with the eternal stream of true love and develop the quality of compassion. They also reveal the aspect of meditation as healing. Here we are going to study the Hindu and Buddhist Inner Cave of the Heart, the Buddhist loving-kindness meditation and Tonglen, the Christian Prayer of the Heart, and the Islamic Dhikr.

From there we move on to the throat chakra chapter, which is all about what I call "vibrations of reality." These throat chakra–related techniques deal with vibrations. *Vibrations* are anything that appears in the form of sound, like echoes of reality. Here we are going to explore basic sounds of creation and the power of the vibrational world. This range of meditations enables us to achieve purification and unite our inner world with the outer world. We will delve into the Hindu aum meditation, Osho's center of sound, the Sikh Kirtan Kriya, the Hindu meditation on the inner sound, and the Jewish method of Hitbodedut.

Chapter 9 focuses on achieving the clarity of truth. It is all about sixth chakra–related techniques that support the opening of our inner eye: the eye of inner wisdom. When we remove the illusions, we are able to perceive invisible realities that only our inner eye sees. Here we will get to know the Zen Buddhist koan, Ramana Maharshi's self-inquiry, the Hindu Sri Yantra, the tantra Buddhist deity yoga, and the Hindu and Buddhist darkness meditation.

The last chapter is the crown chakra chapter, which is all about returning to our original state. By chapter 10, we will be able to easily meditate after going through six other chapters of meditation techniques. We will have built our meditative capacity in such a way that it will be easy to reach these seventh-chakra meditations. Here we are going to move to techniques that return to the original state before creation, and in doing so, we will meet our faceless face. We will enter the world of the yogi: the world of samadhi, deeper states of meditation, self-absorption, and the dissolution of the separate self. We will study the tantra Buddhist empty body and subtle body visualizations, the tantric Hindu kriya yoga, the Tibetan Buddhist Dzogchen, the tantric Buddhist Mahamudra meditation, and Subud's Latihan.

As you will surely have noticed by now, the range of techniques in this book is vast: it includes meditations rooted in Hinduism, Buddhism, Taoist tantra, Islam, Sufism, Sikhism, mystical

Christianity, mystical Judaism (Kabbalah); techniques by Osho and Gurdjieff; New Age meditations; and even one of my own. This is a grand process, and that is why we must follow this law of meditation: *Always be here and now. Do not think too far ahead.* In the here and now, there is already so much to explore; we cannot waste our attention on thinking ahead.

. . . .

PART ONE

The Fundamentals of Meditation

CHAPTER I

The Nonmeditative and Meditative Perspectives

After exploring the fifteen purposes of meditation, it is time to discuss what meditation actually is. I am going to dedicate two chapters to understanding the nature of meditation. There are plenty of techniques out there, but the specific practices don't necessarily help answer the question of what meditation is. If someone asked you, "So what is meditation?" would you reply, "Focus on the air that enters your nostrils," or "Dance wildly until your mind loses all boundaries," or "Sit motionlessly, feeling like you are a mountain"?

It is essential to first understand what meditation is as a principle, not just where it can take us. Do we really know what meditation is? In fact, I would recommend asking yourself this question from time to time, because too often when we try to describe our meditative experience, we simply say, "I felt extremely relaxed," or, "There was a vast space inside me." But what really happens in that powerful moment of closing our eyes? Since the world of meditation is all about increasing our awareness, the more you become aware of what exactly is taking place, the deeper the meditation goes.

What is important to understand about meditation is that it is, first and foremost, a state of mind, a perspective. Generally (this is a gross generalization, just for the sake of conveying this topic), the mind has two different perspectives, two ways in which we can look at our lives, the world, and ourselves: the first is our ordinary perception—the *nonmeditative perspective*, which is our constant experience—and the other is the *meditative perspective*. These perspectives have absolutely no connection to one another; it is as if they are two different worlds, or two different experiences of reality. The whole idea of meditation is to be able to shift to the second,

• • • • • • • •

meditative perspective in no time. In fact, if you are able to make this shift at will, at any point in time, that is an indication of your degree of inner freedom.

The interesting thing is that in the meditative perspective, everything that is real in ordinary perception is gone: it disappears just like that, with the snap of a finger. This makes it like magic; you close your eyes and suddenly shift to another part of your mind. It is an out-of-this-world experience, really. Think of your head as having two regions, one at the front, where ordinary perception is, and the other at the back, where the other perception comes from. By making a slight shift from one region to another, all of a sudden the world as we know it disappears. That is how powerful meditation is.

The Transformative Power of the Meditative Perspective

Now I am going to describe several elements of our ordinary perception and how they transform as soon as we move to the meditative perspective. It is easier to understand what the meditative perspective is by first defining what it is not. Feel free to add more elements from your own direct experience. This is just a basic overview, which is designed to evoke the feeling in us.

Before describing each of the elements, I will invite you to close your eyes for a moment. This makes the moment of decision to enter the reality of meditation more conscious. So, let's close our eyes for just a moment.

Time and Timelessness

The first thing that characterizes nonmeditative, ordinary perception is the feeling of time. Time is probably the most meaningful element: as soon as we open our eyes, we are filled with the sense of time—even without clocks and without a conscious awareness of the movement of time. Time implies what was, what is, and what is going to happen. There is a feeling of moments ticking by, as if one moment follows another. There is a sense of something that keeps building up, a feeling of a brick-by-brick movement that obviously also creates a sense of moving, even rushing, forward, as if we are marching toward a certain destination. Because life is experienced as rushing forward, it must inevitably require constant effort. For this reason, ordinary perception involves a sense of effort, the feeling that life is a constant demand and that we must always be on our toes, in a state of unhealthy concentration.

This also gives us the sense of becoming. Becoming is a crucial element: it means that our sense of identity depends on time. We experience ourselves as something that was, that is, and that will be; a being that is also progressing, improving, and hopefully changing for the better, with great hopes for the future driven by a sense of incompleteness. For example, right now, I don't know what meditation is, but I hope to know what it is. I hope to become a meditation master, and consequently become this and that. *Becoming* means something that I am not already, but that with every moment, I am getting closer to.

The ordinary perception, then, is that our sense of identity is deeply connected with time. There is a linear perception, a conviction that this is how life is: a straight line forward. There is just one direction, and we are moving toward it.

Now, what happens when we close our eyes?

If you become aware of what actually takes place, you will realize that the sense of time disappears. It is like you're cutting out the sense of movement. You do not participate anymore. You are thrown out of time, and with it, all sense of action and effort becomes utterly irrelevant. You might think at that moment, *It feels like time has stopped*. But this is not what has happened—saying that time has stopped implies that it exists generally. The right understanding is that time is nothing more than a mental perception. It is a perspective that you can either have or be free of at any given moment.

Becoming and Being

When we close our eyes and there is no more movement and we are no longer a part of the big project of life, *we move from becoming to being*. Understanding the difference between becoming and being is perhaps the most fundamental insight into the nature of the meditative state. *Being* means that there is a sense of pure existence that cannot change or evolve, and therefore cannot become more complete than it already is. In being, my identity is unchanging. Becoming, however, is exactly the opposite: identity depends on evolution.

This is also the difference between *now* and *time*. Even the present is a part of time, since it is only a part of the line that includes yesterday, today, and the tomorrow already ingrained in today. The now, on the other hand, has nothing to do with time. This is why the words *now* and *being* are deeply connected.

As soon as there is this sense of being, there is also a feeling of a spreading of perception: instead of the ordinary movement forward, there is a feeling of something that expands in many directions, with no one clear pathway. It feels as if life is opening up; life in the now is opening up.

With this in mind, we are going to close our eyes for a moment. But before you do this, pay attention and notice what is happening. Right now, your eyes are open, we are in communication, and you may feel that you are learning, in the process of becoming an improved you. As you close your eyes, realize that by doing this and choosing to enter the meditative perspective, you are disrupting time and becoming, enjoying this complementary half, the very opposite. Of course, these two perspectives don't compete; it is not that one is better than the other. They complete one another, so perceive them as a circle. Ideally, we are meant to have both, and to possess the capacity to choose between the two whenever we feel like it. When, for example,

. . . .

we are tired of becoming, we can immediately close our eyes and, in a second, we can disrupt this movement.

Moods and Equilibrium

Moods are a strong characteristic of ordinary perception. When we are under the reign of this perception, we are susceptible to mood dependency. This means that our moods completely depend on external triggers. There are ceaseless ups and downs, including brief, painful moments of failure and pleasant moments of success throughout each day. We constantly crash or feel elevated. For a moment, we are full of optimism, and a second later we feel completely disappointed and frustrated and that life is no good. It feels like we are on what I call an eternal seesaw: going up and down, up and down, all day long.

In reality, this eternal seesaw is not the result of the events that take place in our lives, but of our thoughts about these events, the way we interpret these events, and the fact that we believe our reactive thoughts. But we are rarely aware of this truth. As a result, we constantly try to improve our mood and to avoid negative situations that might bring us to a bad mood.

In the meditative perspective, we can only have one mood. This is because we move away at once from external triggers, and we are no longer a part of life's ups and downs. It is as if the moment of meditation conveys a statement: "Now I am taking a break from this constant fluctuation. I know that whatever change of mood I might be experiencing can only be the result of me believing a certain thought that then makes me feel this way or that way." With this statement in mind, it becomes clear to me that I am able to control my mood.

Feel how, now that you are about to close your eyes again, you are actually deciding to discontinue your connection to external triggers for a moment.

Bodilessness and Bodily Awareness

Let's take a look at another element that characterizes ordinary perception: a lack of bodily presence.

This may sound surprising, since we tend to believe that when we are in the ordinary perspective, we are completely identified with our body. In fact, we are identified with the *idea* of having a body, but are we in the body? Far from it. We are actually stuck in our head, and our presence doesn't permeate the body at all.

When we do feel the body in ordinary perception, it is mostly through either intense pleasures or disturbing physical sensations. When there is a certain physical problem, signaled by the presence of pain, we become conscious of the existence of the body. But even this is not bodily awareness; it is more like a sense of being disturbed and prevented from doing what we want to do.

We can say that in ordinary perception, it is as if we drag our body with us from here to there: as long as it doesn't complain, we don't even notice the full presence of the body. We certainly don't breathe into this physical presence, and we don't inhabit it. At the same time, we experience heaviness and density. This is a strange phenomenon, since you might think that in not feeling that you have a body, you should actually feel light, airy, and spacious. In actuality, it is the very opposite: the idea of possessing a body makes us feel heavy, but without enjoying its physical presence at all.

On the other hand, when we change this perspective in meditation, we are finally, for the first time, fully present in the body. *We move from head to body.*

People often assume that the physical body is not spiritual. But the only thing that can keep us in a nonspiritual state is our thinking. The body can actually be our direct link to reality, more so than anything else.

So when I move from the head, begin to breathe, and allow my being to spread throughout the body, this immediately leads me to spaciousness and airiness. In no time, I feel as if I have been filled with space, and I lose any familiar sense of heaviness. How can this be? This is the amazing paradox: if you are fully present in the body, its subtle spiritual presence arises, and you realize that it is truly made of space.

More than that, in the ordinary perspective, we are aware only of material reality: it appears as if all that exists is made of dense matter. The universe can only be this hard reality of flesh and blood, machines and substances. But as soon as we close our eyes, we reveal a far subtler world, a world consisting of vibration and energy. All of a sudden, you can come into contact with the dance of life inside you, with life as a flow rather than a rigid reality.

With this conscious view of the body in mind, let's briefly close our eyes. What is happening when we choose the meditative perspective?

Personality and Subjectivity

We gradually come to realize that when we close our eyes, we detach from time, becoming, and the eternal seesaw of our mood swings. We fill our body with presence and begin to feel that being present in the body is actually quite spacious. And we learn that by closing our eyes, we can move our attention away from phenomena and personality.

Usually, our attention is focused on the issues that occupy our personality, all the objects of the world with which it is engaged. This creates in us not only the feeling of time, but also of space.

When we close our eyes, it's like saying, "Now I'm not dealing with my personality and with its complex relationship with the visible world. I am not dealing with the world of objects at all." Just feel how powerful this can be—by making such a declaration, the moment I close my eyes I imply that in an instant, all of this disappears and the sense of being located in the world is no more. When I am no longer in the world, I am not invested in all those things that ordinarily occupy my personality. After all, my personality is made of constant interactions with the outer world.

So, as I close my eyes, I actually say, "Goodbye! It was nice to meet you, and it will be nice to meet you again. But until then, in this shift of perspective, I am no longer my name or my person. I am not in the world and I don't need to interact with it. I can immediately turn all of that off."

Feel how you can turn it off. You may discover that it is much easier than you think. In fact, it is the easiest thing in the world. Because we have these two perspectives available to us all the time, we can choose to leap into the meditative perspective whenever we want.

In ordinary perception, we also believe that "I am my thoughts, feelings, and actions." This is directly related to our identity as a personality in time and space: we feel that we are completely identified with our thoughts, with our feelings, and with what we do. We cannot separate ourselves from this. There is absolutely no existence for us without it.

In the meditative perspective, it is as if all of a sudden, we are undefined. We just are. We realize that we don't need these thoughts in order to be.

Craving and Completeness

One more element is craving and fake need. When we are immersed in ordinary perception, we experience craving. Many things need to happen to satisfy us: we need this, we need that; we want this, we want that. We are intensely hopeful that certain things will come in our life, and that they will come exactly when we need them to come. It is very much like feeling continuously thirsty—a sense of constant dissatisfaction.

All these elements are deeply connected: time, becoming, and dissatisfaction. If my identity depends on time, it is unavoidably incomplete. It always needs something to happen and it is always on the run. But when I close my eyes and shift to the meditative perspective, I don't even remember what I needed. This conviction that I need certain things so badly can disappear in a moment. It simply becomes irrelevant, because I immediately cut off the connection with all that. Instead, there is a sense of wholeness and completeness.

Another characteristic of the nonmeditative perception is scatteredness: we are all over the place. There are so many different things that draw our attention, and this is naturally enhanced nowadays with the intense stimuli of social media and technological availability. We do so many things, think so many thoughts, and have so many contradictory voices inside us.

. . . .

But as soon as we close our eyes, we become unified. It is as if the many have become one simple being. Instead of countless and diverse thoughts and impressions, there is only one state, just as there is only one mood.

When we begin to realize that we can make the world disappear in the blink of an eye, it is the beginning of freedom and real choice. So let's close our eyes for one more moment and simply allow this to happen of its own accord.

. . . .

Is Meditation a Technique or a State?

Hopefully by now it is clear that as soon as you close your eyes, something wondrous takes place, something we tend to reduce the significance of. As a result, we remain unaware of how powerful this moment actually is. But as soon as you understand that by simply deciding to close your eyes, you can make this shift to another perspective, you realize that you have a great power available to you in the act of meditation.

But notice that I just wrote "the act of meditation," didn't I? This entire chapter will be dedicated to the crucial understanding of this phrase. Perhaps at the beginning this will seem like semantics, like I'm merely dealing with choosing the right words. But at the end of the chapter you will understand that our entire understanding of meditation must be very accurate before we approach any technique in this world. We should know the difference between a meditation technique and the state of meditation.

This understanding changes everything: the way we relate to techniques, the way we understand what techniques do, and the way we identify what meditation really is. Because we are going to study plenty of meditation techniques throughout this book—dozens of them, from around the world, from different ages and different times—we could easily get lost in the abundance of techniques.

In reality, there are no "meditations." The very term *meditation* cannot be pluralized. Of course, technically you can pluralize it, but essentially, there is one meditation and many techniques. This means that you cannot say you have tried out many meditations, but that you have tried out many

· · · · · · · ·

techniques. As soon as you manage to reach the state of meditation, it is always one and the same, and it implies only one thing.

Why Carry a Raft on Dry Land?

The Buddha said that the technique of meditation is like a raft that is meant to carry us to the other bank, but we are not meant to carry this raft on our shoulders after we have reached dry land.[6] This makes sense: as soon as you reach the other side of the river, you don't need the raft, because it was only meant to take you from here to there. In this chapter, we will take a step even further beyond the Buddha's allegory: we will realize that in many respects, the other side of the river is completely imagined. In fact, this is exactly where our misunderstanding of the state of meditation lies.

What is the difference, then, between a technique and the state of meditation? I will start by giving three examples.

There is the very well-known transcendental meditation. In transcendental meditation, you are given a so-called individualized mantra (which is not really very individualized) and you are asked to let this mantra resonate within your mind, again and again; to let it work inside you and do whatever it does for a limited time of twenty minutes. However, there are moments in which the mantra disappears. In these moments, you are not meant to bring it back forcefully. It is basically only when you "return," when you come out of the silence, that you are meant to repeat the mantra again. But the entire purpose of the mantra is to lead to these gaps, when the mantra disappears.

These gaps, when the mantra disappears, are what we can call moments of contact with the state of meditation. Thus, the mantra is a technique, and the meditation, in so many ways, has absolutely nothing to do with the technique. They are not connected: the mantra cannot enter, and cannot exist in, the state of meditation. In this space, it becomes completely irrelevant.

Another example is a group of meditation techniques that are sometimes considered preparation techniques. By preparation techniques, I mean a kind of middle techniques that are meant to lead us to meditation. This is the group of pranayama, in which we manipulate and control our breathing, either stopping or regulating it in various ways, in order to attain states of balance, inner quietude, and other qualities that may support and enhance our meditation. Obviously, pranayama is not meditation. It is just a technique that can be used to create the right conditions for meditation to appear—although even the idea of it "appearing" is fundamentally wrong.

---

6. I am paraphrasing; see Batchelor, "When to Let Go of the Dharma, Too."

• • • • • • • •

A third example is Osho's dynamic meditations. These meditations were developed by twenty-first-century Indian mystic Osho when he realized that Western people were so intensely conflicted within themselves and carried such a heavy and complex psychology that they could not be taught meditation the same way as Eastern people, who grew into a rich culture and heritage of meditation. Osho understood that he couldn't simply tell westerners to sit and meditate, because then they would bring their inner madness into their so-called meditative experience. As a result, Osho told westerners to scream, dance, and reach cathartic forms of breathing so that they could bring themselves to the edge of madness in order to jump to the other extreme: authentic silence, relaxation, and peace.

Naturally, Osho's dynamic meditations cannot be considered the meditation itself. They are techniques that prepare you for the moment in which you are finally ready to sink into meditation.

These three examples are enough to begin to lead us to the definition of a meditation technique.

What Meditation Techniques Do for You

A meditation technique is any mental, emotional, or physical structure that is designed to lead us to the state of meditation. But this structure can only create the ideal conditions for the state of meditation to be—and this choice of word is important—revealed. This is the key understanding: the technique is meant to lead us to the state of meditation, but it only creates conditions and prepares the ground. It doesn't create or bring us to a new state. What it does is reveal the state of meditation.

So, why is this word choice important? What is the difference between revealing something and creating or achieving something? *Revealing* means that you simply remove the veils so that you can see something that is already there, while *creating* or *achieving* implies that you are not there yet, that you are moving with ambition and determination in the hopes of reaching somewhere you are not right now.

Consider, for example, these three commons responses to meditation experiences:

- "Yesterday, during my meditation, I reached a state of deep silence. I had a powerful experience, in which I felt bodiless."

- "This technique is so powerful that it can really lead you to silence."

- "I had an amazing experience of silence, but I lost it as soon as my thoughts creeped in."

In themselves, these sentences are quite innocent and harmless, but they actually reveal a big misunderstanding: they expose the fact that people don't really draw a distinction between technique and meditation.

• • • • • • • •

It is important to understand that in the state of meditation, you don't move from X to Y, as if you have taken a walk inside yourself and have finally come to a certain realm. For example, the phrase "I have reached a profound state" implies that this state can be lost, and that I am therefore dependent on the technique to get it back. What actually happens in the state of meditation is that we return to the natural state of the mind. The state of meditation *is* the natural state: a "natural" state means returning to nature, a state that already is.

Techniques of meditation create the opportunity for us to recognize the state of meditation that already is. Obviously, this means that you cannot "do" meditation, because "doing" meditation is based on the belief that meditation is an act. But the only thing in the world that you surely cannot do is meditation. It is just not possible, since meditation is by its nature nonaction.

Then comes the question: *How can I do anything to reach it?* That is exactly the difference between technique and meditation, and why we must never confuse the two. You don't reach the state of meditation, you relax into it. If something is already there, any movement that you make means you are trying to create silence in yourself. You try to make something that is not there come into being. If, on the other hand, you begin to identify the state of meditation as something that you simply ease yourself into, in many respects you don't even need to have the technique.

We use techniques in order to create the perfect conditions. We use them to prepare our capacity for attention and to distinguish the experience from ordinary experiences. But even that can create the illusion that the state of meditation is somehow special, as if it is something so extraordinary that you are meant to experience extraordinary things in it, like fireworks. But actually, the state of meditation is the most natural, nonspecial thing in the world.

Big and Small Silence

This is the secret, and it is a very delicate kind of secret: your mind is already silent. It cannot become more silent, because when you begin to understand that meditation is only a matter of relaxation, you come to realize that the mind, by its very nature, is made of infinite space. The thoughts you have tried so hard to quieten so that you could have silence are truly a miniscule percentage of the vast space of the mind. It is embarrassing how little space our thoughts actually take up in the silence of the mind. When you understand this, no thought can ever become bigger than you or get hold of you in such a way that you are powerless.

This is when we begin to understand that the state of meditation means tuning into the natural state of the mind, into its natural silence. Think of it like this: when you constantly pay attention to certain thoughts within the mind, do you ever examine the space in which they are contained? Thoughts appear and fluctuate within a certain space. They are just like stars within the boundless cosmic space; we only notice the stars when we look up at the night sky, because

· · · · · · ·

this is the way we notice everything. Our attention always focuses on what stands out in space, but very little on the space itself, the space that contains it. This is why the state of meditation is the recognition of the space that is already the nature of the mind. But it is not just the space of the mind that should be recognized. It is the space everywhere.

Here, we need to differentiate once again between two terms: *small silence* and *big silence*. *Small silence* is the silence that we try to create through techniques. It feels like an island on which we have managed to find silence. This is why small silence always depends on the absence of thinking; we are inevitably afraid our thoughts will come back and rob us of this precious silence. As a result, when our thoughts begin to run wild again, we say that we have lost this silence, and for good reason: this silence *can* be lost. It is an experience. You create it through special conditions. This is why I call it small silence: it is a small point in your mind that is the opposite of the general noise. It is the silence that is the opposite of sound and thought. After experiencing small silence, you may think, *For a while, I didn't have any thoughts at all*—which is great, but soon you *will* have thoughts, and you will be in trouble once again.

This is why small silence cannot be the state of meditation. It is nothing more than a technical pause, a point of relaxation in the midst of noise. It has nothing to do with the understanding of what meditation is. *Big silence*, on the other hand, is the understanding that the universe is full of silence, in the same way that the space of our mind contains our thoughts. It is not a silence that you create, but a silence that you recognize, and it is not only inside you. It is everywhere. This vision is beautifully captured by the mystic Jiddu Krishnamurti, who said, "The universe is in a state of meditation and that is the ground."[7] Big-silence meditation is like the ground of the universe.

When the technique ends and the state of meditation begins, what actually happens is that you are tuning in to a meditation that is already taking place—you just weren't noticing or participating in it. I like to compare it to tuning a radio: as long as we tune ourselves in to the state of ordinary perception, all we hear is the noisy chatter of thoughts, but when we switch the station just slightly, suddenly we can hear that the world is full of silence, that there is a deep meditation behind and beneath it all, and thanks to this meditation the universe exists. And thanks to this silence, we can even notice thoughts.

I know this might be quite hard to believe. You might be thinking, *What are you talking about? The world is just noise!* But that is exactly the thing: the noise of the world is enabled by silence. Silence is like the glass that holds water. If you pay attention only to the water, you will miss the obvious fact that the water is contained within a glass, and you will not be able to see the full picture.

7. Jayakar, *J. Krishnamurti*, 424.

• • • • • • •

This is what is so beautiful about the meditation of the universe: it is like a glass that holds water, which means that meditation is not separate from the world. This is also the big difference between the state of meditation and small silence. Small silence is always an escapist silence. It is silence that has nothing to do with the world. When you come out of it, you have lost it and you feel that you were in another dimension; you don't know how to integrate the two. But when you get in touch with big silence, there is no longer the question of integration, because what does it even mean to integrate anything if this is happening simultaneously, and if it is the ground of everything?

Right now, my words are written on the foundation of silence.

This is probably the most liberating point: you can be in a state of meditation while your world of thought goes completely crazy. Your thoughts could be conflicted, negative, and deeply confused, and still you would not lose the state of meditation. How? Think of it like this: historically, humanity has seen many conflicts, and they have given rise to many wars and to horrifying bloodshed, but all this turmoil has taken place on the ground of meditation. Similarly, if you are untroubled by what goes on in the small area of the mind that can be troubled, what could possibly challenge the state of meditation? Big silence is all-containing.

Remember that meditation is discovering our other half. The two halves come together and thus cannot contradict one another. They may appear to contradict each other when we have only a technique, through which we reach an experience that can be lost—an experience that takes place in time.

This is another meaningful difference between technique and meditation: in techniques, there is the feeling of time. "Yesterday I had a very powerful experience." But what does that even mean? As soon as you understand that meditation is not an experience, but a revelation of reality, that is the moment meditation becomes transformative. Then it has the power to change everything. After all, we can have millions of experiences, and in this book, we can easily learn how to create the conditions for thousands more—powerful ones. But if you don't understand this one point, all these experiences will be lost in time, because they are a part of time.

The whole point of the state of meditation is that it has no relation to time. When I declare "Yesterday I had a powerful experience," what I really mean is, "Yesterday revealed to me that which is real now." When we consider it that way, we are already getting closer to a description of reality. This also implies that this state is here, right now, while I am thinking about yesterday's experience. Thus, my connection to meditation begins to be one uninterrupted thread, uniting all moments and all times. This state becomes the ground rather than a moment in time.

By this point in the chapter, I hope you understand that when you engage in a technique, you enjoy certain conditions that make it possible for you to relax into the meditation that already

• • • • • • • •

is. This approach makes meditation so effortlessly natural. And in this way, it also cannot really be lost. You may be unable to recognize it for some time, but it cannot be lost, because it is not something that appears or is achieved; you can lose something only if you have achieved it. When meditation is "lost," that really means that in the moment, you cannot recognize it. Nevertheless, you can trust that it is the present reality, regardless of your current experience. Finally, meditation becomes a matter of joining this silent celebration of the universe.

It is wonderful to have techniques, and as you surely know, this book is filled with them. But don't let the colors and the special tastes and fragrances of all these techniques confuse you—meditation itself has only one taste and one fragrance.

Summary

In this section, I am going to highlight the differences between the two worlds of technique and the state of meditation as clearly as possible.

- Do these two worlds converge? Yes.

- Do you have to go through a technique to enter the state of meditation? No.

- Do techniques lead to big silence? Often they take us to small silence, but when we use techniques with the right understanding and with a depth of intention, they can create the perfect conditions for the revelation of big silence.

- Meditation techniques always feel as if they take us from X to Y: "I am here, and hopefully, I will be there." They also involve a sense of progress and a sense of "there" and "then." The state of meditation, however, is "here": instead of moving even one inch from where we are, we are, finally, not moving.

- Meditation techniques are all about the feeling of achievement, while the state of meditation is available. It already is—you cannot gain it and you cannot lose it.

- Meditation techniques are all about doing ("I'm going to do my meditation now") while the state of meditation is all about relaxing—undoing, really. It is the least doing you can ever do.

- Meditation techniques are about freeing the mind because we imagine that the mind is stuck, that it is in bondage, whereas the state of meditation is all about realizing the true nature of the mind, which is already free.

- In meditation techniques we narrow our attention to focus on a particular object, like the sensations in our body or an image of the Buddha. The state of meditation, on the other hand, is all about unfocusing. It is a state of complete openness.

• Meditation techniques are created by us, while the state of meditation existed long before us. This is a wonderful recognition: silence has always been here. It is not a part of your meditation. You do not contain it. You allow yourself to become a part of it.

• Meditation techniques create the illusion of another world. But the state of meditation is everywhere because it is the ground of being; it holds the world and makes it possible.

• Meditation techniques are all about experience: a variety of new and exciting experiences. The state of meditation, nevertheless, is about reality. You either get in touch with it or you don't. Still, it is right now, as I write and as you read.

• Meditation techniques require the end of thinking, while the state of meditation is inherently uninterrupted.

CHAPTER 3

Improving and Deepening Your Meditation Practice

By now I have explained that techniques are designed to create the ideal conditions for the revelation of the state of meditation. But even the techniques themselves can be practiced in far better conditions in order to fulfill their greater potential.

Sometimes, our meditation practice can be flat and circumstantial: we may have a "good meditation day" in which we are wide awake and present, and a day later, a completely distracted experience during which we fall asleep for half an hour. Fortunately, there are ways to minimize these unnecessary blockages. In this chapter, I will discuss several elements that you can add to your daily practice to make it a fully conscious and realized practice.

Right Posture

This may sound quite technical, but actually it is not. Although we will discuss posture more extensively in the next chapter, in which we focus on the group of grounding meditation techniques, there are some general principles that derive from the understanding of our subtle system.

The fact that the common meditation posture includes keeping the body as erect as possible is not a traditional whim; there is a subtle understanding behind it. When we sit for meditation, we aspire to stimulate the flow of kundalini, the mostly dormant life force that resides in the base of the spine. In meditation, the flow of kundalini begins to travel all the way up to the head—to the brow chakra and the crown chakra. When it finally reaches these higher chakras, we transcend ordinary perception and come into contact with the state of meditation. The way of sitting must not hinder this flow. For the very same reason, the pelvis must be open rather

• • • • • • • •

than locked. This doesn't mean that every meditation is going to be an explosion of kundalini flow, but at the very least, this flow can be generated. In fact, whenever we focus our attention on spirituality—even if we simply long for spiritual transcendence—this flow begins to take place, even if it is not extremely powerful or explosive.

Ancient Hindu, Jain, and Buddhist yogic traditions have recommended the well-known half lotus and full lotus (*Padmasana*) positions. In the full lotus position, one foot is placed on top of the opposite thigh with its sole facing upward and heel close to the abdomen, while the other foot is placed on the opposite thigh as symmetrically as possible. In the milder half lotus position, one leg is bent and resting on the ground, while the other leg is bent with the foot in lotus position. Both positions aim to lock the base of the spine, so to speak, in a way that actually forces the kundalini to flow upward.

However, very few of us are capable of sitting in half lotus position for more than thirty seconds, let alone in a full lotus! Fortunately, this is not a problem at all. What is important is to sit as straight as possible. Imagine this as a proud, dignified position. Open up the pelvis and keep it open. Make sure that you don't press against the area of the solar plexus chakra. The solar plexus is a very important point of energy flow, so don't sit in a way that squeezes it inward and downward. This area doesn't need to be kept frozen either; just make sure that you gently lengthen it.

In addition to the pelvis and the solar plexus, take care of your chest. For many of us, the chest is blocked. Emotionally, we are not used to having our heart open to the world, and we therefore do our best to protect it. In meditation, we do the exact opposite: we gently make our shoulders fall back to allow the chest area to become broader.

Last is the neck. Make sure that the neck remains as long as possible. Again, don't push too strongly—it is not about creating a new type of pressure. Simply imagine that you are enabling a flow; this flow would not benefit from you pressing against it and blocking it. One easy way to lengthen your neck is to imagine that there is a thread that connects the top of your head to the ceiling.

Does this mean that we cannot meditate lying down, or in any other way? No—there are no rigid rules. These are only suggestions for creating better conditions. Other advantages of the erect-back position are that it prevents us from falling asleep, and that it is like making a statement of a much prouder and more present you.

To avoid falling asleep and to have a lucid meditation, it is wise to prepare your body just before entering meditation by using a breathing technique, two or three asanas (yoga postures), or any form of stretching exercise to create a movement of life force and to unblock the flow toward the head, where the higher chakras (energy centers) are.

Consider adding a five-minute practice of this simple technique of full yogic breath:

• • • • • • • •

1. Inhale slowly, drawing breath deep into the lower abdomen, starting from the pelvic floor and slowly allowing the breath to fill upward (toward the navel) and outward (away from the spine).

2. As soon as the lower abdomen has filled completely, continue the inhalation by filling the mid-torso in a similar manner.

3. Continue to draw the breath upward from the navel to the ribs, allowing it to gently expand the diaphragm, the ribs, and the mid-back as it continues to rise.

4. Once the mid-torso feels full, complete the inhalation by drawing the breath into the upper chest, allowing the breath to rise up into the heart, the sternum, and finally into the shoulders and the base of the neck. Feel the collarbones lift slightly in response. This completes the inhalation.

5. Allow a brief, natural pause at the top of the inhalation.

6. During a long, slow exhalation, do the reverse: release the breath from the upper chest as the heart, lungs, sternum, and shoulders all relax, dropping down and drawing in, toward the spine; then expel the breath from the mid-torso, feeling the ribs contract and the navel draw in, closer to the spine; and lastly, release the breath from the lower abdomen, feeling the belly contract and draw inward toward the spine.

Alternatively, you may add any other breathing technique you are familiar with.

As for mudras (hand gestures), these will be recommended only in relation to specific techniques. Presently, we are not concerned with any kind of traditional system that must be followed.

Right Environment

The right environment means, first of all, ensuring that you have a special place for meditation. This doesn't mean you need to set up a shrine in your house; even having a corner that is exclusively kept for meditation, an area that you clearly identify as that special place you go to when it is time to meditate, can be meaningful. This creates a sort of orientation in you and begins to establish a healthy habit: you know that when you sit there, you enter something that is unusual in terms of your ordinary perception.

You don't have to bother purchasing a luxurious or sophisticated meditation cushion. There is no need to aspire to fit yourself into the classical image of a yogi. All that matters is that you are able to sit proudly and comfortably enough on a chair or a cushion.

· · · · · · · ·

Practicing your meditation in fixed hours may prove highly beneficial. This can even be repeated in cycles of just a few minutes. As soon as you tune in to specific times, you start to enter a certain flow. This doesn't mean that you cannot meditate at other times. Indeed, you are most welcome to do so. But it would generally be wise to form this good habit by synchronizing your body and mind. To make this habit even more stable, you can set yourself reminders. If you are not able to follow this habit, do not beat yourself up—there is nothing meditative about self-judging! Go slowly, and throughout the meditative journey you may feel more naturally drawn to a persistent and regular form of practice. It is important to feel the joy of dedicating time to yourself. By sitting to meditate, you intend to take a vacation from the world, including your own personality, and to devote your attention to pure beingness.

Right Approach

The last thing you want to have is an approach that is entirely based on effort, as if you are going to work and to "do" meditation. Remember, this can never be what meditation is about.

The right approach is a combination of several elements. First, it must include enjoyment: the feeling that meditation is joy. Thinking of your practice as one more duty that you should fulfill will cause your mind to resent it after a while. Our brain is tired of duties, so it would strive to avoid meditation and seek out pleasure elsewhere. Instead, remind yourself that meditation not only opens you up and makes you radiant, joyful, and capable of love, but that it is also, simply, a form of supreme joy.

Aside from joy, another vital ingredient is the spirit of totality. Sometimes we enter meditation with low spirits, feeling that *again* we have to practice the same old technique. As a result, we don't bring our entire being to the practice. Instead, do your best to bring your entire being into it by agreeing to leave the world behind.

This is perhaps the most important point: when we enter meditation, our thoughts immediately make use of this time by trying to solve problems and fix things. Fixing things and trying to solve problems is what we do all day long anyway, so when our thoughts notice that we have some available time, they become excited: "Now, let's solve some problems!" Then our thoughts bring up problems, and we find ourselves thinking about relationships, or sexuality, or work, or even how we should better arrange our schedule. It is wonderful to bring awareness to all these topics—but it has nothing to do with meditation.

Leaving the world behind means that you deliberately turn off your connection to the world, as if it has vanished into thin air, while taking into account that you are going to leave problems untreated and unresolved. Remember that when we go to sleep, all of us inevitably leave certain issues unresolved, so we can afford to disrupt this constant flow on occasion. We don't have to be in charge of the world when we are steeped in meditation.

• • • • • • • •

Right Intention

All the recommendations above become easily applicable when practicing with the right intention. Create an intention, even write it down prior to entering meditation. Declaring your intention is probably the best way to give direction to the practice. As soon as you declare why you are going to meditate, you bring totality into the practice. Remember the list of fifteen purposes from chapter 1? You could use one or more of these as intentions, or you could invent your own.

Your meditation could be directed to advancing world peace, or to emanating beauty and purity in the world. You could even meditate with the purpose of enhancing your relationships. Keep in mind that you don't have to cling to a fixed intention; your intention can evolve from time to time. If you don't know where to begin, start with something like: "By entering this meditation, I wish to/I direct my being toward/my focus is…"

Do not think of your intention as a form of prayer. Don't think, "Please God, make it a good meditation!" Setting an intention is not about the hope that the meditation will be good. What is your purpose? What meaning do you give to your practice? You need to have a reason. A purpose is not like a goal: a purpose is planting an intention to make your meditation flower. It is not about *what* you are going to do in the practice, it is about *why* you are going to do it. In this way, the entire practice becomes instantly colored with your intention. Intention is not powerless, but rather one of the most powerful things in life. If you have a motivation, a reason why, this changes the what and the how immediately. It is thus the source of totality.

Your intention could follow this approach: "In entering this meditation, I'm leaving the world behind. I don't care what's going to happen. Right now I'm not going to solve any problems. It's none of my business. This is the time for myself, the time for me to enter a deep intimacy with myself." As soon as you utter these simple words and close your eyes, you will notice that suddenly, the meditation is far more awake and energetic.

In addition, it is wise to create an intention for when you leave the meditation. In this way, you can make your meditation far more effective. For example, as soon as you open your eyes, you can contemplate: "Now, as I leave the meditation, I'm going to take with me a sense of complete presence—the presence I have discovered in the state of meditation—so that it can be the conscious background of every activity and every single breath." This is just one possibility. But as soon as you utter such words, they form a bridge between your meditation and your activity.

In what way do you bring the practice into your ordinary perception? In what way do you integrate this presence into your life? Here, the power of your intention enters: from this ground of being, you can now stand up while still retaining your full presence.

When we come out of meditation, we usually don't trust that the meditative state can actually last. This is the truth: we don't believe in it. We think that as soon as we open our eyes, it

• • • • • • • •

must be gone—that state was then, but now we are here. This is, first of all, because we don't dare to fill up the world with our presence. Thus, as soon as we open our eyes, we immediately shrink back to our cute, kind, or social selves instead of courageously thinking, *This tremendous being is what I am. I'm going to let it out and shine forth.* There needs to be trust that meditation can last, as well as a choice to take up space in the world.

After meditation, you could try to do small and simple things while retaining this presence, even if only for a few minutes. From one practice to another you can extend it a bit—for five or even ten minutes. Don't immediately rush to do something extreme that might diminish the sense of presence. If you focus for a short while on something simple, like washing the dishes or some other mundane task, you will feel more capable of prolonging the meditation. You can act and remain in the state of meditation. This slowly merges the meditative perspective with ordinary perception. Perhaps this is why Zen masters and other spiritual teachers famously hand a broom to students who have just experienced a profound spiritual awakening. The student is instructed to sweep the floor or to pursue other grounding tasks. At first, this seems a bit annoying. The student may feel that they are immersed in such an extraordinary space that this instruction is not reasonable or even possible. Why would they sweep the floor? But these are actually wise instructions, since now that the student has realized they are divine, they can also realize that even as a divine being, they can sweep the floor. Or, in Ram Dass's words, "It takes a while to realise that God can empty garbage."[8] This presence can be perfectly human.

In meditation, it is less important *what* happens to us and much more important *to whom* it happens. Always remember: it is all about realizing your presence and the way you approach everything, not what you experience or observe. Meditation is concerned with presence and being. So even if you experience visions, images, vibrations, and other exciting phenomena, do your best to treat these as fingers pointing at the one who experiences it all.

This is the message that hides behind the noble meditation posture: your meditation is the way you approach everything, the way you choose to give attention to anything that may arise. It is the discovery of the power of attention and the capacity to free it from any kind of dependency on emotions, thoughts, and feelings. This doesn't mean that you should never be ecstatic in meditation. More important than holding on to the experience is the question of how independent your being truly is: Do you rely on such experiences? Do you need them, or do you realize that your being is free enough to depend on nothing?

So, plant an intention before and after meditation to make your practice more conscious and profound.

---

8. Dass, *Be Here Now*, 28.

Right Relationship with Thoughts

When we explored the state of meditation in chapter 2, we determined that we should not be troubled by the presence of thoughts while in this state, and that there is no need to quiet them down. This is for one simple reason: essentially, what we call "our thoughts" are not our own. If they were our own, they would indeed be our business and our problem, and then we would need to take care of them very diligently and thoroughly. But in reality, our minds are influenced by an activity that is commonly termed *the ego* and that I call *the thinking machine*. This activity is not personal at all, and it can be thought of as almost external. We simply take it in and identify with it.

What is the source of the thinking machine? Originally, it was a survival mechanism. It all started thousands of years ago when humans had begun to experience their first thoughts. Back then, thinking had been used for anticipating and predicting dangers, predicting what horrible things might happen based on the thinking machine's capacity to register impressions and events that had happened before. This proved to be extremely beneficial in regard to avoiding predators and the creation of tools, but this capacity has become quite self-defeating the more it has evolved. Now it keeps predicting dangers that don't exist, such as emotional and mental dangers, and scenarios that will never happen. The thinking machine keeps producing worry and anxiety. In its pursuit of the best conditions that you could ever have—the safest, most comfortable conditions—it has become frantic, restless, and eternally dissatisfied.

This is what the thinking machine does: essentially, it tries its best to protect you, but in actuality, it doesn't achieve this aim, because it has gotten out of hand. Presently, it is just an endless stream of thoughts, and beneath it there is an underlying sense of problem-consciousness. This is why we are always trapped in the flow of time: we are always in movement toward fixing something.

When you sit for meditation, try as much as possible to externalize this stream of thoughts. Imagine that it is not happening within your head, but rather around you, like vibrations that come your way from the outside world, or like a collective energy field that surrounds you. You don't have to internalize it. You have the power to not give it attention. This is the law of attention: what you choose to give attention to instantly becomes powerful and meaningful. However, what you do not give attention to becomes completely powerless.

This means that in your meditation, you establish an absolute relationship with thought: none of its contents are interesting or meaningful to you. If you want, you will have all day to treat your thoughts with exaggerated seriousness, but while in meditation, you really don't have to. When you stop making thoughts meaningful, none of them can be independently powerful, and consequently, you don't need to fight any of them.

· · · · · · ·

The worst trap in meditation practice is the temptation to fight thoughts in order to quiet them down. Never enter this strange battle! This only creates a split within yourself. Suddenly you are two: the silencer and the naughty thoughts you observe. This doesn't make sense. Simply begin to treat all this endless chatter just as you would birds singing in trees—nothing more than background noise.

If you feel tremendously attracted to watching one of the highly creative films produced by the thinking machine, watch it, by all means, but then remind yourself that this system does not actually have substantial contents. The materials it offers are neither profound nor true.

Thus, adopt a mode of nonreaction: simply don't react to any given thought. When you no longer react to thoughts, you leave the world behind fully, because the world exists in your thoughts. To be honest, it actually exists *only* in your thoughts—at least the world as we think we know it.

Right Relationship to Difficulties

One last important recommendation concerns difficulties. You may come across hindrances. Despite all the instructions above, you might still find yourself in a state of inner battle or confusion, especially at the beginning.

This is important to understand: difficulties in meditation are good. Remember that meditation helps you create yourself. We don't exist in the fullest sense of the word; we don't have an independent existence, a substantial presence outside our personality and its interactions with the world. The difficulties help you learn to reject and overcome certain automatic forces and to slowly find yourself.

All difficulties arise from the same source: our belief that thoughts, feelings, and sensations have an independent existence and are therefore outside the range of our influence and control. This is not true, but we may still cherish this belief until we decide to stop believing it.

Very often, a difficulty is actually an indication that a breakthrough is about to happen in your meditation. It is a sort of transition through which you are going to leap to a higher understanding or a greater stability. The difficulty, in this context, creates a helpful friction. This is why it is important not to despair when you meditate, or to think, *Oh, this is not at all what was promised to me. Where is my effortless relaxation into the state of meditation?* Remember that meditation practice is a long-term relationship. Sometimes, to attain a deeper love, there has to be a temporary friction and the transcendence of this friction.

Meditate Just Before Going to Sleep and After Waking Up

Try to adopt the habit of sitting for a moment of meditation just before going to sleep. Yes, you may be tired; you may even feel like you are nearly falling asleep. Still, sit proudly for a moment.

· · · · · · · ·

This could last just one or two minutes. Take this time to gather all your energies with the intention of bringing consciousness into the state of deep sleep.

Throughout the day we have so many impressions, and often before we go to sleep, instead of clearing our mind, we watch a movie, check our social media accounts or emails, and generally have scattered attention. Then we bring this mess into our sleep. But we need to try to do the very opposite: regroup ourselves and bring all our presence into a unified attention that is peaceful, concentrated, and awake. The best way to go to sleep is actually to be fully awake.

Then, as soon as you open your eyes in the morning, try to move to a sitting position at once, and again, gather your being for one long moment. If you wake up with the aroma of meditation and go to sleep with it, you will begin to influence your subconscious mind and to create a thread that connects the three states of waking, dreaming, and sleep.

Keep a Meditation Diary

Keep a diary of your exploration of the world of meditations. Such a diary would include highlighting your outstanding insights, reflections on your developing relationship with the state of meditation, and changes in your relationship to life and with other people resulting from the practice. Journaling about your journey may make your evolution significantly more conscious. Of course, keep in mind that evolution in the world of meditation should always be complemented with the nonevolution of the meditative perspective. After all, we can only evolve in the dimension of becoming, but we don't evolve at all on the level of being.

· · · · · · ·

PART TWO

The World of Meditation

CHAPTER 4

Root Chakra Meditations: Ground Yourself and Align Your Body and Mind

Our starting point is the most direct and accessible reality: the physical body. Techniques that make use of the reality of the physical body are the foundation of the meditative journey. It is not a coincidence that most classical meditation techniques work with the physical body. More precisely, they fill the basic activities of the body with consciousness. Therefore, the meditation techniques in this chapter are extremely basic. We are going to sit, stand, walk, breathe, and experience physical sensations. That is all!

The obvious question is: how can the most basic activities that humans (and also animals) perform become a gateway to self-transcendence and the greater reality? That is the purpose of this chapter: to explain how and why focusing on these simple activities can lead us to profound states of consciousness.

These types of meditation techniques are usually what people encounter when they have just embarked on the path of meditation. Why? Because the physical body is the most immediate and undeniable part of their being. There is no imagination involved. There are no otherworldly realities. You don't need to think about God or the divine. These meditation techniques are therefore highly grounding. You simply come into contact with the most persistent dimension of existence, on the basis of which you perceive, think, feel, and act. Nevertheless, because these are nearly unconscious elements of our being, they usually receive very little attention.

· · · · · · · ·

Since the root chakra is the foundation of the subtle body, the beginning of the spiritual journey, and the energetic governor of the physical aspect of our being, I have classified these techniques, for the sake of the explanation, as root chakra techniques.

The Root of Trauma

The first principle that underlies all these techniques is already clear: when the physical body and its different activities are filled with consciousness, they become a gateway through which we can enter the greater reality. The more you focus on the essence of your physicality, the more you will find yourself slipping into subtle worlds of energy and spirit. But there are five more important principles. Each of the techniques in this chapter fulfills at least some of these principles, and together they can be a complete process of root chakra healing and balancing.

The second principle is that the physical body is our most direct connection to the reality of the present, or to what some call the here and now. Often we look for reality in profound and extraordinary states that take us completely beyond what already is. Naturally, such transcendent practices are quite ungrounding, but worse, they might make us overlook the fact that in so many ways, the physical body is already steeped in reality. The core problem has never been the physical body; the problem lies in our thinking, and not even our thinking in general but, as we will discover in the last part of this chapter, a specific layer of it.

This group of root chakra meditations rarely unbalances and destabilizes the meditator (unless they are used excessively). Moreover, because they begin with a very grounding element, the first thing that happens is that they bring us back to the reality of the body. The meditation techniques reveal that the body has already achieved what we try so hard to achieve in meditation: The body is already in the here and now. It is already real. Enter your body deeply and settle in it, and you will instantly find yourself inside reality.

The third principle is that the physical body is the beginning of the development of awareness and presence. Awareness and presence develop through physical presence—through awareness of physical realities and sensations—and from this your presence is expanded. If your awareness is first fixed on the physical body, physical presence can become a greater presence, and awareness of the physical can become a greater awareness. This is the first step to separating awareness and the thinking mind.

The fourth and the fifth principles, which complement one another, deserve some attention: the fourth is that these techniques dissolve existential tension, and the fifth is that they have the power to build inner stability. To comprehend these two ideas, we need to learn something about the world of the root chakra.

The root chakra is the center of our being, through which we need to learn an important lesson. This chakra is deeply related to the legs; thus, when it is stable—and soon I will explain what *stable* means in this context—we feel that our feet are placed firmly on the ground. It is as if we have set foot on planet Earth and have truly and fully agreed to incarnate.

The root chakra represents the purely instinctual level of our being. Now consider for a moment what happens when we enter into this world: the first thing our instinct tells us is that life is full of dangers. Soon enough we realize that we are mortal, so death becomes the ultimate danger. The journey of life itself is filled with threats, hostile forces, violence, and unexpected and uncontrollable changes. There are two ways the root chakra instinctually reacts to this frightening realization. First, it arouses the impulse to always cling to pleasure, and second, it evokes the impulse to avoid pain as much as possible. So, we cling to pleasure not only because pleasure is enjoyable, but more fundamentally, because pleasure signifies security. On the other hand, we instinctively try to avoid pain not only because it is uncomfortable, but also because it signifies danger and insecurity. This establishes our instinctual connection with life.

Once we realize that there are sudden and unexpected changes in life that can destabilize us immensely, we begin to try to avoid change. Change signifies danger, while clinging to stability seems safe. When there are sudden and uncalled-for changes, many experience what may broadly be called *trauma*: the impression ingrained in the root chakra when it is confronted with unexpected and uncontrollable changes that involve pain and intense instability. As a result, the root chakra stores all the possible traumas we have ever had.

Traumas can be very subtle; they don't have to be extreme shocks. They include all the moments in life that have left in us unforgettable impressions of danger, profound disappointment, and pain. These moments, which usually pass of their own accord, become frozen in us. When we resist the pain and the change, we ironically imprint them forever: an impression becomes an imprint. These imprints are the cause of the existential tension in us.

So, it all starts with the pair of pleasure and pain, where pleasure signifies security and pain signifies danger. This pair leads to the opposites of change and stability. Change can be deeply connected to trauma, and traumas create a further chain reaction, leading to the desire to control future events and to make them predictable. This also leads to attachment, which is, in its simplest definition, wanting certain conditions, people, and objects to remain exactly as they are. Attachment is the wish that everyone and everything we are attached to will remain unaffected by time, change, sorrow, and illness. Since this wish is practically impossible to fulfill, we enter a state of existential tension.

This existential tension is mostly unconscious. We actually begin to realize that we have been under so much tension only when we enter our initial meditation practice: as soon as we close our eyes, we grow intimate with ourselves and are thus able to feel that our body is extremely tense and contracted. Ironically, our first meditations emphasize how unrelaxed we are; they alert us that we are in a state of constant war with life.

· · · · · · · ·

Meditation Heals Your Existential Tension

This existential tension literally keeps us on our toes. It makes us feel as if we live in a world of constant danger—and it doesn't matter how relaxed and comfortable our life actually is! Even if our life is pretty stable, this underlying tension will keep producing new dangers. For example, in the absence of physical dangers, it will come up with emotional dangers or fear of experiencing emotional traumas. At this point, even an insult could signify terrible danger that should be predicted and avoided. Since these types of situations are sometimes unavoidable, there is tension caused by not being able to fully control the experience.

Existential tension accumulates within the root chakra—specifically in the area deep within the perineum. This tension extends to the legs and to the base of the spine. Many back pains and muscle aches originate from this tension of the unbalanced root chakra. This is because the root chakra is the foundation of the entire structure of our body and being, including the way we hold our body and the way we literally and metaphorically face reality.

More deeply, this existential tension can be thought of as a resistance to being here, on planet Earth, since life on Earth is dangerous. As a result of this subtle resistance, we never fully incarnate. It is as if only a small part of us is here, while the rest of our being is still negotiating the terms of its presence on Earth: "If life were different, I would happily agree to incarnate! If only life could welcome me with flowers and with the promise that nothing will ever change…" This is how fantasies come into being. Fantasies are the way that we begin to build an inner world; we move into a dark and hidden place within our mind, where we feel safe and unaffected. From this dark place, we give rise to images of alternative realities: how life "should" be.

This is a key understanding in this group of meditations: so many of the thoughts we have in our head really originate from the root chakra. They appear to be cerebral, but they are nothing more than a projection of instinct onto the screen of our mind. That is why when we enter deep meditation, we immediately begin to experience calm. The mind grows quiet, because the first thing that meditation—particularly root chakra meditations—can do is heal and relieve this existential tension. These techniques teach us to return to the body and to truly dwell in it, and from this sense of physical embodiment, we finally place our feet on the ground.

Healing our resistance to life is one of the most important gifts the root chakra meditations can give us. We enter the world of meditation with a bruised root chakra, and these techniques show us how to accept change and pain.

How can we be meaningfully relieved of existential tension? After all, as powerful as meditation can be, it cannot do the one thing your unbalanced root chakra hopes for: it cannot make life perfectly predictable, controllable, and unchanging. But here lies a most beautiful insight: meditation cannot change your life, but it can definitely change you. Life will remain the sometimes-unsafe place that it is—nothing outside will become any nicer or softer—but these techniques will make it possible for you to build the inner stability to face life's harsh reality.

The Secret Power of Inner Stability

This is the ultimate learning of the root chakra: you will never manage to establish the stability you so anxiously hoped to receive from life, but the good news is this was the wrong type of stability. You were confusedly looking for stability in the wrong place. You are better off finding it as an inner structure, a genuine place in you that remains stable and untouched, even in the face of change and pain.

The techniques we are going to study in this chapter do exactly that: they slowly enable us to build inner stability. Prior to the meditative process, we may not possess an authentic sanctuary within ourselves. We may not possess our own solid existence because we are governed by a bundle of instinctual reactions to change and pain; changing circumstances shape our being, and our existence is therefore completely dependent.

The effect of these meditations works in two directions: by beginning to accept change, you build inner stability, and by building inner stability, you become able to accept change. With inner stability, everything in life is permitted to take place and nothing becomes a trauma. There can be devastating moments, but if you let them happen without resistance and draw on the power of your inner stability, these moments don't consolidate into permanent imprints of trauma.

So, our task is to learn how to feel safe, not outwardly but inwardly. That's the shift enabled by these techniques. All five meditations will develop this quality in you in their own ways. Perhaps the most important key will be provided by Body Scan, since by being able to observe and allow painful sensations in your body without intervention, you learn how to embrace negative states in general, while always remembering that they are, after all, fleeting. This quality of silent observance makes you capable of remaining nonreactive during major upheavals in your life as well.

The sixth and last principle of this group of meditations is that these techniques align and unite mind and body. However, the way that they achieve this alignment is by making the mind follow the body—currently, the body follows the mind. In fact, the body is like the unconscious storehouse of the mind. It contains all the conditioning that the mind puts in it. On the other hand, what these meditations show us is that the body is more real than our thoughts, so the process they offer is all about freeing the body from the mind. Whereas some traditions suggest that we should detach ourselves from the body, these techniques tell us that our starting point must be to learn how to settle in the body, perhaps for the first time. After all, we are already detached from the body because we are absorbed in our minds. So why should we become even more detached than that? This is the predicament that the root chakra group aims to change.

· · · · · · ·

When we make the mind follow the body, we are directing our awareness to move as one with the simplest physical realities.

Mindfulness of Breathing

Mindfulness of breathing can be considered the most foundational meditation technique, and for this reason, it opens our journey into the world of meditation.

Historical Background

According to the earliest Buddhist scriptures, the Pali Canon, the technique itself originated in the direct teachings of Gautama Buddha around 2,500 years ago. In Pali, it is termed *Anapanasati*, which literally translates as full awareness (*sati*) of the in- and out-breath (*anapana*).

Although the Buddha taught mindfulness of breathing in several sutras (scriptural narratives containing his discourses), our main source is the *Anapanasati Sutta*. In Theravada Buddhism, which abides by the Pali Canon, this text is considered so fundamental that many monks learn this sutra by heart.[9] This text outlines the Buddha's comprehensive practice of mindful breathing, presenting it as the path that led Gautama Buddha himself to spiritual awakening.

While many Western mindfulness teachers tend to emphasize mindfulness of in- and out-breathing as the core of this practice, the original practice is far more complex and detailed. It actually only starts with mindfulness of the breathing itself, since breathing is our most immediate tool for cultivating mindfulness. However, after this has been established, the practitioner moves to focus on other objects, being mindful of them *with* each in and out breath. These objects include feelings such as calm, joy, and happiness, different states of mind, and various characteristics of the impermanent nature of reality. Eventually, the meditator develops mindfulness of "letting go," the ultimate object that leads to spiritual enlightenment.[10]

Of the sixteen stages of mindfulness of breathing, we will focus here on the first four, which are regarded as the four preliminary methods. According to the scripture, the meditator goes into a forest or sits at the foot of a tree. They should sit stably in an upright meditative position and follow this elementary form of mindfulness:

9. Hanh, *Breathe, You Are Alive!*, 19.
10. Goodheart, "Mindfulness of Breathing."

1. Breathing in, I know I am breathing in. Breathing out, I know I am breathing out.

2. Breathing in a long breath, I know I am breathing in a long breath. Breathing out a long breath, I know I am breathing out a long breath. Breathing in a short breath, I know I am breathing in a short breath. Breathing out a short breath, I know I am breathing out a short breath.

3. Breathing in, I am aware of my whole body. Breathing out, I am aware of my whole body.

4. Breathing in, I calm my whole body. Breathing out, I calm my whole body.[11]

Purpose

Although each of these four preliminary methods of mindfulness can be practiced separately, they also present a progression of insight. The purpose of the first two stages, in which we become aware of our breathing, is to unite mind and breath. In the third stage, we learn how to unite mind, breath, and the entire body: being aware of our breathing is being aware of our body as a whole. Finally, in the fourth stage, we realize how the calming of the breath leads to the calming of both body and mind. The mind, the breathing, and the body calm down together. Thus, through these four simple stages we realize the oneness of body and mind. Even more so, we realize that breathing is the key to this body-mind alignment.

In general, breathing is one of our greatest gateways to reality. Whereas our thinking and feeling processes often become obsessed with unreal things, such as fantasies, unreasonable worries, and emotional dramas, returning our attention to the most accessible and undeniable relationship we have with life can be deeply grounding. Breathing, after all, is real. When we unite our attention with this constant evidence of reality, which literally exists under our nose, we immediately find ourselves inside reality, communicating once again with life rather than imagination.

Breathing is like a love affair: when you are mindful of your breathing, you grow aware of the unbreakable relationship between your physical body and the rest of the universe. This is how you are linked to life in the most fundamental sense. Breathing shows you the degree to which you are already an inseparable part of the whole. You don't need to do anything to earn this oneness! When you center your mind on it, you are already there.

Unlike many systems of yoga that recommend controlling your breathing (see, for instance, vase breathing and kumbhaka in chapter 6), in the Buddha's guidelines you are meant to only be aware of your breathing, without even the slightest manipulation. This is the art of mindful-

---

11. Hanh, "Sutras."

ness: to show you how to let things be as they are, and in this way, you relax into the reality that already is.

However, Anapanasati has one last important purpose: we shouldn't forget that this is a practice that is related to the liberating understanding of impermanence. If you look deeply into the nature of the process of in-breath and out-breath, you will realize that it is the most immediate representation of the reality of impermanence: your breath rises and falls continuously; life enters you with every in-breath, and every out-breath is like a small death. First, then, you realize impermanence by contemplating your breathing itself, and later, you look with your breathing at all other passing phenomena. This is how breathing can lead you to enlightenment: if you experience life not as a solid and fixed reality, but as constant change, you can free yourself from desperate attachments.

Practice

The first phase of this practice, which includes the Buddha's first two stages, is in a sense the most significant, since it helps you to establish a fundamental mind-breath unity. If you have achieved this sense of alignment, the two later phases will follow naturally.

Directing the mind's attention to the in-breath and out-breath may be challenging at first. Remember to rest your attention *lightly* on your breath and let it be just as it is. Realize that you are not "doing" your breathing in any case. In this practice, you are interested in being one with reality, rather than adding anything to your present moment. On the other hand, it is a bit tricky to try to be natural, so don't get caught up in worrying about whether your breath is natural or not.

During the first phase, be mindful of your breathing through either the subtle sensations of your rising and falling abdomen, or the sensation of the air passing through your nostrils and touching the skin of your upper lips. However, remember that in the two advanced phases of this technique, your breathing should gradually become one with your body as a whole. It therefore extends beyond any of these regions.

As you focus on the breath, you will notice that other perceptions and sensations continue to appear. Simply notice these phenomena as they emerge within the field of awareness, then return to the breathing. Gently keep your attention on the primary object of concentration while treating other thoughts, sensations, and sensory perceptions as "background noise." If any of your mind's contents or sensory impressions happen to hook your attention, focus on these objects for a moment or two and label them with a general mental note, like "thinking," "memory," "hearing," or "desiring." Then return your attention to your breathing, until only attention and breathing remain and begin to flow as one.

Instructions

PREPARATION: This meditation requires between twenty and thirty minutes.[12]

1. Begin by closely following your breathing in order to become aware of it: know that you are breathing in and out. Through awareness of breathing, become awake to the present moment. Realize that breathing with full awareness naturally helps your mind stop wandering in confused, never-ending thoughts. When you are there with every in-breath and every out-breath, you become fully present. Simply allow the breathing to take place and be aware of it, without struggle, whether it is long or short, deep or shallow. Don't try to make your breath slower or deeper—it will naturally become slower, deeper, and more enjoyable, since the quality of your mindfulness will affect the quality of your breath.

2. Become aware of your body with every in-breath and out-breath. Start by practicing mindfulness of your body, by taking the different parts of your body one by one, and then breathing with the organism as a whole. You can begin at the top of your head and gradually go down to the tips of your toes. For example, note to yourself, "I am breathing in and I am aware of my head," and then, "I am breathing out and I am aware of my head." After breathing with the different parts of the body, observe your whole body, without discriminating between the different parts: "I am breathing in and am aware of my whole body." Let your breathing, your body, and your observing mind become one. Your mind is no longer an entity that exists outside of your breathing and your body.

3. After practicing the first two steps, realize how the flow of your breathing, your body, and your mind have become naturally calm. When you breathe in, the air enters your body and calms all its cells. At the same time, each "cell" of your breathing becomes more peaceful, and likewise each "cell" of your mind. The three are one, and each one is all three. The calmness of one brings calmness to all three. In the calmness of meditation, discrimination between body and mind does not exist, and you dwell at rest in the state of "body and mind at one."

AFTER THE MEDITATION: Unite full awareness of breathing with your daily tasks. For example, you might say, "I am breathing in, and I am writing an email. I am breathing out, and I am aware that I am writing an email." If you find yourself engrossed in emotional drama or confusing thoughts, unite mind, breath, and body. This is not the same thing as taking deep, relaxing

12. The instructions derive from Hanh, *Breathe, You Are Alive!*, 43–49.

• • • • • • •

breaths—it is a gentle reminder that wherever you are, you have a ground, and this ground is being here and now.

Walking Meditation

Walking meditation is an important Buddhist practice that exists in different variations among various traditions of Theravada, Mahayana, and Zen Buddhism. The practice has also been popularized by the growing mindfulness movement.

Historical Background

In Theravada Buddhism, walking meditation is considered an essential part of the monks' training and lifestyle. In some monasteries, it is not unusual to find monks who walk for many hours as a way of developing concentration, sometimes even ten or fifteen hours a day. This variation recommends walking back and forth on a single straight path. As Buddhist teacher Gil Fronsdal explains, the reason for taking a back-and-forth walk on a single path is to put the mind to rest by no longer needing to consider the route.[13]

Japanese Zen, on the other hand, practices its own form of walking meditation, which is called *Kinhin* (literally, "to walk straight back and forth"). Kinhin is done between sessions of seated meditation (also known as *Zazen*, which we will discuss later in this chapter). The practitioners walk clockwise around a room, moving in a very specific posture and at an extremely slow pace.

Among other notable approaches, the Vietnamese monk and renowned Buddhist teacher Thich Nhat Hanh (1926–2022) developed a less traditional and more simplified approach to the practice, using life-affirming statements following each step. In addition, the modern mindfulness movement has moved away from the concentration-based and laser-focused approach of the Theravada tradition and advocated a form of walking that expands one's attention to include all sensations and perceptions of the present moment. The practice suggested here offers the various options of Theravada, Thich Nhat Hanh, and mindfulness.

Purpose

Like many other root chakra meditation techniques, walking meditation helps you learn how to align body and mind through an often-disregarded, mundane task. In ordinary walking, the task is mainly physical. Based on the notion that our minds and bodies are two separate entities, our

13. Dienstmann, "Walking Meditation."

feet do the walking while our minds are elsewhere. When walking is transformed into meditation, however, we are able to acknowledge the interconnectedness of body and mind. We fill the mundane and earthly with consciousness, learn to walk with full body and full consciousness by connecting the two through breathing and movement, and thus begin to "walk like a Buddha."[14]

In this way, walking meditation is a highly grounding form of practice. Since it involves a familiar but unconscious physical act, it helps you bridge between daily life and meditative awareness. This makes it an excellent preparation for living and acting from the state of awareness. For this reason, walking meditation can complement any form of sitting meditation as a way to continue your meditation in active life. And since this practice still involves movement, it may be the ideal way for a beginner to be introduced to the world of meditation.

Another aspect of the grounding power of this meditation is its ability to help us agree to set foot on this earth and to walk on it with trust. This is a subtle form of therapy, since for many people who struggle with an unbalanced root chakra, it is challenging to agree to fully incarnate and face life as it is. In this sense, this technique may also involve healing your relationship with Mother Earth. Perhaps this is what Thich Nhat Hanh meant when he wrote that "People say that walking on water is a miracle, but to me, walking peacefully on the Earth is the real miracle."[15]

The final important lesson of this technique is how to establish ourselves in the present moment and arrive firmly in the here and now. This learning is strongly emphasized in this practice, because walking is associated in our minds with the concept of destination. After all, you usually walk from one purpose to another: most walks are designed to lead you from point X to point Y. By making the walk itself your ultimate destination—or, even better, each single step—you confuse the goal-oriented thinking machine. All of a sudden, you move not to get somewhere, but to actually be here for each step along your life's path.

Practice

Each of the three forms of the practice—Theravada's, Thich Nhat Hanh's, and the mindfulness movement's—has its beauty and value. Feel free to choose the one that suits your spirit the most. However, I generally recommend starting with the Theravada approach, which grounds you in the technique and helps focus your attention, and only then continuing to the looser forms of Thich Nhat Hanh or the mindfulness movement. (I have excluded the Zen variation, since it was originally designed as a pause between sessions of sitting meditation, and its posture is quite rigid.)

14. Hanh, "Walk Like a Buddha."
15. Hanh, "Walk Like a Buddha."

· · · · · · ·

The Theravada approach centers on the rising and falling of your feet and the contact of each foot as it touches the ground while keeping your eyes lowered to the ground a few steps ahead. You need to be fully aware of your foot, the ground, and the connection between the two, which is your conscious breathing. Since this is a predetermined and limited route, it is wise to choose a safe and comfortable setting, such as your home or a secluded outdoor area. Although this type of slow walking requires a great deal of attention, you can increase your pace the more you establish a relatively stable state of awareness.

Thich Nhat Hanh, on the other hand, suggests a practice "with the appearance of nonpractice" by walking in open spaces, preferably in nature.[16] Like Theravada, his technique involves focusing all your attention on the sole of your foot, printing your Buddha-like stability on the ground, and making the next step only when you are perfectly certain that you have arrived in the here and now. However, he also emphasizes being conscious of your connection with the earth, and he suggests enjoying the practice and keeping a smile on your lips. You walk as if you were the most secure person on Earth. You may also take notice of each breath and the number of steps that you require as you breathe in and out. Alternatively, you can use affirmations. For instance, when you breathe in, say to yourself, "I have arrived," and when you breathe out, think, *I am home.*

Mindfulness meditation is an even more open practice, in which you experience a broadening of your attention to notice all sensations and impressions without grounding yourself in any particular object. Your only anchor is thus the general sense of the here and now.

In all three approaches, it is wise to start by standing and anchoring yourself with several deep breaths and by bringing awareness to your body.

Instructions

PREPARATION: The meditation usually lasts between twenty and sixty minutes. Either be barefoot or wear socks or light shoes. Anchor yourself by standing; stand with your feet apart as wide as your hips and balance your weight evenly on both feet. Feel the stability of the ground. Take a few deep breaths. Close your eyes and scan your whole body, starting at your feet. Make a note of any sensations, thoughts, or feelings and take the time to explore them fully. Bring your awareness to your body, noticing how it feels as you are standing, and become aware of all the sensations going on. (At times of strong emotions or stress, walking meditation may be more relaxing than sitting.)[17]

16. Hanh, "Walk Like a Buddha."
17. Dienstmann, "Walking Meditation."

Theravada Walking Meditation

1. Walk back and forth on a straight, defined path (up to forty feet long). Walk upright, with your eyes cast down about five feet in front of you. Don't look at anything in particular (you may also keep your eyelids half-closed). Shift your attention completely to the soles of your feet, bringing awareness to the sensations and feelings that arise there.

2. As you lift your leg, feel the legs and feet tense, then feel the movement of the leg as it swings through the air and note the sensations. Similarly, as your foot comes into contact with the path, a new feeling arises; note it. At each new step, new feelings are experienced while old ones cease—a feeling arises and another passes away. Eventually you will notice all six components of walking: raising, lifting, pushing, dropping, touching, and pressing. To help keep your mind in the process, you may also mentally note what is happening ("lifting," "moving," "placing," and so forth), or you may use labels such as "stepping, stepping" or "left, right."

3. As you reach the end of your path, come to a stop, turn around, stop again, and then continue to walk. At the beginning, middle, and end of the path, contemplate: "Where is my mind? Is it on the soles of my feet?" and thus reestablish your mindfulness. If your mind wanders, calmly bring it back to your feet. Your speed may vary; what matters is your degree of mindfulness. If you feel like standing still, or sitting down to meditate silently, do so.

4. If powerful emotions or thoughts seem to require your attention, stop walking and attend to them until they are no longer compelling. Similarly, if something catches your eye, you may consciously stop to take a look. You can also simply note: "seeing," "hearing," "worrying," or use a mantra to keep your mind focused and awake.

5. Instead of focusing on the soles of your feet, you can do loving-kindness meditation (see chapter 7) while walking: on each step, focus on the feelings of loving-kindness and think, *May all beings be happy, may all beings be at peace, may all beings be free from all suffering* (or *May I be happy, may I be at peace, may I be free from all suffering*).

Thich Nhat Hanh Walking Meditation

1. Walk slowly and calmly. While being aware of each step, bring your attention to the present moment. Smile and enjoy every step you take. Kiss the earth with your feet, imprinting gratitude and love as you walk.

2. Mentally repeat one of these verses as you walk:

   • Breathing in, "I have arrived." Breathing out, "I am home."

   • Breathing in, "In the here." Breathing out, "In the now."

   • Breathing in, "I am solid." Breathing out, "I am free."

   • Breathing in, "In the ultimate." Breathing out, "I dwell."

Mindfulness Walking Meditation

1. Be aware of the beginning, the middle, and the end of your steps. Maintain full awareness of your bodily experience: the feet touching the ground, the movement of your muscles, and the constant balancing and rebalancing of the body. Pay attention to areas of stiffness or pain in the body and consciously relax them. Allow your awareness to move up through every part of the body, noticing the sensations as you walk. Gradually scan all parts of your body, bringing your attention to the ankles, shins, calves, knees, thighs, hips, pelvis, back, chest, shoulders, arms, neck, and head.

2. Start expanding your awareness to include your location in space, the sounds around you, and the air temperature. Without judgment or control, include your present mental and emotional states in your awareness. Notice your state of mind: Is it calm or busy? Cloudy or focused? Where is your mind?

AFTER THE MEDITATION: Stand and relax. Gather all the energy from the practice into your standing. Remember that even after the practice, you will have plenty of opportunities to walk. Even moving from the living room to the kitchen includes precious moments that can be used for meditation. By the time you are in front of the fridge, you could already be a fully present version of yourself! You can interrupt any activity with mere minutes of conscious walking; slow down your pace and realize that the journey is the purpose.

Standing Meditation

While most meditation practices require a sitting position (with the clear exception of walking meditation), we can also find ancient examples of standing techniques that are just as profound and beneficial. In the world of yoga, for instance, we find the mountain pose (*tadasana*), which is considered to be the foundation for all other asanas, in particular the standing poses. However, the Chinese tradition of meditation practices supplies us with many more examples, such as the Qigong standing meditation, the classical Tai Chi posture Wuji, the Yiquan standing practice, and the technique that will be presented here: the Zhan Zhuang standing meditation ("standing like a tree" or "post standing").

Historical Background

While the origin of Zhan Zhuang (pronounced "Jan Jong") is found in ancient Taoist methods of meditation and health, this practice was later adopted and adapted by the world of martial arts. The term *Zhan Zhuang* was coined by the Chinese master Wang Xiangzhai (1885–1963), who founded the martial art of Yiquan: a method of kung fu that is entirely based on Zhan Zhuang, along with movements that continue the feeling of the standing post in action.[18]

As a result of Xiangzhai's efforts, this technique has become a common practice for powerful chi ("life energy") cultivation. Nowadays, most Qigong schools use a derivative of Zhan Zhuang as a foundational practice, and it is considered to be the most powerful exercise of all the Qigong postures. Although martial artists used this standing technique to develop a martially capable body structure, this form of Qigong, which emphasizes stillness over movement, is now mainly taught for meditative and health purposes. It is often used as a separate exercise to increase leg strength, concentration, deep breathing, and chi flow.

Purpose

Like walking meditation, standing meditation may serve as an effective substitute for more traditional silent sitting meditation. It can therefore be an introduction to the world of meditation, or even an alternative in case you face certain physical or mental difficulties while sitting for meditation. Standing meditation can make it easier to remain mindful and rooted in physical presence, and it is less likely to cause drowsiness than sitting meditation.

According to the researcher Jai Dudeja, standing meditation was sometimes considered superior in terms of its ability to allow a smooth flow of life energy (chi or prana) and to align

---

18. Dudeja, "Benefits of Tadasana, Zhan Zhuang, and Other Standing Meditation Techniques," 609.

our energy centers. This increase in energy flow has something to do with the fact that standing meditation helps correct our body posture. Almost all modern people suffer from improper posture. When in a state of misalignment, the muscles in our body are constantly attempting to maintain equilibrium. The standing practice makes systematic improvements in our ability to maintain proper equilibrium. As a result, the skeletal structure creates a natural vessel for us to maintain and cultivate a reservoir of energy that circulates around the body's subtle channels (meridians). This could be the reason practitioners of standing meditation report not only enhanced energy levels, but also greater mental clarity.[19]

Chi flows throughout the body's energetic pathways or channels. In Chinese medicine, there are eight vessels, twelve primary chi channels, and thousands of secondary channels branching out from the primary ones.[20] The goal of Zhan Zhuang is to unblock stagnant chi and to open and connect all the body's energetic pathways. Additionally, standing meditation can make you aware of current blockages in your body. After just a few minutes of meditative standing, you will become aware of imbalances that need to be corrected in order to continue your practice. Your mind will become increasingly aware of your body and how it should stabilize to find its equilibrium.

Perhaps Zhan Zhuang, which is all about learning to "stand like a tree," owes its power to the fact that we are imitating the intelligence inherent in nature. By standing treelike, we develop a firm foundation upon which we can erect a solid trunk. This proud position keeps us rooted both in the natural world and in the present moment.

Practice

The following instructions include many adjustments before finding yourself in the right position, but the practice is essentially simple: you stand still, in an upright posture, as if you were a tree. The tree metaphor is significant—your feet establish the roots, your legs and torso form the trunk of the tree, and your head and limbs form the branches.

If you want to be able to stand still in a static position for more than a few minutes, you have to hold your body in a relaxed, extended, and open position. As long as you maintain this type of position, your mind will follow and remain empty but alert. Trust that your body will gradually find its harmony. Stand correctly, in the proper body alignment, but allow the practice itself to guide your body toward a state of equilibrium. It is key to feel your center of gravity in the energy center (dantian) that is found two to three inches below the navel, not in the muscles of your arms and legs.

19. Dudeja, "Benefits of Tadasana, Zhan Zhuang, and Other Standing Meditation Techniques," 608.
20. Micunovic, "Zhan Zhuang."

When you first get the impulse to stop the meditation, remain standing for a few minutes longer. Remind yourself that trees stand tall for decades, even centuries. Don't worry if you experience trembling or shaking. This is one of the most common phenomena that many people encounter in the early stages of the practice. Consider this shaking a therapeutic process during which the energy pathways are becoming loosened and unconstricted.

Throughout the practice, you may add a focus on the physical sensations of standing, the physical sensations of breathing, or an enhanced awareness of the world around you.

Instructions

PREPARATION: Start by practicing this meditation for ten minutes. Gradually build your capacity. However, don't exceed thirty minutes. Wear loose clothing. If possible, do the practice in a naturally lit and ventilated setting, whether indoors or outdoors. If it's helpful, your first experience can take place in front of one mirror or several, which allow you to see yourself from several angles to get a better sense of your body positioning.[21]

1. Stand with your feet pointed straight ahead, parallel to each other, firmly on the ground at shoulder width. Grasp the ground with your feet while keeping them elastic, with the tips of the toes slightly extended.

2. Extend upward from the crown of your head into the sky. Feel as if your head is floating above your neck, effortlessly suspended above your spine.

3. Roll your hips slightly forward as if you were sitting at the edge of a high bar-stool. Since most people have a natural *S* curve in their spine, this will straighten the spine in your lower back.

4. Keep your knees bent slightly. Your knees should never be too straight ("locked") or too bent (going beyond your toes).

5. Relax your shoulders. Round your upper back and make your chest slightly concave.

6. Let your arms rest comfortably at your sides. To create a small space, imagine a pea-sized ball under each armpit.

7. Let the palms of your hands face your hips. Due to the small space under your armpits, your hands won't touch your hips, but will hang about two or three inches from them.

---

21. The instructions derive from Dudeja, "Benefits of Tadasana, Zhan Zhuang, and Other Standing Meditation Techniques," 616.

• • • • • • • •

8. Tuck your chin inward. Roll it inward and up toward the top of your head (this opens the area where your spine meets your skull).

9. Keep your eyes slightly open, with a soft gaze ahead. Keeping your eyes just slightly open prevents drowsiness and at the same time removes distractions from your range of vision.

10. Place your tongue gently on your palate with your lips barely closed. Relax your jaw muscles.

11. Breathe comfortably, slowly, and quietly through your nose. With every exhale, let your body relax a little more.

12. Avoid using physical strength. Impatiently "trying" to stand will increase tension. Instead, rest yourself on your skeletal structure and sink all of your muscle tension into your feet and the ground below them. You can place your attention on your feet at the beginning of your practice to achieve this state. As a result, your feet will become heavy, as though they have become glued to the ground.

13. After positioning yourself in this complete standing posture, turn your attention to tense parts of the body. Start at the top of the head and scan your body downward. When you locate an area of tension, breathe into that area and allow the tension to dissolve and sink into your energetic core, two to three inches below the navel.

14. You may experience numbness, tingling, pulsations, warmth, or coolness in your hands, feet, head, or other parts of your body. These sensations are positive indications that the life energy is attempting to flow freely through the body.

15. Do this for between ten and thirty minutes.

AFTER THE MEDITATION: This basic standing posture can become second nature to you. Feel free to use it whenever you find yourself standing in your daily life.

Body Scan

Mindfulness is a moment-by-moment nonjudgmental attention focused in the present. The Body Scan is a body-oriented practice of mindfulness that was first developed for clinical purposes and has since become a widely spread do-it-yourself meditation.

• • • • • • • •

Historical Background

Born in 1944, Jon Kabat-Zinn is one of the world's leading meditation teachers, as well as a prominent meditation researcher at the University of Massachusetts Medical School. Aside from popularizing ancient mindfulness practices, Kabat-Zinn has also developed several techniques, among them the mountain meditation (see chapter 6).[22]

Kabat-Zinn is particularly known for his mindfulness-based stress reduction program (MBSR), which is offered by more than 720 medical centers and organizations around the world. The Body Scan is the starting point of the program's standard curriculum, and it serves to introduce patients to mindfulness in practice.[23]

However, it is clear that Kabat-Zinn was highly inspired by his Buddhist studies and practices when he developed his own version of Body Scan. The insight into the impermanent nature of all bodily sensations is rooted in teachings that date back to the first few centuries after the time of the Buddha and can be found in a canonical body of texts of the Theravada tradition.

Additionally, Kabat-Zinn was inspired by the tradition of Sayagyi U Ba Khin (1899–1971), whose most well-known student was the Vipassana teacher S. N. Goenka (1924–2013). U Ba Khin taught "sweeping through the body," a practice that enhances awareness of the nature of passing sensations by allowing our attention to travel from one body part to another.[24]

Purpose

Jon Kabat-Zinn's intention was to develop a meditation practice that could help people who suffer from chronic pain. The idea came into being while he was practicing U Ba Khin's technique at a retreat that included sequences of long Body Scans in a specific order, during which participants were sometimes not allowed to move. Kabat-Zinn was facing intolerable levels of physical pain while also experiencing spaciousness and the absence of suffering. This experience revealed to him a state in which one could actually "befriend" intense and unwanted sensation. Interestingly, the Body Scan taught by U Ba Khin seemed to be able to offer relief from pain; the reason that S. N. Goenka became convinced of the efficacy of his teacher's method was that the practice cured him completely of his debilitating migraine attacks.

Jon Kabat-Zinn explains that even though the practice of Body Scan can sometimes intensify our sensations, including greater pain in vulnerable or diseased regions of our body, we become significantly more capable of meeting these sensations without emotional and mental reaction. From the state of heightened awareness, we learn to develop a sort of intimacy with bare sensations, and consequently we are less disturbed by their presence. We understand the difference

---

22. Kabat-Zinn, "About the Author."
23. Anālayo, "Buddhist Antecedents to the Body Scan Meditation," 1.
24. Anālayo, "Buddhist Antecedents to the Body Scan Meditation," 3–6.

• • • • • • •

between awareness of pain and being caught up in pain. Kabat-Zinn writes that "It seems as if awareness itself, holding the sensations without judging them or reacting to them, is healing our view of the body…This in itself is an experience of liberation."[25] This view of the body can lead us to a new appreciation of it.

In a deeper meditative sense, Body Scan enables us to experience important Buddhist insights firsthand. Since the sensations we observe pass away as soon as they have arisen, we learn to recognize the momentary nature of life itself. In addition, we can gain insight into the ever-changing, immaterial essence of our body. U Ba Khin used to teach that at the material level, everything that exists is composed of material units much smaller than atoms, which die out soon after they come into being.[26] The more we scan the body's sensations in meditation, the more we can directly confirm that the body is made up of subatomic particles that arise and pass away with great rapidity. This can lead to a state termed *Bhanga*, a transformation of our sensations into pure energy flow and, as a result, a total dissolution of the sense of physical solidity.

Practice

In this version of Body Scan, you systematically "sweep" through your body, starting with the toes of the left foot and moving up to the leg and hip, then shifting to the other foot and the corresponding leg and hip, followed by covering the torso. From the shoulders, your attention shifts to the tips of both hands, then moves up both arms simultaneously and proceeds to the neck and head. Kabat-Zinn suggests considering the process as a way to throw open all the windows and doors of your body's house, allowing the fresh air of awareness to sweep it clean. The emphasis is on being aware without reactivity. However, this nonreactive awareness is combined with an affectionate, openhearted, and interested attention to the body's various regions.

Without moving a muscle, you put your mind anywhere in the body that you choose and become aware of whatever sensations are present at that moment. Remember, there is a big difference between being *inside* the sensation and simply *being aware* of its existence. Being aware is like quietly resting your attention on something. Do this as if you were watching the constant flow of a gushing river. Be aware, without dividing and preferring: don't cling to pleasant sensations and don't push away unpleasant ones. Although sensations come and go anyway, whether you are aware of this reality or not, your awareness may alter the sensations, not because you want them to change, but simply because you create for them a healing space in which to dissolve faster. On the other hand, along the way you may encounter areas of pain that will be felt even more acutely as a result of the process. Observe them as impersonally as possible, remind-

25. Kabat-Zinn, "The Body Scan Meditation," 2.
26. Anālayo, "Buddhist Antecedents to the Body Scan Meditation."

ing yourself that they are impermanent. It is also possible that while you are bringing your laser-focused attention to one region, other body parts will become activated. This may be because the areas are subtly interlinked. Nevertheless, fix your attention on where you are at a given moment.

While traditional Vipassana meditation mostly involves the well-known sitting and walking postures, Kabat-Zinn's version of Body Scan is usually practiced in the prone posture. This posture was chosen as a result of his wish to make mindfulness practice accessible to people who suffer from physical pain. Nevertheless, feel free to practice this technique in either a sitting or a standing position.

You can undertake the process with great precision and detail, or you can scan your body quickly. You can do a one in-breath and one out-breath Body Scan, or a one-, two-, five-, ten-, or twenty-minute Body Scan. A more detailed practice may include sensing how the breath is moving in and through each region and inhabiting it. According to Kabat-Zinn, "Each speed has its virtues, and ultimately, it is about being in touch with the whole of your being and your body in any and every way you can, outside of time altogether."[27]

The Body Scan is an excellent practice to do while lying in bed at night or in the morning.

Instructions

PREPARATION: The meditation usually lasts thirty minutes. Wear loose clothes that will not constrict your breathing. Make sure you are in a protected environment where you can remain completely uninterrupted. Lie down, sit, or stand. Don't try too hard to relax; simply allow things to be exactly as they are. Let your eyes close gently.[28]

1. Begin with awareness of your breathing. In particular, focus on the area of the abdomen: as the breath flows into your body, it fills up your belly, and as it moves out, your belly deflates. If you are lying down, let your body become heavier and sink further into the mat or floor with every exhalation. Do this for two to three minutes.

2. Shift the focus of your attention to the toes of the left foot. Become aware of whatever feelings are in this region of the body. There may be sensations such as tingling, moisture, itching, or warmth. Observe these sensations exactly as they are. If you experience absolutely nothing there, simply experience feeling nothing. Breathe with these sensations. As you breathe in, imagine that the breath is

---

27. Kabat-Zinn, "The Body Scan Meditation," 3.

28. The instructions derive from Kabat-Zinn, "The Body Scan Meditation," 1, and "Jon Kabat Zinn Body Scan Meditation Guided Meditation."

• • • • • • •

moving right down through the lungs and belly to your toes, and as you breathe out, it is moving back up from your toes to your nose. This should feel as if you are breathing into and out from your toes. After a long moment, let go of the toes completely on the out-breath; allow this region of the body to dissolve in your mind's eye.

3. Do exactly the same with all the other body parts. First, move through the entirety of the foot—the sole, the heel, the top of the foot—and then up the left leg, including, in turn, the ankle, the shin and the calf, the knee and the kneecap, the thigh in its entirety (on the surface and deep within it), the groin, and the left hip. Then, shift your attention to the toes of the right foot, the other regions of the foot, and then up the right leg in the same manner as the left.

4. From there, the focus moves (successively, and slowly) into the entirety of the pelvic region, including the hips again, the buttocks and the genitals, the lower back, the abdomen, and the upper torso; then to the upper back, the chest and the ribs, the breasts, the heart, lungs, and great vessels housed within the rib cage, the shoulder blades floating at the back of the rib cage, all the way up to the collarbones and shoulders.

5. From the shoulders, move to the arms (you can often do them together), starting from the tips of the fingers and thumbs and moving successively through the fingers, palms, backs of the hands, wrists, forearms, elbows, upper arms, armpits, and shoulders again. Then move into the neck and throat, and finally, the face and head.

6. After you have covered the entire head with your awareness, move all the way to the crown. Breathe through the top of your head, letting the air and energy move through it. Then breathe simultaneously through the bottoms of your feet and through your head, encompassing the entire length of your body. Experience your entire body breathing and be aware of this flow of energy and breath.

Zazen

Zazen (literally "seated meditation") is the primary meditative discipline of Zen Buddhism. The meaning and method of Zazen vary from one Zen school to another. For instance, in the case of the Japanese Rinzai school, Zazen involves contemplation of koans (see chapter 9). However, the form of Zazen that will be introduced here derives from the Japanese Soto tradition, which teaches a form of the practice called *shikantaza*: the well-known "just sit" approach. In shikantaza, the practitioner does not use any specific object of meditation, but simply remains in the present moment, in a state of serene reflection.

Historical Background

Dogen (1200–1253), the founder of the Soto Zen tradition, considered Zazen a holistic body posture rather than a state of mind. He used various terms to capture this unique physical position, such as "sitting immovable like a bold mountain."[29] Although the Soto's full lotus position doesn't seem so different from that of the Hindu yogis, for Dogen this position wasn't the technical foundation on which you carried out your practice, but the practice itself. This implies that Zazen is not a mental exercise—the body sitting while the mind is doing something else—but learning how to sit correctly, with absolutely nothing to add to it. Kodo Sawaki Roshi, an early twentieth-century Zen master, summarized this principle by simply saying, "Just sit Zazen, and that's the end of it."[30]

Purpose

Shikantaza ("nothing but sitting") is like a physical manifestation of the essence of Zen. Instead of giving you a particular practice, it deprives you of the idea of practice, since it is designed to teach you that there is nothing to add to the here and now or to your true Buddha nature. Practically all other meditation techniques create the feeling that there is a certain direction and goal, but by centering your attention on the correct posture and leaving you to just sit, Zazen shows you that there is nowhere to reach, since you are already inside reality. It cannot become more real than it already is!

In Zazen's unique view, spiritual practice is not some kind of striving to produce an unusual state of enlightenment. It is an expression of the enlightenment *already inherent* in all things. So, the only thing that needs to happen is that you return from the mind's faraway inner journeys to a complete union with the reality of life as it is right now, which is represented by your sitting body. This is the simple genius of the practice: slowly but surely, you dissolve the duality of body and mind, here and there, extraordinary and ordinary, journey and destination, practice and achievement—until you realize that enlightenment was already at the starting point of your practice.

---

29. Fujita, "Zazen Is Not the Same as Meditation."
30. Fujita, "Zazen Is Not the Same as Meditation."

For this reason, as long as you maintain the right physical posture, Zazen is an open state in which you cannot go wrong; wherever you are is absolutely perfect. You don't have to tame your overactive thoughts. Instead, by focusing on a unified mind-body field, the "head" eventually learns to find its proper place inside reality.

Practice

The practice begins with fixing yourself in a stable, relaxed, and wakeful posture. Your hands are folded into simple mudras (hand gestures) and your legs are in one of the standard sitting styles (explained in the instructions section): full lotus, half lotus, a cross-legged posture, or a kneeling posture using a round cushion. However, modern practitioners often choose to practice Zazen on a chair. As long as you sit comfortably but not too comfortably, all of these options are acceptable. In all positions, you are meant to maintain an erect but settled spine while breathing from the center of your belly. Your eyelids are half-lowered, and your eyes are neither open nor shut. With your eyes in this state, you don't turn away from external stimuli, but at the same time, you remain undistracted by them (if your eyes were closed, you might drift into drowsiness or daydreaming).

During the practice, you learn to perceive body, breath, and mind as one inseparable reality that manifests as your perfect posture. As a result of the inherent stillness that you establish through your physical position, the mind's activity will gradually begin to slow down. From that point onward, all you have to do is give yourself to Zazen wholeheartedly and let go of expectations and self-invented goals. Dogen defined this form of letting go as "thinking of not thinking."[31] Be patient and steady and trust that your mind is fundamentally free, spacious, and vibrant. You don't need to transform your mind, but only to create the right conditions for it to uncover its true, illuminated nature.

According to Master Sheng Yen, the revelation of the mind's true nature happens after you have grown aware of everything that was going on in your mind while never abandoning the awareness of your sitting body. At a certain point, you will experience the "dropping off" of sensations and thoughts and, as a result, you will experience that your body has merged into the great reality. In this silent illumination, the boundaries separating your physical body and everything else will be removed and reality will be experienced as one totality.[32]

31. Zenji, "The Principles of Zazen."
32. Yen, *Attaining the Way*, 163.

Instructions

PREPARATION: The meditation usually lasts between twenty and sixty minutes. Avoid sitting when you are physically exhausted or after a heavy meal.[33]

Choosing Your Leg Position

1. **The Burmese Position:** The legs are crossed and both of the feet and knees rest flat on the floor. (It can sometimes take a bit of stretching for the legs to drop this far.) To make this happen, sit on the front third of a round cushion, slightly shifting your body forward. To straighten your spine, imagine the top of your head pushing toward the ceiling and stretch your body that way—then relax your head, shoulders, back, and abdomen without changing your posture. In this position, it takes very little effort to keep the body upright.

2. **The Half Lotus Position:** The left foot is placed onto the right thigh and the right leg is tucked under. This position is slightly asymmetrical, and sometimes the upper body needs to compensate in order to keep itself absolutely straight.

3. **The Seiza Position:** This can be done without a pillow, kneeling with the buttocks resting on the upturned feet, which form an anatomical cushion. Alternatively, you can use a pillow to keep the weight off your ankles.

4. **Sitting on a Chair:** To help ground the body, keep your feet flat on the floor, or place a cushion beneath you on the chair and sit on the forward third of it. To support your spine, sit forward on the chair.

I have chosen to exclude the full lotus position from this list because it is unrealistic for most meditators.

Preparing Your Position

1. Keep the back straight and centered. Don't slouch; allow the diaphragm to move freely. An upright spine allows your breathing to be deep and natural.

2. Breathe through your nose. Don't control or manipulate the breath.

3. Allow your mouth to be gently closed while your tongue is lightly pressed against the upper palate, behind your front teeth.

---

33. The instructions derive from "Zazen Instructions."

4. Keep your eyes lowered, with your gaze resting on the ground about two to four feet in front of you, lowered at an angle of about forty-five degrees. Instead of focusing on your field of vision, bring your awareness to your breath. If you notice that your awareness has moved to your field of vision, bring it back to your breath. (If you face a plain wall an arm's length away, this should remove possible distractions.) With time, sitting with your eyes open will feel easy.

5. Tuck the chin in slightly so that your neck is an extension of your spine, your nose is centered in line with your navel, and your ears are in a line parallel to your shoulders.

6. Lean neither to the left nor right, neither forward nor backward. To achieve this stability, sway the upper half of your body from left to right a few times. Without moving your hips, move the trunk as if it were a pole leaning to one side then the other, so that the waist and hip muscles are stretched. You may also sway forward and backward. Gradually, the movement will grow smaller and smaller, until your body has become centered in an upright position.

7. Let your muscles soften so that there is little or no tension in the body.

8. Fold your hands in the cosmic mudra that helps to bring your attention inward: your dominant hand is held palm up and holds your other hand, also palm up, so that the knuckles of both hands overlap (if you are right-handed, your right hand holds the left hand, and vice versa if you are left-handed). The thumbs are lightly touching, and thus the hands form an oval, which can rest on your thighs.

9. Direct your attention to the breath. Breath and mind are deeply interrelated, so when your breath is deep, easy, and effortless, your mind becomes relaxed, and vice versa. Specifically, center your attention within the breath in the hara, which is an energy center located two to three inches below your navel.

10. Sit and be in this state of open and undirected practice for at least twenty minutes. Gradually, you may come to enjoy sitting for longer periods—between thirty and sixty minutes. Remain as immovable as possible. Remind yourself that you do not hope to reach anything in your sitting, since the sitting itself takes place inside reality. Do not concentrate on any particular object. However, use your position as your anchor; even if thoughts arise, unify body and mind by keeping your attention focused on the posture, and let the thoughts disappear without leaving a trace. Naturally and unconsciously, the ego's willpower

· · · · · · · ·

will become inactive and no longer search for a goal, and all that remains will be the present moment.

Meditate on This: How to Stop Listening to Your Thoughts

There is no better opportunity to explore the principle of "the thinking machine" than the root chakra group of practices. The understanding of the thinking machine is related to this group for two major reasons.

First, remember that these techniques are the most foundational step we can take on the meditative journey. Because they work with the most accessible element of our being, the physical body, these are usually the techniques through which one is introduced to the meditative world. These fundamental techniques are always followed by one essential instruction: "Stop paying attention to your thoughts." The ability to move from mind to body—not to drop the mind, but to make the mind's attention follow the body—is a crucial learning of this group of meditations. However, if we want to develop this capacity, we first need to understand the thinking process. How can we leave behind something that we don't even fully understand?

Second, the thinking machine is actually the outcome of root chakra imbalance. Although it appears as thoughts, it is really the extension of an instinctual process, and we therefore must learn about it in this context. Put simply, the reason we experience a constant stream of thoughts is because of a root chakra imbalance.

Let's focus on grasping how to follow the instruction to stop paying attention to our thoughts. This instruction is added to the guidelines of almost all meditation techniques, but in this group of techniques, the way we approach our thinking is a part of the focus of the practice itself. How exactly should we deal with the contents of our mind, which so easily draw our attention?

The traditions that have developed and taught these five techniques usually recommend *noting* the passing thoughts to yourself and *generalizing* them. This means that you should never fight thoughts, but only notice them as neutrally as possible and then label them using a general term, like "anger" or "fear." This trick makes the content of your thoughts far less special and, therefore, less interesting.

What fascinates your personality are personal issues; if it concerns *you*, it is interesting. Therefore, the biggest distraction during meditation isn't thinking in general, it's thoughts that are relevant to us personally. That is why generalizing thoughts is a good strategy. When, for example, desire is desire, and not *your* desire for a specific object, it is not so interesting. This trick of generalizing thoughts, however, reflects a deeper understanding of the nature of the thinking machine: the thinking machine is not personal in any case. So generalizing is not just a trick to avoid mental distractions in your meditation, but a clear vision of the world of thought.

. . . .

That fundamental meditation instruction "Stop paying attention to your thoughts" would be better formulated as "Stop paying attention to thought." As long as you believe these are your thoughts, it is actually quite difficult not to listen to them—they seem like *your* business, so you are invested in them. It is only when thoughts are just thoughts that they have the neutral presence and neutral value that make it possible for us to detach from them.

Why We Suffer from "Problem-Consciousness"

So, what is the thinking machine? If you understand it, you will also be free from it—understanding and freedom will take place at the same time. You don't grasp it first and then try to practice it; when you see the thinking machine with perfect clarity, you are instantly free. And seeing it is not so difficult either. This is not some kind of superhuman capacity. You have this intelligent function within your mind. The implications of being freed from the thinking machine, however, are enormous. This marks the difference between being a slave to thoughts and a complete master of them, one that could never be persuaded, controlled, or overpowered by any thought. Even if the thinking machine goes on in the background, you will not care any more than you would about a bird chirping outside.

In so many ways, sitting for meditation is the first time we realize the degree that thinking disturbs and influences us. As long as we are taking action, we can imagine that the thinking machine is somehow relevant, useful, and directly related to our action. It appears as if this mechanism actually works together with our action, helps us respond to what is going on around us, and even supports us in accomplishing our aims. For this reason, we are highly invested in our thoughts and identify with the thought process. It seems helpful to have all these thoughts!

But when we sit for meditation, the big deception is revealed. If you sit and engage in no activity, you have absolutely no reason to think, right? When there is no activity involved, thinking is not relevant. There is no reason to solve problems, because you are not currently involved in a challenge that requires problem-solving. Yet we sit and think! This makes the deception absolutely clear: thinking is often not relevant and not useful, since even when you don't need it, it is still there. You don't need the awareness of problems that thinking constantly produces. On the contrary, you are now determined to connect with a state of no problem, and still you have the feeling of a problem, of unease, of discomfort, as if something constantly tries to pull you away from the moment and keep you busy and in a state of agitation.

Meditation begins to crack the narrative of the thinking machine. It makes you capable of noticing that even when there are no problems whatsoever, there still seems to be a problem. Take, for instance, this very moment, in which you are busy reading these lines. Do you have a problem right now? Just take a moment to observe. For this kind of question, you will need to start using your thoughts to remember: *Yes, as a matter of fact, there are some problems that I have to take care of and worry about! Thanks for reminding me!* But when faced with the question *"Right now,* can there be a problem?" you might realize that it is far more difficult to detect one.

Right now, there is no problem. The sense of problem always involves coming out of the now and returning to the continuity of your life by entering a sort of picture in your head. But when you start meditating, you begin to identify more and more holes in the familiar narrative, because you actually come into contact with more and more moments that are perfectly devoid of the sense of problem. The thinking machine thus finds it increasingly difficult to convince you, until at a certain point, it cannot convince you that there is a problem even when you do face challenging situations. So meditation is a preparation: first you break the story, and second, you start becoming capable of not having a problem, even when there seemingly is one. This is because now you are connected to an underlying reality, to a now-ness that also exists when you have challenges.

But why do we have the sense of problem? What is this problem factory? How did it come into being?

The Birth of the Thinking Machine

To answer that question, let's move back in time—to a prehistoric phase in which a peculiar animal on planet Earth attained the capacity of thinking. This animal took a major leap compared to its previous state, which had been primarily instinct- and biology-based. Of course, this should not be interpreted as belittling animals! We are discovering more and more that so many animal species, and even plants, share our emotional capacities. But what made the human animal special is that it received—for reasons we are still not sure of—the capacity to think.

What happens if you take instinct and mix it with the ability to think? This is the type of thinking that evolved back then: a thinking that mainly involved the capacity to plan ahead. All of a sudden, the survival instinct became more sophisticated and could think backward and forward. This means that humans were able to create some continuity, which included the ability to think long-term, based on clear memories, experiences, and learning. Since the incentive was purely instinctual, they made use of this capacity for survival. What would be the first thing an animal would do if it possessed this capacity? Naturally, it would plan ahead based on previous experiences of danger. It would store these memories and use these experiences for further learning: what to steer clear of, where to be, and where to avoid being altogether. It could also improve its conditions in ways that would make it less susceptible to danger and would make its life more comfortable, like storing food in more sophisticated ways.

So this is the beginning of the thinking machine—and it actually started off really nicely! Any animal could use these skills. In that phase, humans could plan ahead, avoid dangers based on previous experiences, and even run scenarios in their heads: "If I go there, these are my possibilities; if I go here, these are my possibilities." This obviously gave human beings power that was unprecedented in the animal kingdom, because this power was more potent than physical power. Humans could actually create patterns of behavior and action. This also led to inventiveness. Human imagination was used to create tools that allowed people to avoid danger and live more comfortable lives.

Of course, this is not a book about history and evolution. Our focus is on what we currently find in our mind when we meditate: the upgraded form of the thinking machine. However, it is really important to understand that the thinking machine is actually a protective mechanism, a survival mechanism that just got out of hand. Let's find out how this has taken place, stage by stage.

1. **As the thinking machine became more sophisticated, it developed a constant wish to improve conditions.** This is what we find in our current world, in the form of technology: constantly making everything more comfortable, easier, faster, and more accessible. This seems to improve our lives, but it actually makes them more frantic. It makes people move faster and also become more restless.

2. **Ultimately, improving conditions means that the thinking machine looks for ways to decrease pain and increase pleasure all the time.** But there is never enough of these conditions! This is why the thinking machine has gotten out of hand: it tries to protect you by helping you look for better ways to avoid pain and find pleasure. Thus, it keeps driving you to hope that one day, you will indeed have these ideal conditions, that your life will become so much better and happier in the future. It works all day and all night to try to create these conditions for you. Think of it like a futuristic robot that malfunctions.

3. **This constant search leads to constant control over every moment.** The thinking machine needs to make sure that everything is going exactly as planned and anticipated at any given moment. Thus, it predicts, then tries to fulfill the prediction. This is a massive reason for existential tension. We are constantly under stress because the thinking machine tries to make sure that conditions are perfect and that there is not even a single disturbance. Control leads to comparison: life is never as it should be because of certain conditions, and then when conditions are not met, something is wrong. The thinking machine places "reality as it should be" and "reality as it is" side by side. And it keeps creating tension, because obviously, how could you like a reality that is never as it should be?

4. **From there, it moves on to constant dissatisfaction.** The thinking machine convinces you that if you only had the right conditions, you would finally be

satisfied. It produces all sorts of mental pictures: if you only found the right partner, or had the perfect career, then you would finally be satisfied according to the prediction of your happiness. This search for happiness is the great deception of the thinking machine. In fact, being free from the search for happiness is probably the only happiness we will ever find! After all, even if you end up going to heaven, if you haven't left the thinking machine behind, it will sooner or later make life in heaven a kind of hell. There is no situation in which the thinking machine can be satisfied because it is by nature dissatisfied, forever searching for better conditions. If you understand this process, you will realize that the dissatisfaction that "you" experience is never going to be fulfilled. It is not meant to be fulfilled, and it cannot be fulfilled. Even more, you will realize that it is not you who is dissatisfied—this is not *your* dissatisfaction. It is this thinking machine that is dissatisfied.

5. **On top of this constant dissatisfaction, there is an additional layer of worry.** Worry is an inseparable part of the thinking machine. Worrying is simply the constant attempt of the thinking machine to predict and its hope that the prediction will be successful. We worry because of this protective mechanism that we obey.

6. **Then, this mental process leads to an expanded experience of danger.** Danger has gradually become so much more than physical survival; an insult can feel dangerous, and it can even feel dangerous when we don't get our perfect holiday! "Dangerous" is now anything that is not our hoped-for perfect conditions. The more comfortable we feel and the more our lives improve, the worse the thinking machine becomes. The thinking machine has become so separated from reality that even people who have so much feel utterly miserable.

7. **This naturally leads us to head-dominance.** What governs our lives is the head, for the simple reason that it is the most convincing part of our being. What could be more important than this stream of thoughts? Eventually, we find ourselves most identified with and invested in the world of our thoughts, and our attention is automatically drawn to it.

8. **Finally, we find ourselves in an eternal search.** The thinking machine causes us to believe that life is always elsewhere, and we are always missing out on something since there is a better life somewhere. Thus, we forever search, and we forever long for that promised reality.

. . . .

The Law of Attention

When we understand how radically fooled we have been by this mechanism, we can move away from it. We begin to notice this mechanism in meditation, since meditation is normally a time when you don't need your survival instinct to be active. While it is generally good to keep some of the survival instinct active, you certainly don't need to have it consistently turned on and so intensely sophisticated. Without a doubt, in meditation you don't need the survival instinct, and you don't need to combat any challenge or use your prediction skills.

In fact, by looking at all these layers of the thinking machine, you can safely realize that you have nothing to do with any of them. This entire mechanism is not who you really are. Noticing thoughts and generalizing them while in meditation can go on for eternity, and each time you will need to free yourself from the specific thoughts that you have at that moment. But if you grasp the mechanism as a whole, you will no longer need to deal with specific thoughts. You will see that all these ingredients of the thinking machine create your entire mental world at any given moment.

The mental world is not all bad. It has three wonderful capacities: intelligence, creativity, and spirituality. So we shouldn't turn against our mental world—we should become aware of the underlying problem-consciousness. We should become fully conscious of all the elements of the thinking machine that hide beneath all our thoughts, even when our thoughts appear to be highly nuanced and special. Our thoughts are actually not special at all. They all consist of the search for increased pleasure and the avoidance of pain; of control over every moment; of comparing every moment to an imagined alternate reality; of eternal dissatisfaction, worry, expanded experiences of danger, and eternal searching. If we look closely into each of our thoughts, we will discover that they all somehow fall into these categories.

The good thing is that we don't have to be identified with any of this. This is what meditation begins to teach us: we can easily separate attention from thinking. Attention, after all, is not thinking. Mostly, we are unaware of this distinction, since our attention is glued to our thinking, as if it were one process. We hardly notice that there is a gap between attention and thinking, but in this gap our entire freedom lies. This is what I call *the law of attention*.

The law of attention consists of two basic principles:

1. Only what we decide to give attention to becomes real. Everything else remains unreal. It is up to us alone. We thus possess the greatest power in the universe: attention.

2. If we place our attention on something for long enough, we become one with it. What we focus on becomes who we are. However, based on principle 1, we don't have to become one with anything we choose not to pay attention to.

. . . .

When you begin to perceive this gap, you understand that *you* give the power to thoughts. There are no powerful thoughts. No one in the world can claim that a certain thought is too powerful and too overwhelming to handle. Thoughts cannot take over you unless you let them do so.

According to the law of attention, when you believe a certain thought, it becomes your reality. But there is more: only thought can make your reality seem conflicted and problematic. What troubles, disappoints, frustrates, saddens, or confuses you are thoughts about reality, not reality itself. For instance, if you believe the elementary thought that life is elsewhere, as a result, you experience longing, sorrow, depression, and an inner split. This has nothing to do with reality. Reality doesn't depress, disappoint, or anger you—only your thinking about reality can do that. Since this is just a matter of believing a thought, it is completely up to you; you can withdraw your power of attention and cease to make it a reality.

If you are immersed in meditation and find yourself believing a thought too much, and are unable to dissociate yourself from it by noting it to yourself and generalizing it, try the following inquiry process. This form of quick inquiry will remind you of the law of attention, your choice of identification, and the fact that *you* give the thought power.

This inquiry consists of five simple questions. However, even answering one of them may be enough to release you from the false sense of powerlessness.

1. Is this thought a reality or just a thought?

2. Do I have to give it attention? (If you are convinced that you have to give it attention, answer: why do you have to do so *now*? Justify your choice.)

3. What happens in my body, emotions, and behavior when I give this thought attention? (This is an important key; answering this will make it clear to you that the experience of suffering is caused by believing a thought.)

4. What could happen in my body, emotions, and behavior if I stopped giving this thought attention? (This is one more way to discover that thought creates problem-consciousness, while reality has very little to do with it.)

5. What happens when I remember that I actually have a choice, that I am completely free? (Now you can decide if you want to be free and happy, or at least consciously decide to be miserable.)

If you are not awake enough at that moment to work directly with a thought, here are four questions to ask when you feel unhappy, dissatisfied, frustrated, angry, or sad. When you find

. . . .

yourself in a negative state, it is because some unconscious thought is controlling you, one that you believe without even noticing it.

1. What is the thought that is making me feel like this? (This is how you expose the mechanism.)

2. Now that I know what thought it is, do I have to give it attention? (This helps to return the power of attention to your mind.)

3. Can I find the gap of choice? (Is there a choice here, or am I in the hands of a powerful monster?)

4. What happens when I move my attention away from this thought?

Realizing that this is all a matter of choice, there is absolutely no good reason for us to experience any of it. The thinking machine will do its best to convince you that it is there to help you improve your conditions and that not listening to it will leave you stuck and miserable. Gently remind yourself that you can always improve the conditions of your life, and you can do so harmoniously, not frantically, because you are free from the thought that if you didn't do so, your life would be a disaster.

CHAPTER 5

Sacral Chakra Meditations: Experience the Joy of Life

If you start reading this chapter with curiosity, thrilled at the knowledge that you are about to delve into a new dimension of meditation, it means that your sacral chakra is already "on." When this chakra is "off," we are pervaded by the feeling that there is not much to look forward to—what could possibly be discovered at this point that is not already known to us?

Physically, this chakra of surprising discoveries and experiences is associated with the lower abdomen, more precisely the area of the pubic bone just above the sexual organs. This chakra includes the sexual organs, the pelvic region, and the kidneys. Learning briefly about its roles and functions can help illuminate the second group of meditations.

Traditionally speaking, the second chakra is often treated as a sort of "bad chakra" because it is generally related to the realm of temptation, desire, and the subconscious. It is mainly discussed for the purpose of inner purification: how can we get rid of all its imprints and transcend obsessions and addictions?

On the other hand, the sacral chakra is also associated with the power of kundalini. Kundalini is a reservoir of life force that resides in the root chakra. It is mostly in a dormant state, and in fact, every meditation draws on this reservoir and activates it more and more. But while this reservoir of life force lies dormant in the root chakra, when it rises to the sacral chakra, it explodes with great intensity. This makes the sacral chakra deeply connected with kundalini energy.

The fact that this is the region of uncontrolled impulses, desires, and unconscious forces in us could understandably make us fear this chakra since it is untamed, like a wild horse. Its elusive ocean of feelings—which include what we sometimes call "gut feelings," but also the well-known "butterflies in the stomach"—is something that the rational mind doesn't know how to deal with and control. As a last resort, the mind represses a great deal of these feelings, hence the sacral chakra being the seat of the unconscious.

In light of this, it is clear why traditional views preferred to transcend this chakra and often considered it an obstacle. However, this chakra is far from an obstacle. In fact, we could call it the chakra of life.

The Birth of Inner Joy

There is no other chakra that better represents the actual experience of life. It is true that the root chakra is also strongly related to a primal connection to life, but the root chakra is our instinct-based center, whereas the sacral chakra is our impulses or urges. It is our connection to life through feeling. It has nothing to do with how we react to life's dangers. It revolves around the questions: Do we dare to fully enter this life with all its experiences? Do we dare to experience with totality, and to feel fully?

From the root chakra's perspective, the universe is either dangerous or safe. But seen from the world of the sacral chakra, the cosmos is a celebration or explosion of energies, shapes, forms, and colors. It is filled with vibrating energy, passion, and desire. The cosmos is like the work of an artistic genius. Why would it need this overwhelming diversity, which includes humans, koalas, giraffes, and over 900,000 types of insects? Why would it need all this creativity? Even though the science of evolution tells us that this creativity is merely the outcome of survival responses to the environment, this doesn't satisfy our poetic nature. Why all the stunning complexity of colors and shapes? This cannot be all about instinctual adjustment, surely. Can't we think of the universe as an incredibly imaginative artist, too?

Through the eyes of the sacral chakra, this creative cosmic burst came into being as a form of divine play. The yogis of the past termed this *Leela*, "God's play" in Sanskrit. The universe is a joyous exploration and experimentation. For this reason, if you wish to be one with this divine play, a powerful way to do so is through your own artistic, aesthetic, and poetic impulses. These connect you with this primal urge for creativity that has no purpose. Naturally, this is a very specific angle to look from: some may think it is rather unfair, even cruel, that the divine created all this, suffering included, just for pure fun. However, perceiving the universe as a divine play is a valid and often liberating perspective.

The question the sacral chakra asks is whether or not we will participate in life's celebration. Are we game? Are we going to allow our own creative urge to be a part of it? Or are we going to stay away from the celebration and remain disconnected? When we choose to remain disconnected, the main sacral chakra feeling is depression. Depression is the feeling of being disconnected from the creative participation in life.

We can identify the elements of the celebration in the creativity of nature and in our own creativity, but also in the great pleasures of the earth. When you eat good food, listen to music, dance, experience your sexuality, or enjoy looking at something beautiful, you begin to get in touch with the different pleasures that the earth has to offer.

On the other hand, if you develop attachment to these pleasures or identify the celebration of life in them alone, you are in trouble, since pleasure is fleeting. Our journey through the sacral chakra should be a much deeper one. It is not about contacting life through its obvious fun parts; it is about contacting life as one movement, one river of life force, and being able to preserve a sense of inner joy regardless of whatever takes place. Just like the root chakra meditations' gift of inner stability, the gift of the sacral chakra is the ability to establish inner joy and a sense of aliveness that doesn't diminish when pleasures and joys disappear.

Feeling alive is very different from being alive. Everyone is technically alive, but many don't really *feel* alive. Aliveness is our level of connection to the life force in us and all around us. And it is a sense that can be enhanced and cultivated, since the life force that bubbles inside our bodies is highly potent and largely unused. Most of us use only a fraction of our life force, mainly for daily functions. Being able to intensify this sense of aliveness, regardless of changing conditions of pleasure or pain, is the achievement of the sacral chakra meditations.

Put simply, sacral chakra meditation is all about being truly joyful, and not because of anything specific that is happening currently or will happen in the future. This joy should exist in you not because of external stimuli, but because of enjoyment that comes from within. This is the enjoyment of life itself. Life itself never loses this enjoyment; it is continuously this vibrating energy.

For this reason, although both the root chakra and the sacral chakra meditation techniques are physical and work directly with our material existence, this is not the same type of physicality. The root chakra meditations aim for stability, balance, strength, and health, whereas the sacral chakra covers techniques that prefer the physical dimension of ecstatic movement, pleasure, sexuality, and life force energy.

The sacral chakra interacts with life through what we may call the juices of life. This is a very good metaphor, because these are actual "juices": the sacral chakra is connected with the water element of the body, with its fluidity. Metaphorically, this becomes a question of whether our life force is flowing, and whether we allow the river of life to flow freely.

Life's juices can be allowed to flow when we fearlessly let experiences happen. Fundamentally, the sacral chakra doesn't care about the future or the past, and more generally, it doesn't recognize the continuum of time. What it cares about is the present: our experience right now.

· · · · · · ·

That is why its purpose cannot be fulfilled through slow building. We may feel "sacral chakra anticipation" when it comes to future experiences we are excited about, but in the deepest sense, this chakra can only be fulfilled here and now. Being the chakra of the here and now, this is also the chakra of appreciation and recognition of the beauty and value in every fleeting moment, like the sunlight caressing your cheeks a second before it is covered by clouds.

An experience is any opportunity we have to contact life's energies and forces through our feelings. This calls for a quick explanation of what feelings are, at least in our context. Sometimes we confuse feelings and emotions. Emotions are actually associated with the heart chakra, in which we have connections between ourselves and others. In these relationships, in the gap between me and others, all sorts of emotions arise: emotions that connect us with other people and beings, or emotions that move us away from them. This is how we experience heart connection and heart disconnection. Feelings, on the other hand, are about our direct connecting points with life's different experiences. They are the way we interact with our experience, not with significant others.

Sometimes we say "This was very powerful" or "I've never felt so alive" or "Just thinking about this experience fills me with excitement." Feelings, then, are the way we evaluate the degree of life that we felt in a certain experience. And when there is no feeling—when our feeling center is numb—this is experienced as depression. Suddenly, life seems terribly dull, flat, and boring, and we don't understand the point of anything. This is a turned-off sacral chakra.

The feeling center needs to be awakened so that we are able to experience very deeply. The depth and intensity of an experience depends on the depth and intensity of our feeling capacity. This is a central element that the sacral chakra activates in us: our ability to feel and experience with totality.

The Different Purposes of Sacral Chakra Meditations

In this chapter we will study five sacral chakra meditation techniques. Each meditation has at least one of the following roles and purposes.

1. **Arousing joy as a healing factor, both physically and emotionally.** Joy is best represented in this group of techniques by the principle of the inner smile. It means identifying an inherent source of joy in us, an indestructible type of joy that hides beneath and behind all our disappointments and frustrations. When we recognize this inner joy, we are able to use it as an effective healer of both our body and our emotional reality.

2. **Contacting and activating our unconditional and unaffected joy.** This is represented by a similar principle: inner laughter. Inner laughter reveals to us that we

can be joyful at this very moment regardless of our current problems, issues, and processes. Believing that we can only be joyful when conditions allow is what is called *conditional joy*, which is an expression of the unbalanced sacral chakra.

3. **Allowing deep catharsis that unravels tensions and pains.** *Catharsis* means physical and emotional release. If the catharsis goes deep, it has the power to uproot tensions and pains that have been accumulated in both body and mind.

4. **Awakening spiritual ecstasy.** *Ecstasy*, a word we use so freely nowadays, is an ancient Greek term that originally meant self-forgetfulness, or being outside of oneself.[34] It comes from the world of Dionysus, the god of religious ecstasy (among other things). A true celebration was considered one in which you could forget yourself, completely becoming one with your experience. While meditation is mostly concerned with learning the art of neutral and detached observation, our ability to be utterly absorbed in an experience is also an important aspect of meditation.

5. **Allowing bodily deconditioning.** Our bodies have been socially adapted to a degree that we no longer remember what it means to experience natural, flow-ing movement, the type of movement sometimes observed in animals. *Bodily deconditioning* means freeing our body from all the social taboos that inhibit its free-flowing movement. Currently, this conditioning controls the way we breathe, stand, and walk, and the degree to which we feel comfortable and set-tled in it. The twenty-first-century mystic Osho developed a long list of dynamic meditations to allow the overly stiff and rigid body of the meditator to shake off this conditioning prior to the practice of silent sitting. His perspective was that dynamic meditations should precede even the fundamental root chakra medita-tions, since the body is just too agitated and unnatural to become immersed in meditative peace. This agitation then takes the form of a highly active thinking machine.

6. **Revealing body-mind unity through joyful movement.** In the root chakra group of techniques, I presented the principle of body-mind unity: being mindful in the sense that my mind is focused on the activity of the body, I become one with my action. Sacral chakra meditations reveal the very same unity through joyful move-ment. They draw the mind to participate in a movement so ecstatic that it drowns

---

34. *Encyclopaedia Britannica Online*, s.v. "ecstasy," last modified October 7, 2019, https://www.britannica.com/topic/ecstasy-religion.

• • • • • • • •

our senses. Even more deeply, we can say that the solution of the sacral chakra meditations is simply to drown the thinking machine in experience—if the experience is intense, the thinking machine doesn't stand a chance because it becomes steeped in it.

7. **Maximizing the experience of pleasure.** According to this principle, we don't really know how to experience pleasure. As long as we experience pleasure in small quantities, we will never know its real potential. Sacral chakra meditations sometimes teach us how to intensify pleasurable moments and sensations and to expand them such that they become a gateway to transcendent states.

8. **Learning to appreciate the depth and intensity of small joys.** Sometimes we look for big joys, big experiences, because we have taken for granted the small joys. A balanced sacral chakra would notice extremely fleeting moments of joy, like the sunlight on your face, the air, the water, certain foods, and the beauty of a jumping squirrel. We need to learn to return to small joys for the simple reason that we don't experience them well enough to be able to move to the big joys. And when you are able to fully experience a small joy, it becomes so explosive that eventually you can move in even subtler directions, searching for the essence of joy itself, where no experience is needed.

9. **Using breathing as a gateway to ecstasy.** We can use breathing not only to center ourselves (as we do in the root chakra meditations) or to control our mind (as we will learn to do in the solar plexus chakra meditations). We can manipulate breathing in a way that makes us feel "high." There are plenty of sacral chakra breathing manipulations that can achieve exactly that.

10. **Learning to access and enhance our life force.** Sacral chakra meditations show us what the life force actually is by way of experience. Moreover, they introduce us to ways we can work with it. This is done by noticing the existence of different expressions of the life force in us and following them. The life force, as the life within us, becomes a tangible element that can be greatly empowered, which implies becoming increasingly more alive.

11. **Learning to face our uncontrolled, unconscious energies.** Yes, the sacral chakra contains unknown energies, which we can befriend. These energies are not really dangerous; they seem dangerous only as long as you fear them, repress them, and make them accumulate in the dark. When, through sacral chakra meditations, you are determined to transcend your fear and meet these energies directly, you

realize for yourself that it is just joy that has been repressed, and as a result has become twisted.

12. **Going through unexplained experiences.** For the most part, meditations are very reasonable and therefore explainable, and when you enter them, you may keep on thinking in order to interpret and understand what is going on. Sacral chakra meditations, however, are not about explaining and gaining clear insight. You may come out of the meditation with some understanding, but only as a by-product. Very often, sacral chakra meditations simply create a perfect setting for a total experience while encouraging you to suspend the obvious need to understand. These meditations invite you to enter an actual adventure.

13. **Learning the spiritual potential of base energies and allowing kundalini to rise through them.** These meditations help us realize through direct experience that our base energies are spiritually potent. When used correctly, our spirituality can emerge from these energies. Thus, what is unique about this group of techniques is that it embraces these energies and transforms them into meditative power.

14. **Learning to transform sexual energy.** We learn how to face sexual energy and how to maximize its potential. After all, the sacral chakra governs the sexual organs and, as a result, our entire sexual experience, as well as sexual energy. Here we need to differentiate between sexual energy and sexual activity: Sexual energy is like the raw power of our sexuality. Coming into contact with this energy is one of the profound revelations of this group of meditations.

15. **Being able to detach from earthly pleasures.** This group is not only about allowing and maximizing earthly pleasures—ultimately, it develops our ability to release the need for such pleasures. This is the final result of our transformation of basic energies. First, we allow them to flow freely, and once they are finally fulfilled, we attain the capacity to go beyond them.

Inner Smile

Inner smile meditation activates the principle of the inner smile to remove all the energetic blockages that inhibit the flow of chi within our body. In this sense, this is both a technique for self-healing and a meditative process that directly connects us to the experience of the inner smile and the state of a fully flowing life force.

Historical Background

The roots of Taoism go back at least to the late fourth century BCE, when Lao Tzu, one of its founders, created his masterwork *Tao Te Ching*. Taoism emphasizes living in harmony with the *Tao* (literally, the "way" or the "path"), which is the ultimate creative principle of the universe. Being aligned with the Tao gives rise to qualities such as action without intention, naturalness, simplicity, and spontaneity.

Inner smile meditation is one of the most foundational and well-known practices of Taoist *Neidan gong* ("inner elixir skill"), also known as inner alchemy: an array of esoteric doctrines and physical, mental, and spiritual practices that Taoist initiates use to prolong life and ultimately to form an immortal spiritual body that can withstand death. These practices offer a systematic and repeatable "science" of changing oneself in accordance with natural law, but far more quickly. This type of alchemy is made possible only when the initiate grasps the hidden essence of life and becomes sufficiently aware of chi flow in their body.

The inner smile was the first step of seven highly secretive inner alchemy "formulas" for accelerating the stages of human spiritual development. However, it also plays an important role in all other "formulas," including the seventh and most advanced one (the union of human and Tao). This implies that the inner smile is both the easiest method for beginners and a key to the highest level of realization.[35]

I have used here a version of the technique transmitted by the Taoist master Mantak Chia.

Purpose

According to ancient Tao masters, the secret of the inner smile is hidden within our innermost heart, which is the abode of the indestructible and forever-unaffected reality within us (see also the Inner Cave of the Heart in chapter 7). Directing this energy into our body may melt stuck or frozen energy patterns without struggle. Since the inner smile is noninvasive, all-accepting, and powerful, it doesn't need to attack sick energies inside us—it softly stimulates the chi, the subtle breath, and thus heals without effort.

Our ability to arouse an internal smiling energy as a way to healing and to meditative presence is not exclusively Taoist. For example, the Buddhist monk and teacher Thich Nhat Hanh, who strongly advocated intentional smiling as a spiritual practice, declared that "sometimes your joy is the source of your smile, but sometimes your smile can be the source of your joy."[36]

35. Winn, *Way of the Inner Smile.*
36. Riggio, "There's Magic in Your Smile."

This claim—that we can enjoy the benefits of smiling by choosing to smile at this very moment—is backed by recent science. Smiling, even without an external trigger, can activate neural messaging that benefits health and happiness: it activates the release of neuropeptides that work toward fighting off stress, as well as the "feel-good" neurotransmitters—dopamine, endorphins, and serotonin. This relaxes our body, lowers heart rate and blood pressure, lengthens our life span, and, thanks to the endorphins, even acts as a natural pain reliever.

Practice

Using visualization and intention, we evoke the smiling energy and channel it through our subtle body, affecting our organs and energy centers. By wrapping our organs and energy centers with loving-kindness and compassion, we transform stored negative emotions associated with specific organs into positive virtues and pure life force. In this way, we prevent these emotions from taking root in the body and turning into discomfort and disease; instead, we harness them for spiritual growth.

This process of successive attention to body parts in order to purify them may seem similar to the Body Scan technique (see chapter 4). But unlike Body Scan, which utilizes the power of neutral awareness, inner smile makes use of the gratitude, appreciation, and smiling wisdom of the sacral chakra. These qualities can also increase our sense of intimacy and communion with our body, since we constantly acknowledge the function of overlooked body parts along the way.

Although our inner smile aims to ultimately cover the entire body, we will focus on five organ systems: the heart, the lungs, the kidneys, the liver and gallbladder, and the stomach and spleen. This focus is directly related to the "emotional intelligence" that the Tao wishes to awaken in us: the wisdom of recognizing the relationship between emotional energies and organ systems.

- The heart is associated with the negative emotions of arrogance and hate and the positive virtues of kindness and love.

- The lungs are associated with the negative emotions of sadness and depression and the positive virtues of courage and righteousness.

- The kidneys are associated with the negative emotion of fear and the positive emotions of gentleness and kindness.

- The liver is associated with the negative emotion of anger and the positive emotions of generosity and forgiveness.

- The stomach and spleen are associated with the negative emotions of worry and anxiety and the positive emotions of fairness and openness.

· · · · · · · ·

Thus, throughout this meditative journey, we turn hatred into love, sadness into courage, fear into gentleness, anger into generosity, and worry into openness.

Instructions

PREPARATION: This meditation requires between twenty and thirty minutes.

1. Sit comfortably near the edge of your chair with your feet flat on the floor. Keep your back straight but not stiff. Stay relaxed, and clasp your palms together in your lap. Gently press your tongue against the upper palate of your mouth. Close your eyes.

2. Create a source of smiling energy in front of you. This can be an image of your own smiling face, an image of someone or something you love and respect, or a memory of a time you felt deeply at peace, perhaps feeling the sunshine, being by the ocean, or walking in a forest.

3. Become aware of the midpoint between your eyebrows, through which you will draw this abundant smiling energy in front of and around you. Let your forehead relax. As the smiling energy accumulates at the mid-brow, it will eventually overflow into your body. Note: you can return to the source of smiling energy to get more energy at any time during the meditation.

4. Allow the smiling energy to flow down from the mid-brow through your face, relaxing the cheeks, nose, mouth, and all the facial muscles. Let it flow down through your neck. You can roll your head slowly and gently from side to side as you do this.

5. Let the smiling energy continue to flow down to your thymus gland, which is located behind the upper part of your sternum, and picture it glowing with vibrant health. Feel the thymus gland become warm as it begins to vibrate and expand like a blossoming flower.

6. You should feel your entire chest cavity filling with smiling, loving energy. Smile to the heart to make it softer. Transmit through your smile the light of the source of life and let the heart radiate in response. Express gratitude for the heart for its most vital activity.

7. The lungs are associated with the negative emotional energies of sadness and depression and the virtuous energies of courage and righteousness. When you

smile into the lungs, dissolve any sadness or negative feelings, creating space for courage and righteousness to expand.

8. Next, direct the smiling energy to the liver, located just below the right lung. Feel the liver become immersed in smiling, loving, joyous energy. The liver is associated with the emotion of anger and the virtue of kindness. When you smile to the liver, dissolve any anger and allow the kindness energy more space to expand.

9. Let the smiling energy flow from the liver across the abdomen into the spleen, located directly beneath the left lung. As you smile into the spleen, see that it is healthy and functioning smoothly.

10. Continuing around to the left, smile into the pancreas, which is just next to the left kidney. Don't worry if you don't know exactly where it is. If you smile in that direction, you will gradually get in touch with it. If you need to, return to the source of smiling energy in front of you, and let the smiling energy flow in through the mid-brow and down to the area of the pancreas.

11. As smiling, loving energy builds up in the spleen, let it flow into the kidneys. Smile down to the kidneys and feel them expand with radiant energy. The kidneys are associated with the emotion of fear. As you smile into them, fear melts away, and the virtue of gentleness can grow. Keep smiling into the kidneys, and let the smiling energy build up until they are full.

12. Next, send the smiling energy down into the urinary bladder, urethra, genitals, and perineum. The collection point for the sexual energy is located about three inches below the navel. Smile the accumulated energies into the sex organs. Bring the combined sexual, smiling, and virtue energies up to the navel, and visualize the energies spiraling into that point.

13. Return your attention to the source of smiling energy in front of you. Be aware of the mid-brow point, and allow more smiling energy to flow in through it like a waterfall pouring down into the organs. Once again, immerse the thymus, heart, lungs, liver, pancreas, spleen, kidneys, urinary bladder, and sex organs in smiling energy.

14. Become aware once more of the smiling energy in your eyes. Let it flow down to your mouth. Become aware of your tongue, and make some saliva by working your mouth and swishing your tongue around. Put the tip of your tongue to the roof of the mouth, tighten the neck muscles, and swallow the saliva. With

your inner smile, follow the saliva down the esophagus to the stomach, located at the bottom and below the left side of the rib cage. Make a promise to your stomach that you will give it good food to digest.

15. Smile into the small intestine in the middle of the abdomen. It is about seven meters long in an adult. Thank it for absorbing nutrients to keep you healthy. Then smile into the large intestine, which is about one and a half meters long. Thank it for eliminating waste and for making you feel clean, fresh, and open. Smile at it and feel it as warm, comfortable, and calm.

16. Return to your eyes. Quickly smile down the midline, checking for tension. Smile into the tension until it melts away. Smile inward with both eyes; collect the power of the smile in the third eye (mid-brow). With your inner eyesight, direct your smile into the pituitary gland, and feel the gland blossom. Smile into the thalamus, from where the truth and power of the smile will be generated. Smile into the pineal gland and feel this tiny gland gradually swell and grow like a bulb. Move your smile's eyesight like a bright, shining light up to the left side of the brain. Move the inner smiling eyesight back and forth in the left brain and across to the right brain and cerebellum. This may balance the left and right brain and strengthen the nerves.

17. Move the inner smiling eyesight down to the midbrain. Feel it expand and soften and go down to the pons and medulla oblongata and to the spinal cord, starting from the cervical vertebrae at the base of the skull. Move the inner smiling eyesight, bringing this loving energy down inside each vertebra and the disk below it, all the way to the tailbone. Feel the spinal cord and the back becoming loose and comfortable. Feel the disks softening. Feel your spine expanding and elongating, making you taller.

18. Return to your eyes and quickly smile down the entire back line. Your whole body should feel relaxed. Attention to the back line increases the flow of the spinal fluid and sedates the nervous system. Smiling into a disk can keep it from hardening and becoming unable to properly absorb the force and weight of the body. Back pain can be prevented or relieved by smiling into the spine.

19. Start at the eyes again. Direct your inner smile's eyesight. Quickly smile down the front line. Follow the smiling down the midline and then the back line. Now, feel the energy descend down the entire length of your body, like a waterfall—a waterfall of smiles, joy, and love. Feel your whole body being loved and appreciated. Allow a full body smile!

• • • • • • • •

20. Store the smiling energy in the navel. The navel area can safely handle the increased energy generated by the inner smile. To collect the smile's energy, concentrate on your navel area, which is about one and a half inches inside your body. Then mentally move that energy in an outward spiral around your navel. Then, reverse the direction of the spiral and bring it back into the navel. The energy is now safely stored in your navel, available to you whenever you need it and for whatever part of your body needs it.

AFTER THE MEDITATION: There are two ways to continue with this meditation. Either smile deliberately and physically whenever you can, especially when it is unrelated to your current situation, or keep on visualizing this smiling presence or energy in front of you and let it flow through your third eye into your body.

Note that you may also apply the inner smile principle to your chakras; this could release the healing and soothing power of the seven energy centers. Place your hands on the area of the chakra and allow the smiling energy to flow into it and permeate it. When the chakra smiles, it begins to function optimally.

Mystic Rose

Mystic Rose, considered by Osho to be his most essential meditative therapy, is a three-hour-a-day process that lasts for three weeks and is done under experienced guidance in his meditation centers around the world. Osho named it "Mystic Rose" because he believed the process may lead the individual to a state in which their being "blossoms and opens all its petals and releases its beautiful fragrance."[37] The following active meditation is a highly condensed form of the technique, which derives from Osho's book *Meditation: The First and Last Freedom*.

Historical Background

Born as Chandra Mohan Jain and also known as Bhagwan Shree Rajneesh, Osho (1931–1990) was an Indian mystic and the founder of the Rajneesh movement.

One of Osho's most significant contributions to contemporary spirituality has been his innovative approach to meditation. He designed more than a hundred meditations in total, some of

---

37. Osho, *Meditation*, 188–96.

which were a development of a vast range of techniques that he gathered from various world traditions, while others were completely original (see chapter 9's Center of Sound technique).

Among Osho's original techniques, the most notable ones are forms of active meditation, characterized by stages of physical activity (including catharsis, wild dancing, and rapid breathing) and culminating in silence and the state of "witnessing," or pure, nonattached awareness. This type of active meditation came into being as a result of Osho's observation that modern people were too tense and conditioned to simply sit and enter meditation. Thus, many of his meditations can be perceived as both meditation practices and techniques that prepare the individual for meditation. In addition, Osho's meditations were developed with awareness of Western psychotherapy and often integrated elements of psychotherapy into the practice.

In a later stage of his life, Osho introduced a series of meditative therapies, among them Mystic Rose.

Purpose

I once met a spiritual teacher who belonged to Osho's tradition of meditation. He briefly summarized his journey of spiritual awakening with these words: "For nine months I was only laughing; then, for nine months, I was only crying; and later, for nine more months, I was laughing. After these three cathartic cycles, there have been no more tears and no more laughter; only silence has remained."

This principle of transformation is both powerful and simple: if you follow your laughter to its end, and then follow your tears to their end, you will naturally go beyond these two emotional extremes and find not only relief but also profound silence. The conditioned sacral chakra forever pursues pleasure and seeks to avoid pain; it clings to the former and fears the latter. But the enlightened sacral chakra embraces with totality these two seemingly opposing experiences, and as a result, leaps beyond both to a state of unconditional, transcendent joy.

According to Osho, both laughter and tears have been considered culturally unwelcome: we have been taught not to cry too much, but also not to laugh too readily. Consequently, we conceal our agony and prevent our true ecstasy from fully taking place. For this reason, Mystic Rose is both meditation and therapy, or, in Osho's language, meditation and medicine: we free our body, mind, and heart from cultural inhibitions and dissolve the two psychic layers that are the major hindrance to the ultimate state of silent witnessing.

In Osho's view, skipping to the transcendent and detached state without cathartically releasing our stored laughter and tears would only lead to an "automatically suppressive" type of witnessing. On the other hand, if you first thoroughly empty your being of these suppressed energies, your mind will effortlessly blossom into a vast state of meditation.

• • • • • • •

Practice

This hour-long, condensed form of Mystic Rose consists of three consecutive stages: you start with laughter meditation, move on to crying meditation, and end in a natural state of silent witnessing. However, you may also divide the process into two separate meditations, practicing either "laughter meditation" or "crying meditation" and culminating in deep silence. Both have been taught by many meditation teachers as independent practices. Interestingly, you may realize that even when you separate the processes, your laughter will occasionally transform into tears and your tears into laughter. Allow this to happen; in a sense, these are complementary opposites, two ends that meet and converge when followed all the way.

In both processes, Osho emphasizes the importance of finding the laughter and tears that are already inside you rather than attempting to produce them. All you have to do is to allow the mysterious and completely unreasonable inner laughter to arise in you, here and now, like a flower blossoms on a tree. In this way, you establish a connection with the quality of independent, authentic joy that is hidden in your depths. Similarly, in your crying, you simply provoke the tears that have accumulated in you for years. The power of intentional tears lies in their ability to melt away suppressed feelings. Thus, concealed layers of pain may be revealed as soon as the superficial layers are expressed and removed.

Instructions

PREPARATION: This meditation requires sixty minutes.

Stage I: Laughter (Twenty Minutes)

PREPARATION: Start by relaxing your being through some movement or stretching. Massage your jaw and yawn widely at least twice to loosen your mouth and relax your jaw muscles. Find a comfortable sitting position (for some, lying down may relax the stomach muscles and allow laughter to flow more easily). Since the emphasis is not on generating laughter but on *finding* your inner laughter, keep your eyes closed.

1. Contact the inner laughter that awaits you at the depth of your being. Start by smiling slightly, and then begin laughing without too much effort. From giggling like a child, gradually move to deep belly laughs. Try different types of laughs to encourage your true laughter to come through. Even if it begins as a forced, artificial feeling, most people find that the forced laughter catalyzes authentic laughter in no time. Simply follow it until it becomes natural. The sound of your attempt to laugh will cause genuine laughter. Let your body roll about in a light, playful, and childlike way. At times, you may come up against

blockages, like anger. Laugh them out or make some nonsense sounds. Let laughter flood all that prevents your ecstasy.

2. As you progress, lose yourself in laughter. Be possessed by it. Let it drown everything in you, all thought, all emotion. Allow it to melt away all tensions. Let all boundaries between you and existence disappear.

Stage II: Crying (Twenty Minutes)

Preparation: You may want to have the room slightly darkened to help you to tap into sadness. Darkness brings out the hidden and the unconscious. In addition, soft background music can support this practice. Either sit or lie down.

1. Surrender yourself to sadness. Close your eyes and move deep into all the feelings that make you cry. You can focus on your own current frustrations, a certain memory, the suffering of someone you love, or suffering beings you have witnessed or heard of. You can even think of a song or film that makes you sad. However, trust that the tears are there; you only need to avoid preventing them.

2. Once you are crying, let the tears flow. Allow yourself to cry really deeply, cleansing and unburdening the heart. Feel the dam of all your pent-up hurts and sufferings break open and let the tears flood out. Don't wipe your tears away; let them flow instead in whatever form they express, and stop worrying about how you will appear, both to yourself and imaginary others. You can cry either happy or sad tears.

Note: If you feel blocked or sleepy, rock your body back and forth a little. You can also be assisted by your breathing: with every in-breath, move into your chest to contact the hidden pain, and with every out-breath, let it come out to be released. If you reach a layer of anger, there is no need to get stuck in it. Let it be expressed with sound or body movements and then return to the tears. Remind yourself that anger is the avoidance of pain, a transformation of your sense of powerlessness.

Stage III: Witnessing (Twenty Minutes)

Now sit or lie on the floor in stillness and silence. Gather all the energy within you. Move to a state of silent witnessing. Feel how this state is much more natural now that there is little left to push away or transcend. Rather than a state of detachment, it is the outcome of your sincere cleansing. Let your witnessing be like an open sky, and be mindful of whatever thoughts, emotions, and sensations appear in it. Remember that it is the watching that is important, and not *what* you are watching, so don't become identified with or lost in any of the contents of your mind and body.

Expansion of Positive Feelings

The expansion method is the youngest system of meditation among this book's practices: I developed it in 2010 as a part of my wish to offer a systematic and quick path to broader states of consciousness.

Historical Background

While most meditation techniques require long, persistent, and sometimes arduous practice until breakthroughs are made, I sought to provide even fresh beginners with a taste of the ultimate meditation. In addition, my hope was not only to lead the meditator to the subtle fields of their consciousness, but also to demonstrate the way that this subtle consciousness can be applied to create changes in life itself. For instance, when an individual is firmly established in these broader states, careful guidance may help them unravel difficult memories and resolve stubborn mental and emotional patterns.

The expansion is thus both an essential practice and a vast range of techniques, which include meditations as well as therapy-based and empowerment processes. The method has been researched at the Charité in Berlin, Europe's leading university hospital, and has an app of its own and books dedicated to it in several languages. Thousands of meditators from all over the world have practiced it, and hundreds have undergone professional training to become facilitators in the system. The following meditation is an expansion technique that focuses on the broadening effect of positive emotions and feelings.

Purpose

While the method is young, the *principle* of expansion is not new at all. Even the ancient Hindu concept of the absolute reality, called Brahman, derives from the root *brh* ("expand") and therefore means "that which expands."[38] Any meditative practice is designed to bring our consciousness back to its original unlimited state, which implies moving from narrow identity back to a broader sense of being. In the words of the twentieth-century yogi Paramahansa Yogananda, meditation is "an expansion of your being beyond the boundaries of the mortal form."[39]

---

38. Easwaran, *The Upanishads,* 339.
39. Yogananda, "Self-Realization."

According to the expansion principle, moving from contraction to expansion implies moving from suffering to happiness. Our spirit feels happy and healthy only when it regains its boundless nature. Everything in us consciously or unconsciously longs to be expanded, and everything can be expanded: positive or negative emotions and feelings, memories, situations, dilemmas, questions, identities, and chakras. However, it is easiest to begin with our positive emotions and feelings, since their starting point is already somewhat expanded.

The renowned positive psychologist and researcher Barbara Fredrickson speaks of the "broadening effect" of positive feelings, meaning their ability to enlarge the scope of our thought, action, and behavior.[40] In the expansion, however, we not only focus on the inherently expanding nature of the feeling, we also learn how to allow it to spread within our being and reveal its greater spiritual potential. While positive feelings, like magnificent butterflies, tend to be fleeting experiences, the purpose of this technique is to gently hold them in our hands and meditate on them. Yogananda put this beautifully: "When a little bubble of joy appears in your sea of consciousness, take hold of it and keep expanding it. Meditate on it and it will grow larger. Keep puffing at the bubble until it breaks its confining walls and becomes a sea of joy."[41]

Even quickly disappearing positive feelings and pleasurable moments are messengers and echoes of the great sea of joy. These are, in fact, our most immediate and effortless connection to life's true nature. But to fully realize this potential, we need to agree to feel powerfully and maximally and to follow the emotion all the way to where it came from. In this way, our feelings become our reliable guide to bliss, freedom, and limitless consciousness.

Practice

The process consists of two simple and repeated stages: first you characterize, then you expand.

Characterizing means giving a vivid and tangible form to your elusive feelings. It can be challenging to try to expand an abstract feeling like love. So, you require a subtle form that can be easily enlarged through your visualization. In general, whatever you wish to expand is stored and reflected in your subtle body as a defined pattern. So, using your five inner senses—the same senses you use in dreaming—you first capture the defined form of your positive feeling.

To successfully identify the subtle form, always start with your body. After you have located a specific body part, go on to identify a shape or image that is associated with your object of attention. Look also for a related color, a general sensation, and a fragrance. However, you don't need to find *all* of these elements to achieve a tangible pattern.

Holding a clear inner vision of the defined pattern of your feeling (for instance, blue ripples springing from a mysterious source deep inside your chest), you enlarge it to its maximal limit

40. Celestine, "Broaden-and-Build Theory of Positive Emotions."
41. Ortner, *The Tapping Solution*, 238.

until it "explodes," almost like a balloon that has been overinflated. Another metaphor is that of ripples in a pond: your intention to expand is like a stone dropped in a pond, generating waves in a beautiful, changing pattern, a rippling ring radiating outward from a center that gradually returns to quietude. To support this expanding movement, use focused intention and intentional breathing. As soon as the subtle form has expanded as much as it can, you will realize that the initial pattern is airier and subtler. This implies that you have reached a broader state of consciousness. By continuing to expand even this subtler form, your feeling gradually shatters its defining borders and limitations, leading you to vast states of consciousness.

Instructions

PREPARATION: The meditation usually lasts between twenty and thirty minutes. This practice can be done either by yourself or with another who walks you through the process.

1. Sit in a comfortable position and close your eyes. Allow your entire being to relax gradually. Breathe slowly and deeply. From this relaxation, let a moment or a time in your life when you experienced the highest level of happiness, elevation, and limitlessness rise to the surface of your mind. (This can be any event that comes to your mind in response to this invitation.) Let that moment become alive in you now: Where were you? What were your feelings? What were your physical sensations? Give a name to the general feeling and get in touch with it. First feel it as it appears in the situation. Then let go of the situation and remain only with the general feeling.

2. Breathe into the general feeling. Move into its depth, into its very core. Try to communicate it—what does it feel like? Look for the area in the body that is most connected to it…a shape or an image…a color…a general sensation or a fragrance…

3. Now breathe into the general feeling and feel it from within. Let it spread further, permeating your entire body and being. Breathe into the shape or image and into the area in the body; breathe into it and let it expand more and more until it reaches its maximum limit, until it cannot expand anymore. Say, "[General feeling], show yourself completely to me!"

4. Breathe into the expanded feeling. Move into its depth, into its very core. Try to communicate it—what does it feel like? Look for the area in the body that is most connected to this state…a shape or an image…a color…a general sensation or a fragrance…Finally, give a name to the expanded feeling.

· · · · · · ·

5. Now breathe into the expanded feeling and feel it from within. Let it spread further, permeating your entire body and being. Breathe into the shape or image and into the area in the body; breathe and let it expand more and more until it reaches its maximum limit, until it cannot expand anymore. Say, "[Expanded feeling], show yourself completely to me!"

6. Breathe into this new expanded state. Move into its depth, into its very core. Try to communicate it—what does it feel like? Look for the area in the body that is most connected to this state...a shape or an image...a color...a general sensation or a fragrance...Give a name to the new expanded state.

7. Now breathe in the expanded state and feel it from within. Let it spread further, permeating your entire body and being. Breathe into the shape or image and into the area in the body; breathe and let it expand more and more until it reaches its maximum limit, until it cannot expand anymore. Say, "[Expanded state], show yourself completely to me!"

8. Breathe into this new expanded state. Move into its depth, into its very core. Try to communicate it—what does it feel like? Look for the area in the body that is most connected to this state...a shape or an image...a color...a general sensation or a fragrance...Give a name to the new expanded state.

9. Now breathe in the expanded state and feel it from within. Let it spread further, permeating your entire body and being. Breathe into the shape or image and into the area in the body; breathe and let it expand more and more until it reaches its maximum limit, until it cannot expand anymore. Say, "[Expanded state], show yourself completely to me!"

10. Breathe into this state. Move into its depth, into its very core. Try to communicate it—what does it feel like? Can you see how the essence of this memory empowers and supports your present? Notice how you've transformed the caused positive emotion into an uncaused one—now it is truly yours. Express gratitude toward the initial event for leading you to this most expanded state... As much as possible, allow this expanded state to permeate your physical body from head to toe...Before you open your eyes, you can choose to remain in touch with this state through your heart, even in your ordinary state of consciousness. You may open your eyes, slowly and gently.

· · · · · · ·

Forest Bathing

The practice of *Shinrin-yoku* ("forest bathing" in Japanese)—or Shinrin-therapy ("forest therapy")—came into being in Japan in 1982. Its initial purpose, however, was not to serve as a mindfulness meditation.

Historical Background

The concept of forest bathing was developed by Tomohide Akiyama, the director of the Japanese Forestry Agency, who hoped to establish a national health program that would associate forest visits with wellness-oriented ecotourism.[42] Forest bathing encouraged people to escape urban life more frequently and to "bathe" in the forest air. Akiyama's initiative was part of an even broader campaign to protect the forests by making people more mindful of their natural resources and their effects on human well-being.[43]

Although this practice is clearly not "ancient," as some would like to think of it, it is not a coincidence that forest bathing emerged from Japanese culture. In Japan, the belief in the healing powers of forests has been influenced by the Shinto religion, which maintains that sentience exists not only in humans but throughout the natural world. According to the Shinto worldview, forests, old trees, and also mountains and rivers have indwelling spirits (*kami*). In particular, every tree has its *kodama*, a spirit that resembles the dryads (tree nymphs) of Greek mythology.[44]

The initiative turned out to be successful beyond Akiyama's wildest imagination. Forest bathing provided a deeply immersive tourist experience, which has attracted the attention of wellness and health guides, as well as researchers, from all over the world. By now, a wealth of studies demonstrating the positive effects of forest bathing (primarily focused on its medical benefits) have accumulated. Moreover, numerous therapy-based programs connecting alternative medicine, ecotherapy, forest wellness, and forest therapy have spread in the United States and other Western countries. In addition to the enthusiasm about the method's therapeutic benefits, mindfulness teachers have come to recognize the potential of forest bathing as a profoundly mindful experience and have developed "forest mindfulness": focusing on the more spiritual values that forests hold.

42. Clifford, *Your Guide to Forest Bathing*, 5.
43. Farkic, Isailovic, and Taylor, "Forest Bathing as a Mindful Tourism Practice," 2.
44. Clifford, *Your Guide to Forest Bathing*, 6.

Purpose

Forest bathing is not comparable to hiking: its destination is being "here" rather than reaching "there." In fact, it challenges the very concept of "making good use of our time." Instead of feeling rushed, it encourages us to allow the moment to be what it is.

However, forest bathing is not the same as taking a leisurely walk in a nearby forest. It is a practice that is designed to teach you the art of stillness in nature. You make use of your senses to bring yourself into the present moment, where you can absorb all that the forest kingdom has to offer.

When the forest is allowed to settle within your being, it supports your body's innate capacity for healing and well-being. Beyond the physical benefits, the forest's energy field, which is the collective consciousness of many trees, can relieve you of mental and emotional imbalances and evoke feelings of gratitude, selflessness, and wonder. Among their many meditative gifts, forests seem to decrease the tendency to ruminate, which may be at least one reason for the development of the spiritual forest civilizations of ancient India, and the age-old phenomenon of forest monks who sought solitude under the trees as part of their path to spiritual enlightenment.[45]

Forest bathing's emphasis on being completely still in nature and broadening the senses has brought many forest bathers to identify this quality time in the woods as a form of mindfulness meditation. Mindfulness meditations are known as practices that help us leave behind discursive thinking and expand our awareness of immediate sensory experience. In mindfulness, the more we are expansively aware of the direct and unfiltered experience of our senses, the more we are present.

The author M. Amos Clifford claims that the difference between these two methods is that mindfulness emphasizes equanimity, whereas forest baths welcome pleasure and delight: our sensory experience becomes sensual enjoyment, and this sensual enjoyment makes us feel intimate communion with the forest.[46] But this description is perfectly in line with the tendency of the sacral chakra group of meditations to use pleasure as a gateway to meditative states.

Perhaps the most profound meditative state that you can experience while immersing yourself in the forest's field of intelligence is a unity experience—your sense of self dissolves and you no longer experience yourself as separate from the natural world. This opens you to a lost sense of belonging to the more-than-human world or to life as a whole. Moreover, since our subtle body seems to be patterned on a similar spiritual template to that of trees, it may be that by meditating so openly on trees—on their solid roots, upright trunks, and blossoming branches— our subtle body becomes aligned with this fully embodied representation.

45. Clifford, *Your Guide to Forest Bathing*, 6.
46. Clifford, *Your Guide to Forest Bathing*, 35.

Practice

This practice involves walking in a forest while immersing your senses in the unique qualities of the energy field formed by woodlands. First, choose a trail that is accessible and easy to walk on. Ideally, your meditative walks should take place in a richly wooded environment, perhaps even with meadows and streams, and with minimal intrusion from human-made sounds such as traffic or construction. Avoid bringing along any technological devices, such as your cell phone or headphones, that can put a barrier between your senses and the forest.

If possible, allow your walks to last between two and four hours; this will provide enough time for the mind and body to slow down and become deeply relaxed. This should be a slow-paced (sometimes extremely slow) type of walk, which invites you to focus your senses on the myriad ways in which the living forest communicates with you and affects you. During your walk, you are not expected to go too far; often, in fact, less than a quarter mile will do!

From time to time, you may combine forest bathing and one of the foundational root chakra practices (walking, sitting, breathing, standing, and sensing). However, don't overburden yourself with concepts such as "mindfulness" or "walking meditation," since these can cause you to make efforts to experience something other than what the forest actually has to offer. In general, minimize efforts to achieve anything—think of this practice more like playtime with a meditative flavor. If you find yourself making an effort, pause for a moment of stillness and proceed again slowly.

The focus is on your vivid sensory experience rather than an objective and scientific observation of nature. The Japanese recommend utilizing all five senses for forest bathing.[47] Open your senses widely to receive the gifts that the forest bestows on you, including its sounds, sights, and subtle energies. When you know how to receive, you begin to communicate with the more-than-human world. Another dimension of this communication is reciprocity; the process is not only about taking from the forest—in this case extracting wellness and pleasure from it—but is more like a partner relationship, a give-and-take exchange. Step by step, you grow aware of what it means to be a part of the web of planetary interconnectedness.

Throughout your walk, include awareness of your body as the receiver of the forest's transmission in your mindfulness. Like in any other mindfulness practice, your body awareness leads you away from mental occupation and directly into the immediate present. Be attentive to the movement of your body and the attendant sensations. Through these two gateways of the forest and your body, contact the felt sense and quality of the here and now.

47. Clifford, *Your Guide to Forest Bathing*, 9.

• • • • • • •

Let yourself be guided by the forest's invitations. Work with the forest as a partner rather than as a setting for an activity. Trust that when you open yourself to its intelligent energy field, it will work with you constructively.

Instructions

PREPARATION: The meditation usually lasts at least sixty minutes. Before entering the forest, have a firm intention to be silent and attentive to it and to your senses. Then, begin by standing on a "threshold" that ceremonially marks the start of your forest bathing walk and sets it apart from other experiences.

1. Stay in one place for at least fifteen minutes, using your senses to explore it. Be mindful of your surroundings, scan your body's sensations, and notice how your senses bring you into contact with the forest. The first fifteen or twenty minutes shouldn't involve walking anywhere. Simply stand or sit in one place to establish a mental framework for the pace of the entire walk. It is also possible that you will not even move beyond this starting point due to the richness that you discover in this spot.

2. Walk slowly for twenty minutes, noticing what is in motion around you. While walking, silently notice what is in motion in the forest, and "notice what you are noticing."[48] There is always movement, even when things seem utterly still. Perhaps trees move in the breeze, birds fly by, squirrels scramble in the branches, insects crawl, grasses bend, or creeks change their shape and tune. Inside you there is also motion. Your inner motion cannot avoid mirroring the motion of the world around you, and vice versa.

3. Spontaneously respond to the forest's invitations. The forest offers many possibilities for participation and play. For instance, the grass may invite you to lie in it, the clouds may draw you to gaze at them, or a tree may suddenly call you for an energetic exchange.

4. Sit in a spot for twenty minutes. A "sit spot" is one of the best methods of nature connection; it will deepen your relationship with the more-than-human world. Although the best time for a sit spot is toward the end of the walk, it is not a review of your journey. In your already relaxed and attentive state of mind, simply find a place that feels right and sit there, without considering this a formal meditation practice and without expectations. Become aware of the many things

---

48. Clifford, *Your Guide to Forest Bathing*, 76.

that look to make themselves known to you. The longer you sit, the more you notice. After fifteen minutes, you may all of a sudden "reveal" tiny flowers right in front of you, or perhaps after twenty minutes, a small turtle will move deep in the grass. Allow an inner stillness to emerge as a result of your silent and patient communion with nature. Don't seek to capture observations; rather, let the forest reward you with new perceptions when it chooses to do so.

5. End by identifying another threshold that marks the end of your forest bath and your return to ordinary experiences.

Breathing into Your Sex Organs

This technique, originally called "Testicle/Ovarian Breathing," was designed in a historical period and under cultural conditions that considered there to be only two genders: male and female. While I have chosen to retain some of the original instructions (sections 2 and 8) to honor the traditional wisdom, it should be made clear that sexual energy can be generated by everyone, regardless of gender identity. In addition, don't worry if the region of your ovaries or testicles is less physically functional; you will still be able to engender sexual energy in these areas, since the energy is essentially not physical. Thus, the more detailed instructions can easily be replaced with a general sense of the sex organs.

Historical Background

Under the reign of the Chinese Imperial Han dynasty (202 BCE–220 CE), some early Taoist sects performed sexual intercourse as a spiritual practice called "joining energy" or "the joining of the essences."[49] These transformative sexual arts reached their peak between the end of the Han dynasty and the end of the Tang dynasty (618–907 CE). The Taoists believed that by performing these sexual arts, they could attain not only supreme health and longevity, but also spiritual heights. In fact, Taoist adepts considered intercourse a way of creating within themselves a divine embryo from which the transcendent spirit would emerge.

However, as restraining Confucian attitudes toward sexuality grew stronger after 1000 CE, the Taoist sexual practices and literature were suppressed and disappeared from the public eye. As a result of this cultural oppression, for a long time scholars had no idea that such a radically different concept of sex ever existed in early China.

---

49. Wile, *Art of the Bedchamber*, 6.

The contemporary Taoist master Mantak Chia (1944–) has published and taught many of these ancient practices as part of his wish to introduce to the West a working model of the subtle energy systems of the human body and their healing and spiritual potentials (see also Inner Smile, discussed earlier in this chapter). Chia has devoted his life to studying martial arts, kundalini yoga, and esoteric Taoist practices with several masters in Thailand and Hong Kong. The following meditation technique derives from his books *Taoist Secrets of Love: Cultivating Male Sexual Energy* and *Healing Love through the Tao: Cultivating Female Sexual Energy.*

Purpose

This practice enables us to identify a meaningful and powerful dimension of our sexuality: we learn to distinguish our sexual *energy* from our sexual *activity*. Sexual energy is a latent force that lies within our sexual organs and sexual passion. It can be tamed, redirected, and refined, and thus goes beyond its familiar use for sexual activity. As a matter of fact, Taoists, like tantric Hindu and Buddhist traditions, have argued that we mindlessly waste this precious substance on sexual activity, whereas we could harness it to speed up our spiritual growth.

The second purpose of this practice is to learn how to direct and transform the procreative physical substances into refined energy that can elevate us. The sexual organs are a powerhouse of creative energy that is closely related to the brain. In Taoist terms, our sexual organs are a tremendous source of *ching chi*, the life force essence that underlies all procreation. Since this creative energy is subtly related to brain energy, it may instantly enhance our mental power and clarity. But more than that, when we master the process that refines this denser energy and channels it to the higher centers in our head, this can be a catalyst for meditative elevation and experience.

As a consequence, "breathing into your sex organs" is a simple but accurate method of guiding the kundalini through the central column. In Taoist terminology, this practice opens the *microcosmic orbit*, an energy channel that loops up the spine to the head and down the front to the navel, genitals, and perineum, and is therefore the main energy channel that links the organs, glands, and brain.

Practice

All sexual energy is *yin* (cold and calm) in its latent or resting state. Most people experience their sexual energy only when they are aroused and the ching chi is hot, but in reality, it is always present. In this meditation, you use your mind to draw the cold, potentially creative sexual energy up the spine to your head. Of course, you only draw the energy generated by the sex organs. The energy is easy to deal with, since it is cool. At first it may be slow going, but later, a mere thought can send a refreshing cool wave of energy up your back to your head. When your head becomes filled with sexual energy, the excess ching may spontaneously combust with the chi in your higher centers and spill over into the microcosmic orbit. This is a form of bliss!

• • • • • • •

The cerebrospinal fluid is circulated by two pumps in the sacrum and in the upper neck. In this practice, you get these pumps working and can feel a big bubble of energy travel up your spine. The sacrum is the pump that holds the sexual energy and gives it a push upward. In doing so, it refines the ching chi.

When you have grasped the mechanism of this meditation, you can perform it anywhere, even while waiting for the bus or train. Alternatively, you can use this practice as the starting point of an effortless but profound silent meditation.

Instructions

PREPARATION: This meditation requires between twenty and thirty minutes. Mantak Chia believes that the easiest and most effective way to practice breathing into your sex organs is to sit on the edge of a chair with your legs supporting your weight. For men, this keeps the testes free to allow maximum air energy down into them.

1. Raise the tongue to the roof of the mouth (this completes the loop between the front and back channels). Plant your feet firmly on the floor. Rest your hands palms-down on the knees. Hold your back straight, but slightly round at the shoulders and neck (to help the flow) and tuck the chin slightly in. Allow the body to relax.

2. *Men:* Allow your attention to center around your scrotum and feel the cold energy there. Inhale slowly and pull the testicles up. Hold for a while, then exhale slowly and lower the testicles. As you inhale, think of the breath going down into the testes and filling them up. Continue inhaling and exhaling until you feel a lot of cold energy in the scrotum. Use the mind alone to cause the movement of the testes up and down—don't flex your penis or anus muscles. After some time, you may observe the actual rise and fall of the testes, and the lower abdomen will move less. Do this nine times, then rest and practice again, doing three to six sets of nine.

   Women: First, locate your "palace": Bring both thumbs together on the navel, and stretch both index fingers down and bring them together, forming a triangle. Your energy palace is located where your index fingers meet on your stomach. By spreading the little fingers a little and laying them on your stomach, you find the place of the ovaries. Rub these points until they warm up, and feel the ovaries. Focus on these points, continue rubbing gently, and generate more energy. At the same time, use mental power to open and close the vagina with the help of the pelvic floor muscles. The energy may be felt through sensations such as warmth,

· · · · · · · ·

tingling, or swelling. As soon as you feel this, breathe in and bring the energy to the palace—the place where your index fingers meet. By gently opening and closing the vagina, you can gradually collect and store the energy of your ovaries in the palace. When you inhale, squeeze the vagina, close it, and pull up. Then draw the energy to the middle line between the ovaries; use your mind to draw the energy into this middle line, right into the cervix—and then exhale.

3. Put your mind at the perineum and guide the cold feeling there by inhaling. Feel how it flows, and hold it there. It is like you are using a straw to draw up the fluid.

4. Begin to draw the energy up the back channel, as if sipping on a straw. Draw it up to the very bottom of your spine. To support this, slightly arch your lower back outward, as if you were standing with your back against a wall and flattening against it. Tilt the sacrum downward and hold it down to activate the pump action. You can also rock your sacrum back and forth. There may be a sensation of pain, tingling, or pins and needles.

5. Move the sexual energy to the area behind your solar plexus. You can flex this part of your back in and out to straighten and loosen it for a freer passage of the cold energy.

6. Keep on pumping up the energy to the base of your skull.

7. Continue to move the energy to the crown of your head. Fill the straw to the top. Tilt the sacrum to the back to straighten the curve and at the same time, tuck your chin and squeeze the back of your skull.

8. *Men:* Feel the energy spinning at the top of your head. Allow it to spin in a clockwise direction. Let this refreshing energy enhance your creative power and clarity. Let the sexual energy be converted into pure life force. Remember that sexual energy and brain energy are closely related.

   Women: Continue to visualize the energy flowing through the front line all the way to the navel, where it is safely stored.

9. Bring the sexual energy up to the head in one sweet draw up the straw. Note: you may experience a certain taste on your tongue.

10. Repeat this process seven times and then meditate silently.

· · · · · · · ·

Meditate on This: Discovering Happiness in Your Meditation

This second insight complements chapter 4's insight into the thinking machine. Remember that the thinking machine is the force behind our mental activity; our thoughts are only the result of this force. If you understand this force, you understand what keeps you in the prison of thoughts, and this is a major part of what meditation is all about.

You may also remember that the thinking machine is a mechanism that produces problems and an underlying sense of "problem-consciousness" that we internalize and subjectify. As soon as we make it ours, it becomes very difficult to get rid of. On the other hand, if you understand that this problem-consciousness is not yours, you also come to realize that it is not yours to solve. But aside from problem-consciousness, the thinking machine creates another great source of suffering: it ceaselessly produces alternate realities.

One of the roles of meditation is to ground us. This may sound a bit strange—after all, many people tend to regard meditation as ungrounding. But what meditation really does is finally bring us back to real reality, to this life. It reveals to us that in a sense, for most of the day we are in a highly ungrounded state of daydreaming, caught in a perpetual dream about alternate realities even though our eyes are wide open. Meditation rechannels the energy wasted on this daydreaming and returns this precious life force to our body and to our energy system.

We require this life force to face our actual life. However, we often feel that we have too little energy, and this is because the thinking machine is a thief inside us who steals our power away. All this happens quite unconsciously, so we need to take a look beneath our ordinary stream of thinking and illuminate this hidden activity with the light of awareness.

The Should-Be Universe

We all have a blessed capacity for creative imagination. Even if we don't consider ourselves to be creative, all of us have a creative spark. We can say that we share in the creative intelligence of the universe. Even a small quantity of this intelligence is enough to endow our mind with creative and imaginative faculties. We can use these capacities constructively, by writing poems or making music, and in this way we contribute our own creative expression to an already-creative universe. The problem is that the thinking machine exploits the mind's capacity for imagination by creating alternative and parallel universes. I call these the "should-be, could-be, and would-be universes."

These self-created universes run parallel to the universe in which we really are. What the thinking machine does is constantly compare the real universe to the could-be, should-be, and would-be universes. It does this at any given moment—except when we are in deep meditation, or when we happen to be immersed in happiness because somehow, the should-be universe has

• • • • • • •

merged with the real universe and we momentarily feel as though we are in the right place at the right time.

Mostly, the comparison leads to disappointment, since the universe in which we are is never as perfect as the could-be universe. Thus, this kind of collision between the two universes gives rise to suffering. This is why we can also call the thinking machine the "comparing machine." This tireless comparison has kept humanity in an inner prison since the beginning of thought. The delusion has been so successful because the thinking machine convinces you that your suffering is because the universe is not as it should be. As a result, your attention is always on how to correct and improve life, quarreling with life for not being able to follow your imagination.

Meditation Puts an End to Waiting

Because we are so invested in the delusion of comparison, we find ourselves in a state of waiting: waiting for our lives to become as perfect as the thinking machine wants them to be. We believe that if we try hard enough, at a certain point these unconscious images that guide our way will become fully satisfied. But since this rarely happens (and never permanently), we find ourselves in this state of waiting until we breathe our last. Every day we think "tomorrow," and tomorrow never comes. This is a form of imprisonment!

As soon as you understand that it is comparison that makes you suffer, you will stop wasting your energy on this habit and instead begin to take a look at the real cause of suffering. The problem is not that you don't manage to fulfill the image, but rather that you have this image in the first place. You don't suffer because your life hasn't become as perfect as the thinking machine would want it to be—it is holding on to this dream that prevents your life from being perfect.

Since the thinking machine is in a state of delirium, this must be stated, even if it sounds obvious: This is the only actual life we have. Not only technically, but also essentially, *we don't have another life*. For the thinking machine, there is always a tomorrow. Of course, it is not the tomorrow of the calendar that disturbs our peace of mind, it is the psychological tomorrow: the one that makes every day of our lives only a step toward the next day, as if we are building toward some redemptive day on which everything will be perfect, when the would-be universe will finally become our universe.

Conversely, the liberating perspective of meditation is that happiness comes only when tomorrow dies. The meditative definition of joy is a state in which you are no longer waiting. Thus, joy is the end of waiting. Meditation reveals to us, through direct experience, this peculiar paradox: when we are no longer waiting, we are happy. Similarly, it shows us that when we stop searching, we experience immediate satisfaction.

The thinking machine creates the feeling that you should be on your way toward satisfying experiences, and that you will only ever be satisfied once you reach these moments. Based on our actual experiences, it's evident this is a false promise: no matter how many deeply satisfying moments we've had, they have all failed to bring us to the end of our search. This is for the simple reason that the thinking machine's sense of search is not really about finding anything.

The thinking machine is not really concerned with achieving the satisfaction of finding something. It is, by nature, all about dissatisfaction because it is busy cultivating the sense of building toward satisfaction; that is how its mechanism is built. As long as we follow the thinking machine, we seem to move toward a great promise, but after we have finally reached the moment of satisfaction and experienced relief, the thought process begins again, creating a different goal of satisfaction: "Yes, this is wonderful, but…" The thinking machine is based on the "not yet," the "still." It is forever characterized by a feeling of "just a little bit more, and we are there."

How can we be fooled in such a way? How can we not understand at this point that what the thinking machine does is based on unquenchable thirst? This is the type of thirst that cannot be satiated even when you imbibe what you longed for. It is a perpetual state of thirst, and that's what it is all about. This is what Gautama Buddha discovered in his own meditation practice 2,500 years ago: the core of suffering is this state of eternal thirst, and you can only liberate yourself by shutting down the very mechanism of thirst.

Don't Identify with This Dissatisfaction

If you are now considering shutting down this mechanism of thirst, please pause and remember that this is not *your* thirst. You are not thirsty—the thinking machine is thirsty. In fact, it is thirst itself, a thirst that is not interested in its own satisfaction. It is about forever seeking, in a search that can never be completed.

Under the spell of the thinking machine, we believe that if life's conditions changed, we would feel differently in an instant. But we carry the thinking machine with us, regardless of our lives' conditions, so wherever we go, this machine will produce alternate realities for us. It doesn't matter where we are.

Take the imaginary example of going to heaven. You have reached the longed-for religious heaven, and everything is as promised: angels pamper you, you dine at the heavenly table, and you are in a state of bliss for several good days. But you were transported to heaven with the thinking machine, and this is eternity. Sooner or later, you will produce an alternate reality and begin to complain even there!

For the thinking machine, even if the conditions are perfect, it doesn't really matter. Comparison is going to take place, and as soon as it does, suffering begins. In meditation, on the other hand, we discover that our lives' conditions can remain exactly as they are *and* we can feel completely alive and joyful. How come? What is the secret?

· · · · · · · ·

In meditation, we let go of the alternate reality and become rooted exactly where we are. When we learn to renounce the thinking machine and the alternate reality is no more, we remain in the only life we truly have, and we finally find joy. Instead of suffering from double vision—seeing life as it is, and next to it something else, always better—meditation unifies our vision. It inspires us to move into a state of complete appreciation of the universe we really have: hundreds of billions of galaxies, the vast blue sky, real people and actual experiences. Meditation helps us realize that there is so much to discover in this universe, while our daydreaming flattens our existence and makes it one-dimensional and depthless, sometimes to a degree that it seems futile to live. This is probably the greatest danger of the thinking machine: it can make us turn our backs on the only life we have.

How to Spot Tormenting Alternative Realities

For the most part, we are not conscious of our alternate realities. To unveil these suffering-producing realities, we need to learn how to turn over our frustrations, complaints, and negative emotions. Behind and beneath any negative emotion, frustration, or complaint that we have is a hidden alternate reality. In this way, we quickly realize that the thinking machine produces countless alternate realities for us on a daily basis!

Negative emotions such as anger, sadness, and depression are the powerless expression of our protest against reality. It is as if we refuse to be a part of this life and to accept it unless we get to fulfill our alternate reality—we will do nothing until reality changes. Instead, ask yourself in a moment of negative emotion, complaint, or frustration: *What would it feel like if I were without an alternate reality right now?* It is useful to do this simple exercise from time to time, especially if your mind becomes filled with negative emotions during your meditation practice. This can quickly wake you up from the dream and make you available again.

Draw two columns in a notebook or a Word document, the first titled "Real Life" and the other "The Should-Be Life." In the "Real Life" column, describe life as it is right now, factually and plainly. Make sure that you do not describe it through the lens of the should-be life. At first, you may find yourself describing it in a biased, twisted way. Capturing real life in a balanced way is literally impossible for the thinking machine. Next to this factual description, fill out the column of the should-be life, describing how you imagine the universe should be. What does a perfect reality look like? Be generous. Let it all come out. It is important to expose the dream. In this way, you don't remain stuck on the level of the negative emotion or the complaint, since they are really the result of a comparison.

For example, say you are standing at the bus station. It is wet and cold, and the bus doesn't come on time. In your parallel universe, you draw a perfect image in which buses always come on time. So, the left column will say "buses are sometimes late" (reality) whereas the right column will say "buses should always come on time" (imagination). Then take a look at this comparison and see for yourself what causes the conflict and annoyance.

The conflict is the thought. As soon as you hold on to the thought, it begins to create agitation, anger, restlessness, and tension. Then ask yourself, *Who would I be without this should-be, without this fantasy? What would happen? What would my moment look like?* Take a good look at the sentence "Buses should always come on time" and tell yourself: *This is a dream; this parallel universe doesn't exist.* Wake yourself up. In reality, your problem is not that buses are sometimes late, but that you have a thinking machine, which you believe so strongly that it has taken over your mind.

· · · · · · · ·

CHAPTER 6

Solar Plexus Chakra Meditations: Build Your Presence and Inner Power

The sacral chakra group of meditations had two distinct characteristics. First, it was all about merging into life and experience, disappearing in ecstatic self-forgetfulness, becoming one with the senses and the body, and allowing the center of feeling to flow freely. Second, it taught us how to follow the juices of life to the point at which pleasure actually takes us *beyond* pleasure.

Instead of merging into experience, the solar plexus chakra group of meditations is focused on the experiencer: the self that is distinguished from, and masters, the experience. And instead of following the juices of life, this group shows us how we can control our senses, impulses, and urges.

Here we return to the meditative task that we started in the root chakra group of meditations. The root chakra techniques helped us establish a solid and unaffected center within us, a core that is free and stable enough to release our existential tension and fear of life. Now, on the basis of this inner stability, we will be able to discover the element of inner power, presence, and authentic individuality, which begins with our basic sense of self-existence, the feeling of "I am."

In terms of the chakra system, there are three chakras that are involved in creating and revealing a sense of presence and a feeling of indestructible self: the root chakra, the solar plexus chakra, and the brow (or third eye) chakra. Together they reveal and create a sense of center, a core that is a true, rocklike self. In this context, this chapter begins the second phase of this great task.

. . . .

Meditations for True Inner Power

The solar plexus chakra has profound teachings, and its meditations are powerful and essential for the process of meditative development. Why is this so? We can think of the solar plexus chakra as the center of our own inner sun. This chakra is where our sense of radiating presence springs from.

Most people have little presence, since they exist mainly in the mental realm. Without the solar plexus, our sense of self-existence is largely mental: we think, therefore we are. The solar plexus, however, is the starting point of the development of a very different type of existence, which is presence-based. Presence means fully existing, possessing a profoundly felt realization of the feeling of "I am." There is a huge difference between *feeling* "I am" and *thinking* "I am." As soon as this thought becomes a feeling, the solar plexus begins to awaken.

If you were to sit in the presence of deeply evolved practitioners of meditation, you may sense that they have a sort of emanation. They don't just talk about what they have experienced—it is not what they say that convinces us of the truthfulness of their experience, but the way they *are*. This quality begins in the third chakra; their solar plexus emanates presence.

So this is the first thing we will do in solar plexus chakra meditations: we will begin to focus on the sense of "I am" in order to build our presence. From this perspective, we learn how to *be* in the full sense of the word. According to this group of meditations, we only start to exist when this chakra essence begins to flower and to release its dormant capacity of "I am"-ness.

This also entails a realization of a far more authentic sense of individuality. An individual in the meditative sense is one who possesses a truly fulfilled self-existence that has its own resources of power; one feels independently powerful, without needing to rely on the world for the experience of power or control. This is highly important, because usually our sense of power greatly depends on the external world, like when someone or something validates our own existence. This could be achieving a certain status in the world, a social recognition, being a part of a certain group of people, or meeting a special someone. On the other hand, if you don't receive this confirmation, you are in danger of undergoing a complete collapse of self-identity, since you won't know who you are. Your entire self-existence was woven around this particular relationship, social group, or occupation, and now the carpet has been removed from under your feet.

But when we are empowered by solar plexus chakra meditations, we begin to develop a sense of independent self-existence that draws on its own sources of power. This is what we can term *true inner power*.

Relying on false external power, we depend on empowering experiences, situations, people, and social status. This dependency causes us to try to control the external situation, and when we can't control it, we fall into a near-traumatic sense of either powerlessness or anger. These

· · · · · · ·

are the two imbalances of the solar plexus: anger is the complementary half of powerlessness. We are angry when we try to control something that we know we cannot control. Thus, anger is our last resort: when we raise our fist, we feel our last sense of power.

When we have true inner power, we don't need to control the external situation. We don't depend on the world to grant us this sense of empowerment; we have it. And the first expression of having it is feeling that our power lies in our presence: before anything else, we are, and even if the world collapses around us, we still are. It is a type of presence that precedes experience and the world.

These meditations enable us not only to build true inner power, but also to regain the power we have lost in the past. In this sense, they also heal our wounded solar plexus. From this perspective, the very experience of trauma—shocks we have had in our lives—is caused by an extreme sense of powerlessness. We may have felt that our power was taken away from us by external forces, or even forces from within that seemed to take over our being in an unrestrained manner. The extraordinary gift of solar plexus chakra meditations is that they give us back this lost power in such a way that it cannot be lost—they give us true inner power, which is neither lost nor gained as a result of life's experiences.

Effort and Effortlessness in Meditation

How do we succeed in both revealing and creating this genuine, nonmental self-existence? These techniques offer an unusual contribution to the world of meditation. They tell us that profound presence cannot simply be gained by effortlessly falling into something that is already there. An effortless freefall is overemphasized in the contemporary spiritual world. Some argue that you shouldn't make any effort, and even more so, if you expend even a tiny bit of effort, you should drop it, or you might stray from the path of true meditation. *But this is only half of the truth.*

Solar plexus chakra meditations emphasize the other half of the truth: that of the importance of effort. We shouldn't refrain from effort, since the very process of meditation includes both effortlessness and effort. Sometimes meditation strains our powers, pushes our limits, and moves us beyond our comfort zone.

This is a meaningful realization: we build our genuine, nonmental self-existence both by *revealing* it—becoming conscious of our dormant presence—and by *creating* it. The latter requires going against the natural stream of our thoughts and emotions, since what we call "ourselves" right now is not really our self. Our present selves are mainly a bundle of automatic reactions and fragmented feelings, impulses, and urges. This cannot be regarded as an integrated self. Thus, the self that may feel challenged has very little to do with the self that we aspire to create.

This implies that we do need to go against some of our feel-good tendencies. However, spiritual conventions nowadays consider *effort* a no-go word, as if it were the nemesis of meditation.

• • • • • • •

While everyone knows that real life involves a great deal of effort, doing things we don't necessarily find comfortable, and sometimes going against our urges and impulses, meditation has become the perfect opposite of all that: if life involves effort and going against ourselves, spirituality must involve no effort and is only about going with the flow. Both perspectives are true and beneficial: we need a healthy measure of effortlessness, but relying only on effortlessness can actually be quite damaging. Similarly, a healthy degree of effort is required, but too much might prove harmful.

So, why do we require a healthy degree of effort? Consider the process of meditation: any techniques, including the most relaxing ones, involve going against yourself. You fall asleep, become distracted, or start drifting in thought. Then you need to bring yourself back. This means that you have to go through a little struggle to establish this lasting sense of awareness.

In fact, even deciding to meditate every day is a struggle. You might wake up in the morning and not feel like sitting for half an hour, or you forget all about it, or you feel there are far more important tasks to complete. You may have started your meditative journey with great enthusiasm, and you may still be fascinated by the meditative experience, but you can no longer find sufficient energy to gather your forces and sit on your meditation cushion. Why is this?

The reason is that we are not integrated beings yet. Whereas one part of us wants to focus on the meditative experience, another part wants to think about daily matters. And while one part declares, "From now on, I'm going to meditate every day," the other part says, "I agree, this is a good decision, but…Not now. Not today." So we have different parts, each of them claiming to represent the "right" perspective. In a very subtle way, we are different people, or different voices, in one body.

Meditation is a process in which we begin to consolidate one being, one presence, one "I am." Nevertheless, we shouldn't think of this one presence merely as a pure, nonactive presence simply because we are "just being" in that state. This pure presence also develops our active capacities of willpower: we learn how to want, choose, and decide as an integrated being. We become able to transcend all our diverse voices and behave as masters in our own home.

So, from the point of view of the solar plexus chakra meditations, the struggles we experience in the meditative process are not hindrances and disruptions, but highly beneficial challenges we need to embrace. Put simply, your struggles in meditation are an important—even crucial—part of your practice.

One Will to Rule Them All

The ability to go against yourself and to transcend your urges and impulses can take you very far. Yogis and monks have demonstrated unbelievable abilities thanks to solar plexus chakra meditations. For example, practitioners of the tantric Buddhist Tummo (Inner Fire) meditation have managed to sit naked in the snow, covered by wet blankets, while retaining their body temperature and feeling warm and well.[50] There are many other examples in the world of meditation of what individuals can achieve when they become fully integrated beings.

None of the five techniques presented in this chapter will be too ambitious, even though some of them do aim to strain our capacities. What matters here is the essential learning that as a result of possessing a genuine, nonmental self-existence, we become truly capable of exercising our willpower. When you want as an integrated being, there is very little that can stop you. Having a unified presence and one voice inside you is a form of tremendous power. For instance, achieving high concentration and the ability to focus your attention should already be considered a supreme form of self-mastery.

In general, these meditations help us come into contact with our raw and primal power. This is somewhat similar to the sacral chakra techniques, which also connected us to the raw and primal life force that has been concealed and suppressed due to cultural conditioning. With the solar plexus chakra, we realize the innate power of our being, as well as the greater cosmic powers we can draw on.

The beautiful thing about the power we cultivate and harness in this chapter is that it has no relation to the feeling of power we may gain from resistance and fighting. On the contrary, this power is strongly associated with flow. Remember, only false external powers require fighting. When it comes to inner power, we don't have to fight, since our only purpose is to learn how to govern our own being.

One of the ways we learn to govern our being is through the ability to direct the flow of our life force. This implies governing not only the various forces of our mind, but also the subtle forces of the body, and determining their direction and purpose. In this sense, every type of pranayama (breath control) falls within the scope of solar plexus chakra meditations. In pranayama, we harness the life-sustaining force of prana and use it for higher developmental needs. Instead of breathing naturally and becoming aware of the rhythmic process of our breathing, as we did in the root chakra meditations, we become masters of this process and guide it in a different direction.

Breath control is what yogis have used to develop *siddhis*, or spiritual powers and abilities. Siddhis are a very rich phenomenon and may include powers like walking on water, but they can also be more modest abilities, such as the ability to fast, observe silence for long periods, or spend twenty-one days in a dark room for meditation. Siddhis are therefore expressions of solar plexus chakra capacities; they are living evidence that humans can govern their urges and automatic impulses, like hunger, cold, sleep, or the need to talk, deriving from the powers of self-existence and self-integration.

---

50. Malinowski, "Advanced Tibetan Buddhist Meditation Practice Raises Body Temperature."

This is a great teaching of the solar plexus chakra: before willpower can be crystallized, you need to have a solid sense of self-presence. You cannot want if you don't exist. Prior to the appearance of our presence, our wanting is more like urges, impulses, desires, responses to outer pressures, and needs for confirmation. Real wanting, however, is when your unified being says, "I want."

In the five meditations that await us, we will focus on building self-presence, establishing a sense of inner core, contacting our raw, primal sense of power, and learning how to harness and guide the life force inside us.

Mountain Meditation

By meditating on the image of a mountain and identifying with it until we become one with it, we unveil our own inner mountain: our unchanging, rocklike essence.

Historical Background

Born in 1944, Jon Kabat-Zinn is one of the world's leading meditation teachers, as well as a prominent meditation researcher at the University of Massachusetts Medical School. A student of Zen Buddhist teachers in his past, Kabat-Zinn has been driven to integrate his Buddhist education with scientific findings. He has become a major player in the mindfulness movement and is particularly known for his mindfulness-based stress reduction program (MBSR), which is offered by more than 720 medical centers and organizations around the world. Aside from popularizing ancient mindfulness practices, Kabat-Zinn has also developed several techniques, among them the Body Scan (see chapter 4) and the Mountain Meditation.[51]

Purpose

Mountains have been perceived as sacred sites by many traditions and peoples. Some mountains, such as the Greek Olympus, the Egyptian Mount Sinai, and the Asian Himalayas, have been depicted as the dwelling places of the gods. The twentieth-century yogi Ramana Maharshi openly spoke of the mountain on which he lived, Arunachala, as a god. More generally, we can find references in almost every culture and tradition to mountains as mothers, fathers, protectors, allies, and guardians. Since ancient history, meditators have sought spiritual guidance in mountains.

But why have mountains been elevated to such a degree in people's minds? Jon Kabat-Zinn suggests that it is difficult to think of any other natural phenomenon that can better represent

51. Kabat-Zinn, "About the Author."

our own dormant qualities of enduring resilience and majestic silence.[52] In fact, of all natural phenomena, mountains reflect what it truly means to take our seat for meditation. If you think about it, when we sit cross-legged and our back is erect, we actually resemble a mountain!

Ordinarily, we tend to experience ourselves as vulnerable and sometimes even fragile beings, susceptible to change and harm. When we learn to replace this fragile self-image with a mountainlike presence, we finally tap into a sense of true inner power. Consequently, we can draw on this inner vision for support when facing challenges and stress.

Practice

In this adaptation of Jon Kabat-Zinn's meditation, we learn to become like a mountain by employing two methods: we hold an image of a mountain in our mind's eye and let the image merge with our sitting body, and we sit in as immovable a position as possible.

This meditation's source of power is the vivid image of a particular mountain. Choose a mountain whose form speaks to you personally. Through it, you will be able to contact the universal quality of mountainness, ultimately transcending any particular shape or form.

The ideal posture is sitting cross-legged and keeping a straight back, since in this way you not only feel mountainlike but also resemble one.

For deeper results, I have added an emphasis on physical immovability to establish the mountainlike presence even more. By sitting immovably, we use our body as a reminder of the unchanging, stable core of our being. It is important to clarify that an immovable position is not a rigid posture. It does entail resisting the temptation to scratch an itch or shift position, but when we relax into it, we realize that the body can sit this way for hours. It is easier and more natural than you would initially expect! Bear in mind that what "needs" to move is not really our body, but our restless thinking.

Instructions

PREPARATION: This meditation requires between twenty and thirty minutes. Read the instructions carefully and simply sit to meditate without worrying about the details, which are only meant to inspire your practice.

POSITION: Sit with your back straight, allow your head to be gently held on your shoulders, keep your shoulders relaxed, and place your hands on your knees. Make sure you sit in a comfortable position that allows you to remain as immovable as possible without needing to change your position. The only movement you should allow is breathing and swallowing, but even these can be gentle and conscious. Feel how you can remain in this position softly and effortlessly. Feel the

---

52. Kabat-Zinn, "Jon Kabat-Zinn - Mountain Meditation."

contrast between the thoughts that may still run around and your own fundamental choice to be in this immovable position. Relax into physical immovability. Let this physical stillness influence your mental stillness: as the body follows the mind, so the mind follows the body. As you allow the body to be still, feel the sense of dignity, resolve, and being complete; you are whole in this very moment. Your posture reflects this sense of wholeness. Bring your attention to the surface beneath you and the support it provides. Root your body in its strength and become aware of your connection to it.

1. Start with attention to the flow of breathing, without attempting to alter it.

2. Now picture the most beautiful mountain you know or can imagine. Hold the image and let it come into greater focus. Observe its shape and its points of contact with the earth and the sky. Notice how massive it is, how solid, how unmoving. Notice how its base is rooted in the earth's crust. Perhaps your mountain has snow on its peak and trees on the lower slopes, a peak or a series of peaks, or a high plateau…Sit and breathe with the image of the mountain, noticing its qualities.

3. Bring the mountain into your own body so that the image and your body become one. You share the massiveness and the stillness of the mountain. You become the mountain, rooted in this sitting posture, your head a lofty peak, your shoulders and arms the size of the mountain, your legs the solid base, rooted to the chair. With each breath, you become more like a breathing mountain, unwavering in your stillness: a centered, rooted, unmoving presence. Experience the uplift, the elevated quality of being a mountain, deep in your spine and pelvis.

4. As the sun travels across the sky and night follows day and day follows night, so many changes of light and shade take place. Through it all, the mountain just sits, experiencing change at each moment, yet always being itself. It remains still as the seasons flow into one another and as the weather changes moment by moment. It is calmness abiding all change. Perhaps in the summer there is no snow, and in the winter a blanket of snow and ice covers the mountain. It may be shrouded in clouds or fog, and people may or may not come by to behold it. None of this matters to the mountain. It remains its essential self. Clouds may come and go. The mountain's magnificence doesn't change. It just sits, being itself. At times, violent storms, snow, and rain occur, but through it all,

the mountain continues to sit, unmoved by the weather, by what happens on the surface, by the world of appearances.

5. In the same way, you can embody this unwavering stillness in the face of change over hours, days, or years. We constantly experience changes of mind and body and of the outer world. We have our own periods of light and darkness. We experience storms of various intensities. We endure periods of darkness and pain and moments of joy. Even our appearance may change. Realize that as a mountain, you can have an inner smile of knowing inside you, like a soft Buddha's smile: the smile of knowing that whatever happens, there is this unchangeable, unaffected center in you. The emotional storms that affect us are very much like the weather on the mountain; mistakenly, we take them personally. Instead, notice how now, as the mountain, the thoughts feel external, more like birds flying around your mountain form. Sit in silence and notice the changes with neutrality, thinking of your breath as your foundation.

6. Finally, from this mountainlike state, start reanimating your body and the ordinary function of the mind. Breathe the presence of the mountain into the body and the mind. Prepare yourself for the first movement…Gently shake your head a bit from side to side, then allow the shoulders to move very softly, then move the hands, pelvis, and knees. Let the life force reach your feet. Slowly and gently come out of the meditation and open your eyes.

AFTER THE MEDITATION: Hold the image and feeling of the mountain whenever you remember to. Bring it in front of your mind's eye and feel how this presence affects your own presence—how it instantly reminds you of your own mountainlike element. Remember to do this during times of emotional distress, tension, or challenge. How would you respond to the situation from your mountainlike state?

"I Am" Meditation

The purpose of this meditation is to move your self-identity—your sense of "I am"—from the head, the mental center, to the solar plexus, the presence center.

Historical Background

George Ivanovitch Gurdjieff (1877–1949) was a Greco-Armenian mystic and philosopher. Gurdjieff founded an influential global movement based on his Fourth Way, which combines and transcends the traditional paths of the fakir, the monk, and the yogi. Gurdjieff inspired the formation of many groups after his death, all of which still function today and follow his ideas faithfully.[53]

Gurdjieff's most fundamental assertion was that ordinarily, humans live in a state of hypnotic "waking sleep" and thus cannot claim to possess actual "souls" and will.[54] However, if one ardently practices a conscious self-remembrance, one may eventually transcend this unconscious, automatic form of existence. The title of one of his books, *Life is Real Only Then, When "I Am,"* succinctly conveys this message: when you are fully present, everything around you becomes truly alive, but when you are not, life feels like a passing dream.

One of Gurdjieff's most notable disciples was the philosopher Pyotr Demianovich Ouspensky. Ouspensky's *In Search of the Miraculous* introduced Gurdjieff's radical teachings to Western readers in an understandable, intellectual form. This meditation is an adaptation and synthesis of two of Gurdjieff's exercises that appear in Ouspensky's classic work.

Purpose

According to Gurdjieff, when most people pronounce the word "I" aloud, they tend to experience the word as if it is sounding in their heads. But as long as your "I am" resides in the head, it is just a thought, and it is therefore nonexistent in reality.[55]

On the other hand, an individual who already has a real "I" would pronounce the word and experience it reverberating in their solar plexus. This would not be a mere thought—it would be more like a vibration or a profound feeling. Therefore, by shifting your sense of self-existence to the solar plexus in this practice, you are able to make your "I am" more and more real: an integrated presence that includes a genuine feeling of existence and vibration.

Gurdjieff based his meditation on a practice which, according to him, had been preserved in the monasteries of the Greek Mount Athos. In this original practice, he claimed, a monk would either kneel or stand in a certain position and, lifting his arms, which were bent at the elbows, he would say "Ego" aloud, prolonging the sound while listening at the same time to where the word is sounding. The purpose of this ancient exercise was to feel "I" at every moment in which one thinks of oneself and to move the "I" from one center to another.[56]

---

53. Britannica, "George Ivanovitch Gurdjieff"; "Part V: The Fourth Way."
54. Ouspensky, *In Search of the Miraculous*, 66.
55. Ouspensky, *In Search of the Miraculous*, 304.
56. Ouspensky, *In Search of the Miraculous*, 304.

• • • • • • • •

The solar plexus is about two fingers below the lowest point of the chest. It is a region that is indistinguishably associated with the navel chakra, the energy center that contains your individual presence and power. The reason for the location of the solar plexus is explained by Gurdjieff only indirectly when he says that the exercise increases the strength of "I am." He was not the first to recommend this in Western culture: the Desert Fathers (the early Christian hermits) practiced bringing their thoughts into the region of their navels (hence the origin of the phrase "navel-gazers").

Gurdjieff claimed that after mastering this practice, you can intentionally concentrate this reverberation and self-presence in any part of your body in order to stop physical disharmony. For example, you could cure a headache by concentrating the reverberation on the part of the head from which the sensation of pain arises.[57]

Practice

The process is divided into two parts. In the first part, we evoke presence in the solar plexus through breathing and thought. We draw on these two sources and store the gathered energy in the solar plexus. Gurdjieff calls it "a preparation to have an 'I.'"[58] In the second part, we finally attach the sense of "I am" to the solar plexus. We intone "I am" and try to sense a resulting reverberation or flow of energy in the solar plexus.

At first, you may pronounce "I am," but the words will feel empty and you will need to use your imagination. Nevertheless, through frequent repetition, you will gradually begin to experience how this pronunciation settles in your solar plexus and leads to an energized sense of self-presence.

Instructions

PREPARATION: This meditation requires between twenty and thirty minutes.

Stage I

1. Focus on your breathing. Recognize what is happening to the air that you breathe in: part of it goes in, part goes out, and a part remains. Your body, through your lungs, takes a part; a part leaves, and another part remains. Feel what is happening in your lungs: when you breathe in, part of the air is assimilated, and you feel its flow all over the body. It goes everywhere. Feel how this air is assimilated in you and how it flows into and enhances your presence. As your attention is

---

57. Gurdjieff, *Life Is Real Only Then, When "I Am,"* 143.
58. "Possible Foundations of Inner Exercises."

occupied with this—breathing, assimilating, and flowing of the air—your thinking should already be relatively weak.

2. While remaining attentive to this breathing process, notice how, as a result of the process, a thin, small, light air or energy arises within your brain. Direct your attention to help this energy flow toward your solar plexus. Feel how it flows. Consciously let this flow of assimilated air, and this energy that arises in your brain, flow into your solar plexus. As your solar plexus takes in this prana more intensely, feel that "I AM."

Stage II

1. Pronounce the words "I am" inside your being. Try to remember to keep this reverberation in your solar plexus. When pronouncing the words "I am," imagine that this reverberation flows and settles into the solar plexus. Simultaneously concentrate your attention on the words themselves, "I am," and on your solar plexus, and the reverberation should gradually become synchronized by itself.

2. Go deep into this feeling—*I exist, I am.* Don't think it; feel it. Remember that just saying it in your mind is futile, so don't go on repeating in your head, "I am, I exist." Instead, as you let the "I am" reverberate in your solar plexus more and more, feel how this sense of presence sinks into your bones. Feel it all over your body as a total unit, not only in the head.

3. When you start feeling self-existence and being grounded in it, notice how the whole world becomes alive to you in a totally new way. You are one with the whole. While you are feeling this sense of self-existence, don't create a limit to it: existence has no beginning and no end, and neither do you. Let this presence expand to include the entire sense of everything existing in the universe, beginning from the atom and ending with everything existing as a whole.

AFTER THE MEDITATION: As you open your eyes, try to keep this sense of presence that starts within your solar plexus and expands infinitely. Whenever possible, think *I am* and connect this thought with a deep feeling in the solar plexus. Feel how each time you do this, you enhance and deepen your sense of presence. Feel how you encounter many moments of your day from this solar plexus presence, and observe what the experience of life is like in this state.

· · · · · · · ·

Sufi Whirling

The dance ceremony of the whirling dervishes, whose precise rules are followed to this day, was designed by Rumi as a form of ecstatic self-pivoting dance, during which the disciple enters a trancelike state, forgetting the world around them and uniting with their "beloved." Annemarie Schimmel, a scholar of mystical Islam, writes that this dance is the "most widely known expression of mystical life in Islam."[59]

Historical Background

Sufism is a mystical form of Islam that has existed as an individual inner practice since the early days of the Islamic religion. Sufis seek to establish a direct connection with God through the experience of identifying and uniting with the One. Dervishes ("mendicants" in Persian), who are the members of Sufi fraternities, are spiritual seekers who have committed to abandoning the illusions of ego in order to merge with the divine. The dervish hopes to access the state of *wajd*, a term for spiritual ecstasy that literally means "finding"—finding God and, as a result, becoming eternally peaceful.[60]

The Sufi Mevlevi order was founded in 1273 in Konya, Turkey, by the followers of the greatly famous mystic and poet Jalal al-Din Rumi (1207–1273) soon after his death. Rumi, originally from Balkh in Persia (today Afghanistan), fled Mongol persecution and settled in Konya around 1226. He wrote 30,000 verses of lyric poetry that were entirely dedicated to the theme of love and spiritual bondage. His most venerated work, the *Mesnew* (also spelled *Masnavi*) is considered by many the second Koran. Rumi's Mevlevi dervishes practice music, visual art, poetry, meditation, and mystical rituals, but they are primarily known as the "whirling dervishes" due to their famous practice of whirling (Sama) as a form of *dhikr* (remembrance of God; see chapter 7).[61]

The Mevlevi order continued to practice in Konya until the foundation of the Turkish Republic in 1923, which prohibited public religious performances. However, after 1956 it was permitted to be performed on certain occasions, and since 1964, supported by UNESCO, the Mevlevis have begun to spread their practice throughout the world. Nowadays there are dervish centers and communities that train Western students as well. In the past, dervishes used to endure 1,001 days of training to become a Mevlevi member, but the order is now open to people of all backgrounds, and the training offers spiritual teachings adapted to modern times.[62]

---

59. Erzen, "The Dervishes Dance."

60. Erzen, "The Dervishes Dance."

61. Erzen, "The Dervishes Dance."

62. Harel, Czamanski-Cohen, and Turjeman, "The Spiritual Experience of Sufi Whirling Dervishes," 2–3.

Purpose

Sufi Whirling uses rhythm, chanting, and focusing of the mind to spin toward the center of existence and become one with it. The physical spinning is a metaphor for having the mind, heart, and body entirely centered on the supreme Self—any movement you make can only take place from the center outward. As the spinning intensifies, the world literally fades away and withdraws to the background. The rotational movement separates your consciousness from what is alien or superficial to it, to the point that your body is in the world but your spirit feels far away from it. It is only you and your "beloved" at the unmoving core of the world of change, united in an ineffable ecstatic embrace (wajd). This unusual form of dance meditation can also be described as a ritual that celebrates the finding of divine love, or in Rumi's own words, as rising above the world, "tearing your heart to pieces and giving up your soul."[63]

Rumi also explained that the dancing dervishes imitate the solar system and the planets that revolve around the sun. The dervish dies to the world and revives in the eternal dance of the free spirits around a sun that neither rises nor sets. By joining this cosmic choreography and uniting with cosmic powers, your mind and soul become separated from physicality and earthly bondage, extend from the earth to the universe, and move to concentrate on the axis of existence. Through this dance, you feel and understand the possibility of the eternity of the soul.

The twentieth-century mystic and meditation teacher Osho, who helped to disseminate Sufi Whirling, believed that when the body moves in all directions around one point, the contrast between the body and this point becomes far more noticeable, and it is easy to identify the element within our being that is not moving at all. He wrote, "Every circle has a center, but we are always living on the periphery of this circle. Personality is our periphery, our real source of life is at the center of our being. This center is connected to the center of existence, to the center of the whole universe."[64]

Practice

In the traditional ceremony, the dervishes whirl in a circle group through four phases (called *salams*). Each salam lasts between eight and eighteen minutes, with a two- to three-minute break between salams (for a total time of about forty minutes). The whirling is a self-pivoting, rhythmic, counterclockwise rotation on the left foot, with the right foot propelling the rotational movement.

While they are vividly aware of the moment, themselves, and their surroundings, the dervishes maintain an open but unfocused gaze to blur their sight. Their eyes look without seeing so that they can look into their own interior world. Arm positions vary between closed across the

---

63. Harel, Czamanski-Cohen, and Turjeman, "The Spiritual Experience of Sufi Whirling Dervishes," 1.
64. "Osho No-Dimensions Meditation."

chest and open, with the right arm and palm positioned upward and the left arm and palm downward. This arm position symbolizes being a funnel: receiving from the heavens and giving to the earth. The dervishes begin to move very slowly around themselves and around the center. The soft music gradually changes its rhythm to encourage accelerating speed.

If you have not whirled before, start out very slowly, and generally whirl at your own speed. Your confidence will grow after trying it for a while. Once your mind and body become attuned to this type of movement, you will naturally rotate faster. If you experience nausea or dizziness, stop for a moment and then start again. These symptoms should go away after a few tries. However, if severe discomfort remains after several initial practices, avoid this meditation altogether.

Instructions

PREPARATION: This meditation requires forty-five minutes. Choose an uncarpeted, smooth floor. Make sure you have sufficient space to move around and that there are no sharp edges nearby in case you fall. Wear loose clothes; socks can be helpful. Consider selecting a piece of music that lasts fifteen minutes so that you don't need to be conscious about the time. Ideally, look for tracks that have been designed especially for Sufi Whirling. There are many options available online.[65]

1. Take some time to build up to the whirling. Any meditation technique can ensure that you are centered in your body before you start, so consider taking the first fifteen minutes to sit and meditate. Alternatively, you can prepare yourself by having fifteen minutes of free movement.

2. Enter your starting pose by folding your arms over your chest with the hands on the shoulders. Place your right big toe over your left big toe. In this state of self-embrace, feel love toward yourself. Kiss each hand as they rest on the shoulders. When the music starts, take a moment to bow in an expression of gratitude for the moment, the music, the masters of this practice, and the universe that has led you to this meditation.

3. After a few spins with your arms still hugging yourself, move them down from your chest to the hara (two inches below the navel). From there, put the backs of your hands together and unfold your arms upward. Traditionally, the right palm will face toward the sky, while the left faces the earth. This signifies the receiving and giving of divine energy.

65. The instructions derive from Henrike, "Meditation in Motion."

4. Whirl! Your body knows how to whirl, so just follow your feet. Whirl like small children sometimes do. Try to really spin on the foot that is providing a center point to avoid "stepping in circles," which is a little different from whirling. Traditionally, you should spin toward the left, into the heart center. But if it feels more natural to spin to the right, try that. (If you whirl to the right, start with the right foot and right arm to the right and extend the left arm in the opposite direction.) Additionally, while you are whirling, you can change your hands to any position that feels more natural to you. Remember to connect to your breath. At a certain point, you will find that magical center line that connects your body to the earth, and you will start feeling a natural flow in the whirling. You might also notice that when your energy goes back to the mind—thinking and perhaps even worrying about falling—you create more instability in this center point. It is really a matter of feeling it out.

5. When the music ends, slow down, bringing yourself back into the starting pose and folding your arms across your heart center. Dervishes sometimes end the whirling by simply letting themselves fall, but this may not be ideal for a home practice. Another option is to lie on the floor on your belly to be in contact with the grounding energy of the earth. Take fifteen minutes to relax like this with your eyes closed.

Vase Breathing

Vase breathing is a technique of tantric (Vajrayana) Buddhism. Originally, it was designed as a preparatory practice for, and a vital component of, the far better-known Inner Fire meditation—a powerful solar plexus chakra meditation that is too complex and demanding to be presented in this book. Fortunately, vase breathing is an excellent initiation into the world of Inner Fire.

Historical Background

Inner Fire meditation, or the Yoga of Inner Heat, is famously considered the first of the "Six Yogas of Naropa." Although it is attributed to the lineage that started with the great yogi Tilopa (988–1069) and his principal student Naropa (1016–1100), the system of the Six Yogas brought together earlier techniques and elements from diverse tantric sources. During the ninth century, hundreds of Buddhist tantric systems had been developed. Tilopa and Naropa's practices drew from the systems that were classified as *maha-anuttara-yoga*, or the "great highest yoga" tantra, whose ultimate stage—the "completion stage"—consisted of meditations on the subtle body.[66] At a certain point, the Tibetan Marpa (1012–1097), who came to Nepal in the hope of attaining the highest knowledge, became Naropa's student and received from him numerous transmissions, among them the six instructions. Marpa integrated the system even more, and was responsible, along with his renowned spiritual successor Milarepa (1052–1135), for its dissemination throughout Tibet.[67]

Purpose

Vase breathing is a form of intense pranayama (breath control) that harnesses the inner heat stored within the solar plexus chakra for the generation of physical and spiritual bliss. The blissful experience is achieved by concentrating all the subtle airs (prana) of your body deep inside the solar plexus chakra and releasing them into the central channel, all the way to the crown of your head. This technique is probably one of the easiest and quickest ways to settle in the core of our subtle body, which is the central channel, and to realize meditative bliss. Since it is a bliss meditation—utilizing bliss to attain knowledge of reality—it is a close relative of the crown chakra group of meditations. (Note: Another set of preparatory meditations from the world of Inner Fire—the Empty Body and Subtle Body Visualizations—can be found in chapter 10. I strongly recommend combining the two, starting with the crown chakra set, to form an even more successful practice.)

Practice

Vase breathing is so called because it is as if we hold all the air from above and below in a sort of vase. The vase is the solar plexus chakra, which is considered the source of inner heat and the place where the "red kundalini" drop lies dormant. Tantric Buddhists represent this drop with a flamelike syllable whose image is also used as a part of the vase breathing visualization.

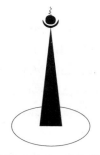

Navel Chakra Syllable

66. Mullin, *The Six Yogas of Naropa*, 25–26.
67. Mullin, *The Six Yogas of Naropa*, 28.

The principle is simple: Place your entire attention on the solar plexus chakra, in its deeper location within the central channel, and guide all your being toward that point. Take a deep breath and hold it, concentrate on the syllable within the solar plexus chakra, and push all the subtle airs of the body, from both above and below, into the chakra. As soon as you slowly exhale, the subtle airs will be released directly into the central channel and effortlessly shot into your crown.

ATTENTION: If you are pregnant or have heavy menstruation, strong breath retention and pressing of the abdomen—both of which are used in vase breathing—might be damaging. In this case, it is better to apply vase breathing using visualization only, without any physical pressing.

Instructions
PREPARATION: This meditation requires between twenty and thirty minutes.

Stage I: Visualization
Visualize the central channel, close to the spine. Visualize how it goes all the way from the crown chakra, deep inside the brain, down to just below the sexual organs. See the side channels, which branch from their point of confluence just behind the meeting point of the two eyebrows. Perhaps you can even visualize them as they intersect in the throat, heart, and navel, forming three knots. Feel how with every inward breath, you are filling the side channels, inflating them. After all, they start in the nostrils; they are conductors of prana. And now, bring up the syllable, burning red, and place it within the solar plexus chakra, four fingers' width below the navel, deep inside the body, and close to the spine. Feel how as soon as you bring in the solar plexus chakra syllable, the airs from the two side channels become magnetized. Everything flows there; it is like the center of your being, the powerhouse.

Stage II: The Pranayama
1. Sit as straight as possible in order to enable optimal flow. Using the visualization of the subtle body—the side channels and the central channel—breathe through your nostrils and imagine and feel how the two side channels become inflated with air and pranic flow. At the same time, place your being and awareness inside the tiny, burning syllable. To move the air that is flowing through the side channels into the point below the navel, hold your breath gently, without contraction. Swallow and follow the saliva as it goes down in the direction of your digestive system, and give a slight inward push of the abdomen to indicate that you are aiming to move the air into the navel syllable; if the air remains at that point, it has nowhere to go. A second later, contract your pelvic muscles in

order to close the openings of the anus and the sexual organs in order to force the energies from below to reach the very same point. Your aim is to unify the airs from above and below, inside and around the syllable. Centralize inside the seed syllable. Just be there, with all your energy focused.

2. When holding your breath becomes uncomfortable—since our lungs are not used to it, and our body and mind do not yet fully rely on prana—just release it very slowly (don't open your mouth; you want to keep the energy in). Do this elegantly, because then the airs go very deep through the central channel. Send the energy upward in one shot of deep, deep pleasure. Relax for a moment.

3. Do this at your own pace; when you can't hold the breathing in an unforced way, just breathe out through your nostrils, deep inside the central channel. Repeat the process for several rounds. This technique is not about counting or moving quickly. When you reach a highly energized state, continue to a deep meditation.

Kumbhaka

Pranayama—the practice of breath control—is an ancient Hindu yogic technique. In his *Yoga Sutra*, Patanjali (between the second century BCE and the fourth century CE) considered pranayama to be so essential that it constituted the fourth of eight stages intended to lead the aspirant to the supreme state of samadhi. The significance of pranayama was also highlighted by scriptures such as the *Bhagavad Gita* and many later Hatha yoga classics.

Historical Background

Swami Sivananda explains that there are three kinds of pranayama: when the breath is expelled, when it is drawn in, and when it is suspended, which is the state of kumbhaka.[68] All nine of the classical pranayamas are actually different ways of regulating the processes of exhalation, inhalation, and the in-between state of kumbhaka. The word *kumbha* means "vessel," and thus it implies holding something—in the context of pranayama, holding the breath.[69] This state can be found and practiced either after inhalation (inner retention) or after exhalation (outer retention). However, yogis past and present have clarified that originally, pranayama was synonymous

---

68. Sivananda, *The Science of Pranayama*, 30.
69. Saraswati, *Prana and Pranayama*, 118.

with kumbhaka. This is because the ultimate goal of all pranayama practices is the cessation of breathing. When we direct our inhalation and exhalation in certain ways, it is only a means to achieve kumbhaka.

Lastly, there are two types of breath retention: when we deliberately hold our breath, and when our breath is suspended spontaneously. Reaching this type of spontaneous breath retention (*kevala kumbhaka*) is, in fact, the aim of all pranayama practices; in the yogic view, when your breath has effortlessly ceased, this is equivalent to the state of the ultimate meditation. Since this retention takes place as a natural state, it involves no risk. On the contrary, the resulting state is said to be a spreading of inner light and a leap to a superconscious state of perception.

Purpose

In general, the practice of pranayama is considered by yogis to be essential for spiritual progress. The reason is subtle: if you can control the motion of the respiratory organs, you can control your vital energy (prana), and if you can control your vital energy, you can easily control your mind. In the early stages of pranayama, you learn to control your in-breath and out-breath. This improves your overall health and vitality, but also prepares you for the techniques that involve kumbhaka.

The secondary benefits of kumbhaka also include vigor and longevity. In fact, some scriptures speak of kumbhaka as the cure for all diseases (if you concentrate on your navel while practicing it), and others even consider it a source of great power of manifestation. But naturally, kumbhaka's most significant role is in the field of meditation.

Swami Niranjanananda Saraswati writes that while inhalation is the active or positive breath and exhalation is the passive or negative breath, kumbhaka transcends this duality of active and passive, positive and negative.[70] In this way, it is a powerful key to silent meditation. We can think of this gap between the in-breath and the out-breath, and between the out-breath and the in-breath, as similar to the space between one thought and another that is practiced in Dzogchen meditation (see chapter 10). Just like the space between thoughts, kumbhaka exists in normal respiration, but only for a split second, and it is not conscious or controlled. It therefore needs to become conscious and expanded.

When you enter the state of kumbhaka, subtle meditative processes begin to take place. First, the amount of vital energy (prana) increases as the body, breath, and mind are brought into a state of stillness. Saraswati compares this process to a pressure cooker: the intensity of energy and heat increase since they are not released from the body.[71] The expansion of prana also has a powerful impact on the mind. Your mental power and level of awareness are greatly enhanced.

---

70. Saraswati, *Prana and Pranayama*, 116.
71. Saraswati, *Prana and Pranayama*, 123.

The mind becomes perfectly focused and one-pointed, and you enjoy a total cessation of mental patterns. This intensity of practice enables you to maintain the concentration and focus that you require on your way to samadhi. Even more deeply, your perception and subtle body disconnect from the physical body. In this state of unconstrained awareness, it is easier to achieve a greater understanding of the true depths and dimensions of your being. All this immense activity takes place in your internal spheres, while from the outside you seem as still as a rock.

In scientific terms, the practice of kumbhaka causes the oxygen levels in the body to drop and the carbon dioxide levels to rise. In training the nervous system to tolerate higher levels of carbon dioxide, many dormant blood capillaries in the brain are opened up to improve cerebral circulation. Moreover, kumbhaka restores the levels of carbon dioxide in the brain tissues and consequently allows the system to fully extract oxygen. Since increased carbon dioxide levels in the blood can lead to expanded states of consciousness, moderate practice of kumbhaka may be a sort of self-administered CO_2 therapy.[72]

Practice

When you practice kumbhaka, retain the breath without fear or shaking of the body. After you have completed the retention, exhale steadily and slowly, without anxiety. Although you definitely need to apply willpower to retain your breath, the air should not be forced to remain inside by continuing the inhalation. In general, don't push your limits. Follow the prescribed ratios of inhalation, exhalation, and retention, and if you realize that you are unable to maintain these ratios, avoid the practice.

To enhance your concentration during the practice, consider focusing on a symbol, preferably the symbol of light. When you hold your breath, visualize the light at the eyebrow center. In general, visualize your inner space becoming more and more illuminated after practicing kumbhaka.

Kumbhaka may be challenging for beginners, especially if you haven't followed any other yogic practices such as asana (postures) and pranayama. However, systematic and regular practice, irrespective of initial experience, will make your breath retention easier, smoother, and longer, and thus reveal the full meditative potential of this technique. If you seek to develop your kumbhaka skills beyond the suggested practices, look for competent guidance and establish yourself firmly in the practice of asana and pranayama. Practitioners of breath retention usually take on certain lifestyle limitations, such as dietary regimens and sexual moderation. It is advised to avoid the practice altogether if you are pregnant or suffer from cardiovascular problems, high blood pressure, vertigo, cerebral diseases, or mental disorders.

72. Saraswati, *Prana and Pranayama*, 119–20.

There are three types of breath retention: internal retention (*antaranga kumbhaka*), external retention (*bahiranga kumbhaka*), and spontaneous retention (*kevala kumbhaka*). Here are three preliminary practices that can help you to develop the awareness of kumbhaka. The first two center on internal retention, whereas the third adds the practice of external retention. Since external retention is more difficult to master, be aware of signals of tension in the body or mind. Either release these tensions before proceeding to the next round or technique, or return to the previous stage. Don't exceed your natural capacity. Remember that internal retention should be mastered first, so avoid skipping the first two techniques. Approach the practice slowly and move systematically so that your foundation will be solid.

Instructions

PREPARATION: The meditation usually lasts thirty minutes. Sit in a comfortable position or lie in shavasana (lying on the back, with your legs spread as wide as a yoga mat and your arms relaxed at your sides). Relax the whole body. Practice yogic breathing for a few minutes (see chapter 3).

Internal Retention

1. Begin by inhaling while counting to four, then exhaling while counting to four (without breath retention) for a few minutes. Make sure that this is done without any tension in the body or mind.

2. Then, move to your practice of internal retention: inhale for a count of four, hold the breath inside for a count of two, and then exhale for a count of four.

3. When you hold your breath, visualize light at the eyebrow center or simply feel how you are falling into the space of kumbhaka.

4. If you experience any strain, go back to normal breathing. On the other hand, if the breathing is rhythmic and you feel generally relaxed, your practice is correct.

5. Do this for eleven rounds (you may gradually increase to twenty-one rounds). Then, sit for an effortless meditation for as long as you wish.

NOTE: If and when this practice becomes comfortable, you can extend the count of internal retention to three, and later to four (giving a ratio of 1:1:1 for the practice as a whole).

Extended Internal Retention and Exhalation

1. Practice the ratio of 1:1:1 until it becomes stabilized.

2. Gradually extend the exhalation to a count of eight (a ratio of 1:1:2).

· · · · · · · ·

3. If the feeling of breathlessness arises, breathe normally between each round. And if you experience strain, simply return to the ratio of 1:1:1. When the ratio of 1:1:2 feels comfortable to you, continue the practice without breaks for normal breathing in between.

4. Practice eleven rounds (you can slowly increase this to twenty-one). Then, sit for an effortless meditation for as long as you wish.

NOTE: If and when the ratio of 1:1:2 becomes comfortable, the count of inner retention can be increased slowly to the count of eight (giving a ratio of 1:2:2).

External Retention

1. Sitting in a comfortable position, relax your body and mind. Become aware of the spontaneous rhythm of your natural breath.

2. For a few minutes, count to four on inhalation, to four on internal retention, and to four on exhalation.

3. Then, after exhalation, hold the breath outside for the count of four.

4. Take several normal breaths in between each round. Drop the normal respiration between rounds only if you no longer experience breathlessness after external retention.

5. Practice eleven rounds. Then, sit for an effortless meditation for as long as you wish.

Meditate on This: Reclaiming the Lost Power of Attention

This entire chapter has been devoted to meditations that build true inner power. However, the greatest power in the universe, at least as far as we are concerned, is something we take for granted: the power of our attention.

In many respects, the process of meditation is the discovery that we don't know what attention is, and that we certainly don't know how to use it. But our meditative insight into the heart of attention goes even deeper than that. At first, we learn to acknowledge the value of this tool, but at a later stage, we come to realize that attention is what we are. To avoid awkward language in this text, I will use phrases such as "when you use your attention" or "direct your attention." But in reality, I mean that attention is what you are. So, what is attention and why is it the greatest power in the universe?

Attention consists of two elements. The first is awareness. Right now you are turning your attention to these words. Attention, in this sense, is like the light of awareness. In its purest

• • • • • • • •

meditative form, it is just awareness, but attention in action includes a second element: choice. When you turn your attention to these words, you do so because of a choice you have made; you have chosen to endow this book with meaning. In the same way, you could choose to pay attention to the mental chatter that goes on in your head. If you choose to do that, your mental chatter will become meaningful, and my words will recede into the background.

So, attention is a combination of awareness and choice.

However, as it is right now, what we call attention is almost completely conditioned and automatic. Therefore, the process of meditation is the beginning of deconditioning and freeing our attention. Second, in terms of choice, we are unable to redirect our attention at will. Being able to do so is actually a great achievement; it's a genuine feeling that we can freely decide how to direct our attention. We can say that this is the beginning of inner freedom and true will: if you are able to guide your attention at will, you will be able to disengage from all the elements you are no longer interested in focusing your attention on.

Your Attention Is Stronger than Any Thought or Feeling

Presently, the process of directing our attention is so automatic that we are not even conscious of it. We are not aware of the gap in which we can make a conscious choice. For this reason, we experience many types of thoughts and feelings, like sexual fantasies or fears, that we believe are just too powerful and overwhelming to overcome. We tend to think that when a given thought or emotion takes over us, we are powerless. We say things like "This thought gives me no rest" or "This desire ruins my life." We experience being taken over by emotional storms, panic attacks, and destructive thoughts. But what does it mean for a desire to ruin your life? How can the desire do anything to you? Does it force itself on you? Why do we speak of these things as if we have absolutely no choice?

Now, what would happen if you were aware of this choice and could therefore consciously choose? That would give you the greatest power in the universe, because nothing—no inner force or energy—could ever take over you again. This is what has been traditionally captured in the term *Buddha*: becoming master of your own attention. You are then able to control the chain reaction that rapidly follows the choice of giving attention to something. To better grasp this chain reaction, we should understand an important law called the law of attention.

The Law of Attention

The law of attention consists of at least four aspects.

1. **Between your attention and any thought, emotion, or feeling, there is a gap.**
   The reason we don't feel we have a choice is that we are unable to notice there is a difference between us and the thought or emotion. We are not aware of

the existence of a gap. Why? Because in the past, when we still had a choice but were unaware of it, we decided to direct our attention to certain internal forces and, convinced of their reality and their being a part of us, we made the choice to give them our attention.

Attention is like the food that mental and emotional entities, such as self-destructive thoughts or fears, require. In the same way that our body needs water and food, these energies feed on attention. The very nature of attention is to act as the light that shines on something. When attention shines on something, it instantly becomes a reality.

2. **Whatever attention focuses on becomes a reality.** Now, this is an immensely powerful principle, because it implies that things are not real unless you focus on them and decide to accept them as a part of yourself. It is only your decision that can make them real. In actuality, thoughts, desires, or emotional turmoil cannot do anything to you if you don't accept them as a part of yourself. If attention looks at these things and is not convinced of their reality, these energies disappear for the simple reason that they can no longer feed on your attention.

The chain reaction works like a closed circle: we turn our attention to a thought, emotion, or interpretation of reality, and immediately it appears to be our reality. Then we begin to feel—physically, mentally, emotionally, and energetically—according to the reality we created through our attention.

For example, I may encounter the thought *I hate myself*. This thought sounds quite convincing, especially since it uses "I" and "myself," which makes it appear personal and intimate. People suffer from this kind of thought all over the world. It is not a small matter: this is the reality of many. Then they find so-called reasons to hate themselves. As soon as they decide that this thought is a part of their being and identity, it becomes a reality. Now this thought becomes like a toxin that infiltrates the body, and as a result, a complete emotional reality and self-destructive behavior begin to emerge.

Thus, in reality what we suffer from all the time is thoughts—thoughts that pretend to be reality. We make them our reality, and then we begin to respond to them and to feel according to our response. When you think about it, this is our true source of trouble: the thoughts we believe and give power to. Everything else is quite manageable.

When you don't have thoughts, interpretations, and reactions to situations, the situations are pretty manageable. In Byron Katie's words, "Reality is always

· · · · · · · ·

kinder than the story we tell about it."[73] Reality is easier to handle without thinking: you encounter a situation, you face the situation, and that is all. This is what seeing things as they are is really all about.

When you detect a thought or an emotion, start experiencing the gap. Ask yourself: What would happen if I identified and embraced this thought or feeling? What would I feel right now? What would my body feel like? Imagine what it would feel like if this became your reality. And then, after realizing what it would feel like, choose whether or not to focus your attention on it to a degree that it becomes a reality.

Realizing that your principal suffering is caused by thoughts is a tremendous power—more precisely, not even by thoughts, but by your *reactions* to thoughts. After all, it is not that we need to control these thoughts; in fact, we cannot control them. We are not meant to control fear or desire and make it go away. Any attempt to control these elements will only get you caught in another conflict. The only thing you can control is your attention, which means owning your own mind and not letting anything in. If you start being convinced by any of these elements, they will enter you and become a part of your mind.

So, this is one of the first things that meditation does for us: it teaches us that our attention is separate from all thoughts and feelings, and that consequently, it always involves a choice. In meditation, we begin to create a gap, and then we train ourselves to maintain this gap and to even remain in it for a while. If you are able to do this consistently, you can then return to life and decide, on the basis of your newfound freedom, what you are going to choose as your reality.

The Next Step: Remain as Awareness

The deeper layer of meditation is the discovery of the freedom of awareness itself: a place where you can just *be* attention.

All day long we turn our attention to objects. Right now your attention is turned to the understanding of my words. We constantly turn our attention to objects and make these things our reality. But there is a third component of the law of attention.

3. **Whatever attention identifies with, it becomes.** This means that if you constantly focus on something and identify with it—if you decide that something is a part of you—at a certain point, it becomes you.

73. Katie, "Reality."

• • • • • • •

This third component is the reason most people cannot even imagine that there is a difference between their core identity as attention and all the things that they identify with: their thoughts and emotions, their body, life circumstances, life story, and memories. Everything they think they are is, in reality, something they have consistently focused on, identified with, and therefore become.

This third aspect of the law of attention, however, points at a magnificent reality: it shows you that in a sense, you are already free. This is because there is already—right now—an inherent separation between attention and everything that you have ever identified with. Right now, as you are reading these lines, you are, at the core of your being, pure attention. All your past conflicts and stories are just things that you have decided to attach your attention to. The two have become so glued to one another that they now appear to be inseparable.

The solar plexus chakra meditations evoke and enhance the sense of "I am" as pure presence that precedes anything else. Prior to "I am hungry," "I am sick," and "I am going to have a baby," there is "I am," a primordial self-presence. Allowing yourself to be pure attention in meditation is no different from this sense of pure presence.

Ultimately, being wide attention with no object is the essence and purpose of all meditation. And this is what the fourth component of the law of attention tells us.

4. **We don't always have to focus on objects and identify with them.** There is absolutely no reason to focus on thoughts, emotions, and objects all day long. We can do what meditation suggests we ought to do: keep our attention unfocused. Unfocused means pure attention. It means that you are fully attentive, but not attentive toward anything in particular. The result is that attention becomes a concentrated energy, an awake presence, because it is not wasted on focusing, identifying, and making anything a reality. In a way, this means that attention returns to its original state, before it became identified with or focused on anything.

If you meditate in this way and truly free your attention—or rather, free the attention that you are—from any focus, you can later return from this state to life and choose to redirect your attention at will. At present, our attention is extremely narrow because it is exclusively focused on the needs and wants of the body and mind. As a result, all that it perceives and notices in space and time

. . . .

are those things that correspond to the wants and needs of the body and mind. It has become highly selective, picking from life's magnificence only those elements. Life has been divided into two: whatever the body and mind like, and everything else they don't like.

Being so focused in this way, your attention has become extremely limited. But when attention returns to pure attention and regains its choice of focus and identification, it becomes not only awake but also sensitive. It notices so many other things in life. It is available. It is vast.

This is an even deeper layer of meditation: when your attention becomes this wide and spacious, it finally relaxes into the ocean of consciousness. Consciousness is like the mother of attention: attention sprang from it. Consciousness is what permeates the entire universe, while attention is like a drop of consciousness. And when this drop is reabsorbed into the ocean, your meditation obviously reaches its fulfillment.

So, attention is not just a capacity of your mind. It is the power that determines who you are, who you become, what your reality is, and whether you suffer or not. This is the key: if you understand the law of attention, you can be free from suffering—and only you can free yourself from suffering, because *you are attention.*

CHAPTER 7

Heart Chakra Meditations: Open Your Heart to Love and Compassion

Imagine your developing being as a tree consisting of roots and trunk, branches and crown. In this metaphor, the previous three groups of meditation were devoted to building your roots and trunk. Unlike a natural tree, our trunk, in the sense of self-empowered existence, doesn't exist yet. We have to create ourselves through the meditative process. Having our being supported by strong roots and a solid trunk is of utmost importance because this means leading a life based on inner stability, inner joy, and inner power.

But there is an even greater reason we require this sense of indestructible self: to be able to move beyond the trunk and to spread our branches toward heaven. And the first act of spreading outward and upward takes place when we turn our attention to the realm of relationships.

We tend to use the term *relationships* in a limited sense. We may think of romantic connections or, in a slightly more expanded context, our personal relationships. But in reality, relationships are everywhere in life, and to a certain degree, they are the very core of it—*they are life*. Nothing exists in isolation. Everything exists in relationships, and one could therefore say this is what we do all day long: we relate.

The Seven Types of Relationships

Relationships are any kind of space that is created between yourself and others. As a matter of fact, even as I write this book, I form a relationship with it. In this space between me and something else, there is a sort of tension. This space can be either a unifying space, leading to connection, or a dividing, separating space.

There are at least seven types of relationships that we engage in:

1. **The Relationship with Oneself:** An intense and complicated relationship, which includes our relationship with our body, personality, patterns, life circumstances, and past, among other aspects.

2. **The Relationship with Loved Ones:** Those who surround us and constitute our closest circle. These are the people who we probably spend most of our time with.

3. **The Relationship with Strangers:** Unfamiliar or nearly unfamiliar people who are everywhere around us. They may be neighbors, bus drivers, or people we meet on the train. Although we may not develop any meaningful connection with them, we still relate to them since they arouse certain thoughts and feelings in us.

4. **The Relationship with Our So-Called Enemies:** These are the people that we don't like, or even worse, hate. They may be people we are afraid of or those who have victimized us. They are people we find it extremely hard to open our hearts to because whenever we think of them, we experience an immediate mental and emotional contraction.

5. **The Relationship with Suffering Beings:** We encounter suffering people, animals, and plants. How do we relate to their suffering?

6. **The Relationship with the Cosmos:** This includes, of course, our relationship with the planet and with everything that lives on it. This is a more abstract, all-inclusive type of relationship with all sentient beings and with all that is.

7. **The Relationship with God/the Mystery of Life/the Source of Life:** If we consider any of these at all, this could be generalized as our interaction with that which is beyond our comprehension and that which is our origin.

. . . .

That's a lot to handle! When we embark on the meditative journey, we slowly discover that it is all about illuminating these different types of relationships, from the relationship with oneself all the way to the relationship with the transcendent or divine reality.

Meditation as a Healer

Heart chakra meditations are, naturally, dedicated to the awakening of the heart. In the process of heart awakening, two remarkable developments take place.

First, these meditations heal the break between yourself and the other in every relationship. They help us melt away the wall we have erected around our hearts. The good thing is that since *we* have erected this wall, we can also remove it, and that is why meditation is all that is required to do so. This has nothing to do with anyone else: it was our decision to create this sense of separation in the first place.

Second, these meditations increase the *unifying element*, the element that tears down the walls between us and makes us one. Thus, all five meditations that will be explored in this chapter have been designed to heal and unify relationships.

There are two helpful heart chakra principles that can illuminate this path of heart-opening meditations. The first principle is headlessness, which has been taught by twentieth-century meditation teachers such as Douglas Harding and Osho. In a way, the ultimate heart meditation is simply walking in the world and interacting with people while imagining that you are headless. If you do this, the feeling of headlessness moves all the mental energy to the heart quite effortlessly. When a sense of spaciousness replaces the solid head, the energy flows to the heart center and you begin to feel how your whole way of communicating with the world—and with yourself—changes radically. You will not be able to look at the world or at yourself in the same way because the heart has its own perception. The most important element of the heart's alternative way of looking is that it is holistic and inclusive. Instead of creating divisions and conflicts, it embraces and connects. If, for instance, you have a problem or you find yourself in a crisis, just imagine yourself as headless and look from the space of the heart at this challenge. How does the heart perceive this challenge?

A second key principle is the inner cave of the heart. Many think that their energetic heart is located in the surface of the chest, close to the skin. However, as we are told by ancient Hindu and Buddhist traditions of tantra, this is only the frontal and superficial extension of the heart. Instead, we should seek to establish a connection with the heart by visualizing ourselves moving from the lower chest inward and backward until we reach the point closest to the spine. This is a tremendous energetic trick. When you reside there, you finally discover the heart's true location—the innermost part of the heart, which in the *Katha Upanishad* is termed its inner cave.[74] This is what is really called the heart chakra.

The Sanskrit term for the heart chakra, *anahata*, is meaningfully translated as "unbeaten" or "unstruck."[75] This contains a striking implication: the heart is the element in us that cannot be beaten, struck, or defeated. This may not sound like a quality of hearts; hearts often tend to cry, get offended, become disappointed, feel betrayed, and, above all, break.

In the yogic tradition, however, hearts are the most unbreakable part of us. This cannot be understood as long as we communicate with the heart chakra from its surface layer, which is easily beaten and struck. The superficial layer is indeed vulnerable to pain and sorrow since it resides close to the skin, exactly in the space between you and the world. To grasp the deeper nature of the heart, you will need to sink backward and inward and to experience for yourself how unaffected the innermost part is. The five meditations that we will be studying in this chapter derive their power from this core of our heart.

Achieving Unity Consciousness in Meditation

Generally speaking, we can consider ten main purposes of heart-oriented meditations. Each of the five techniques in this chapter fulfills at least some of these aims. The first purpose has already been introduced: healing and unifying all our relationships.

The second purpose is profound and it requires some elaboration. Heart-based meditations reveal and establish unity consciousness—at least, almost all of them do. To come into contact with the principle of unity consciousness, let's use for a moment the prevailing scientific theory of cosmic evolution, according to which around 13.8 billion years ago, the universe began as a spacetime singularity. This implies that all that is was just one concentrated point of mass and energy that included all time and space. Impeccable unity was our beginning. The overwhelming diversity we now see is but an explosion of this one concentrated point.

In this explosion, two very strong forces, which are still active in the psychological and spiritual dimensions of our reality, came into being: individualization (or separation) and unification. The force of separation was so strong that it actually moved apart all this mass and energy, causing them to take different forms and creating this space that we now call relationships.

There is no question that we were all there together fifteen billion years ago, but our sense of vision is naturally designed to be guided by the force of separation. Thus, it focuses on the differences: here is a flower, and there is a man. This force of separation sets us apart, and it still works in us strongly in our wish to become strong, independent individuals and to establish our own unique perspectives and paths.

74. Easwaran, *The Upanishads*, 77.
75. Saraswati, *Kundalini Tantra*, 163.

At the same time, the force of unification is active as well. This is the force in us, and in all matter, that strives to return to the original, blissful unity. There is great power and beauty in becoming separate; consider all the countless different faces you have ever met in your life! But from the perspective of the force of unification, something is missing. So this force creates a longing in us, which may take the form of romantic relationships or the parent-child sense of unity. And because of this longing, some experience the odd feeling that they are not fully at home when they are only separate individuals.

The force of unification is what this group of meditations aims to awaken and intensify. When we are in a state of unbalanced heart chakra, the force of separation is much stronger. Moreover, in this unbalanced state, these two forces exist in us in a conflicting way: one moves us apart and the other makes us long for closeness. As a result, we may experience a struggle in our life as well. For example, in our intimate relationships, we wish to disappear into the other person, but we also want to have our limits and boundaries.

On the other hand, when the heart chakra begins to become balanced, the force of unification is stronger. This doesn't mean that we are meant to lose the force of separation altogether, only that the force of unification becomes the leading force in us and begins to guide us toward unity consciousness. Unity consciousness means recognizing and preferring sameness. Instead of focusing on the differences—on what sets us apart—we begin to look for the common ground, energetically, spiritually, and emotionally. But which part in us can do this? The mind? Obviously not. The mind, by its very nature, categorizes and makes judgments. The heart, however, is fit for this challenge.

There is a beautiful quotation by Osho that captures unity consciousness:

> The heart synthesises; the mind can only dissect, divide. It is a divider. Only the heart gives unity. When you can look through the heart the whole universe looks like one unity. When you approach through the mind, the whole world becomes atomic. There is no unity: only atoms and atoms and atoms. The heart gives a unitary experience. It joins together and the ultimate synthesis is God. If you can look through the heart, the whole universe looks like one. That oneness is God.[76]

When Osho uses the term *God* here, this should simply be read as a total heart perception that doesn't divide but instead perceives the universe in its underlying original state.

Unity consciousness is recognizing sameness while on the surface there are manifold creatures. This is what is so special about the heart and what makes it human and divine at the same time. Your heart has the power to include all the differences—the boundless uniqueness of form

---

76. Osho, *Meditation*, 110.

and personality—without losing sight of the reality of oneness. The heart can even include separateness, since even the force of separation does not really separate; it is a part of the broader ecstasy of unity. So, the heart prefers to emphasize sameness while embracing the reality of the many.

This is unity consciousness: seeing the one Self at the heart of every living being. When the heart chakra awakens in meditation, it makes it possible for you to behold the wonder of the many and the One, and to be aware of the sameness of everyone's core. Based on this powerful vision, true love comes into being, and soon after, compassion follows. That's what compassion really is.

As we will discover in some of the compassion-oriented Buddhist meditations in this chapter, compassion is not empathy. It is not a coincidence that we have more than one Buddhist meditation in this list of heart techniques; Buddhist traditions have ascribed great importance to the element of compassion. The practice of compassion can lead to unity consciousness, and unity consciousness can lead to the manifestation of compassion.

Compassion can be considered the active aspect of the recognition of sameness. When we recognize sameness, we inevitably recognize the sameness of suffering as well. Being one in suffering is a part of unity. Unity is not only the fun part of being one with the trees, the sky, and the beautiful planet—it also includes being one with the suffering of humanity, plants, animals, and the planet. That's why compassion is the flower that comes from unity consciousness. Naturally, all this implies that unity consciousness is universal by its very nature, and this universal, all-inclusive nature of love and compassion is an important element of the heart chakra group of meditations as a whole.

Other Roles and Purposes of Heart-Oriented Meditations

The third purpose of heart meditations is that they help us to mature psychologically and spiritually on our way toward unity consciousness. This is highly important: these meditations don't just make us leap elegantly to unity consciousness for the simple reason that we are unable to do so. We all start with certain inhibitions, the greatest of which is our selfishness, which is greatly challenged by the extreme selfless nature of unity consciousness and compassion. In this sense, heart chakra techniques are soothing and comforting, *and* they are intense awakeners that pull us out of our comfort zone. Ultimately, their task is to genuinely evolve our hearts.

In addition, these meditations help us to realize true intimacy, which is the intimacy of the one heart: the experience of sameness in the space between yourself and others. It is true that as long as we are in the body, we can never return to the original state and attain perfect oneness with others. Doing so is not only impossible but also unhealthy. We all need the force of separation to be active in our lives in order to maintain our unique perspectives and individual boundaries. But the profound intimacy enabled by some of these meditations opens the space for us to also achieve a realization of the underlying reality of the one in the many, and to even communicate with each other from this space.

The fifth function of heart chakra techniques is meditation as a healer. Generally speaking, meditation is also a therapeutic process, and at least in some respects, it may replace certain therapeutic processes when used correctly. This group of meditations reveals to us the healing power of meditation. They activate the heart as the element of our being that experiences an unbreakable connection with life and every living soul. Energetically and essentially, the heart is forever connected by an unbroken thread to all others, to the divine, and to one's self. So with the aid of these meditations, we are able to melt away the pain of separation and loneliness that has been caused by the excessive activity of the force of separation in our life. Put simply, these meditations show us that deep down, we are never alone and we are never really separate. They also help us to wipe away memories of the past, develop forgiveness, overcome disappointments and betrayals, and dissolve the protective wall we have erected around our hearts. The last aspect of their healing power lies in their ability to facilitate self-love.

In addition to healing power, these meditations reveal our heart power. This is the secret of the heart's innermost layer, the inner cave of the heart: an indestructible, unbeatable presence, which has nothing to do with the well-known fragility of the human heart. Based on this discovery that the heart is our greatest source of power and motivation, one more purpose is to make the heart the active leader of our life, first by centering ourselves in the heart, and then by being able to make heart choices.

The last, most spiritual role of this group of meditations is to arouse our attraction to the divine and to encourage final merging with the greater reality. The final destination of these meditations is to bring us back to a state of unity, driven by our heart's longing. In fact, the entire spiritual journey starts not in the mind but in the heart; any kind of spiritual passion completely bypasses our rational mind and relies instead on an unexplainable heart knowing.

The Inner Cave of the Heart

The principle of the inner or secret cave of the heart was first indicated in the *Upanishads*, ancient India's Hindu textbook on self-liberation through meditation.

Historical Background

In the *Katha Upanishad* (dated back roughly to the fifth century BCE), the Lord of Death declares:

> The wise, realizing through meditation
> The timeless Self, beyond all perception,
> Hidden in the cave of the heart,
> Leave pain and pleasure far behind.[77]

This is not only a metaphor that describes our innermost being; the sages pointed out that we should actually find our true self in the depths of the heart chakra. If we know how to penetrate into this dark, hidden territory and meditate on it, we can reveal a source of illumination there. Although this source of light is but a small lamp, it contains within it the entire universe and the supreme Self, and it has the power to dispel darkness and to brighten up all and everything.

Versions of meditation on the inner cave can be found not only in Hinduism but in Buddhism as well. The simplest version is to learn to identify the deepest location of the heart chakra and to meditate on a source of light there, or to allow the mantra Aum (see chapter 8) to reverberate in that location. We can also visualize a glowing white drop, as tiny as a sesame seed, which represents the kundalini fluid that lies dormant inside the heart chakra (see the meditation in chapter 10 titled "The Empty Body"). This fluidlike substance is called the "indestructible drop of the heart" in Vajrayana Buddhism since it is considered the element that survives death even after everything falls away, and it is therefore the key to immortality. In this sense, this region can also be regarded as the seat of the soul.

The most advanced form of the practice of the inner cave is the Clear Light meditation of Vajrayana Buddhism, in which the meditator visualizes the entire universe, including their own body, becoming absorbed in the drop until only the drop remains. Here, however, I loosely rely on the version taught by the Tibetan Tsoknyi Rinpoche and written down by Tias Little.[78]

Purpose

This meditation has two major aims. First, it is designed to heal the heart profoundly. The healing power of focusing on the inner cave is that in this way, you can tap into a layer of your heart and being that has never been hurt or damaged, and that is actually a source of great, indestructible power. This is even more meaningful if we consider the ordinary experience of the heart as the most vulnerable part of our being, which requires protection and a safe environment. We tend to

---

77. Easwaran, *The Upanishads*, 77.
78. Little, "Awakening the Power of the Heart."

associate the heart with emotional pains and perhaps even difficult memories. Thus, by learning to trust that the heart is invincible, we identify it as our resting place, where we can abide in inner completeness. Moreover, we may feel even more empowered to deal with our heartaches and heartbreaks.

The second purpose is realization of our deepest spiritual self. The inner cave is the most accessible point that links us to our subtlest consciousness. It has remained unaffected by human experience and changing circumstances and conditions, and it even transcends death. Instead of contemplating the supreme Self or the transcendent reality in abstract terms, we can simply merge our awareness with this point deep within our subtle body.

Practice

The key to this practice is identifying the exact location of the inner cave of the heart. First, place your attention midway between the breasts, right at the bottom of the sternum. This area is the outermost layer of the heart chakra and the closest to the skin. From this point, using your inner vision, pierce deep into the chest and move into the frontal part of the spine. Just before this part of the spine, and facing inward as if toward the spine, you find the heart chakra's true location, deep within the central channel of the subtle body. Remember, this point is no longer our familiar emotional heart, where we find heartbreak and heartache. This inner cave is the heart's true, untainted nature.

During this meditation, we will journey into this point through the heart's two outer layers. The outermost layer, which is close to the skin, is the one that looks outward and faces the world. Given its location, it can easily be hit and emotionally bruised. It is subject to our daily experience of pain, hurt, insult, changing circumstances, and passing impressions. This makes it highly vulnerable, and for this reason we erect a protective wall around it to help prevent direct hits.

A few centimeters into the chest we can identify the middle layer, which contains deeper emotional impressions and the challenges of the heart. This includes the way we evaluate our self-worth, as well as complex emotional patterns and deep-seated memories.

As we move deeper, we leave the superficial experience of the heart behind, until we land in the heart's inner cave. However, you cannot reach this deepest element through effort or volition; you need to surrender and fall back into your heart, as it were. Then, you rest inside this cave for as long as you wish, and through it, you stay in communion with the greater reality. This restful experience is silent, sweet, and mysterious, but it's also powerful and highly energetic.

Instructions

Preparation: This meditation usually lasts between twenty and thirty minutes.

1. Sit in a comfortable position and close your eyes. Feel that you are drawn to discover and to contact the heart's mystery. To allow your attention to drop into the heart and settle there, visualize your head disappearing completely so that instead of the head, there is empty space. Having the head as the center of your perception makes it overloaded; feel how light this area feels now. As a result, your center of gravity can naturally move down to your chest. Feel how your head is now your heart. As soon as you shift the center of gravity, the heart's space begins to operate.

2. Now begin to journey into your heart chakra. With every in-breath and expansion of the chest, feel how you are pulled into the center of the heart, first moving through the outermost layer, the part that is easily hit in life's ever-changing play; the part that experiences the most immediate pains and joys of the heart. Then, pass through the wall of the outermost heart to find the heart's inner world: its more concealed and intimate thoughts and feelings, self-image, and past impressions and conclusions.

3. Now, aim to reach the source of the heart's inner light, the very spring of your heart's energy. Simply let go and fall back into the heart chakra's vibrating core. What do you find in this innermost darkness? Move your consciousness into this heart of hearts while momentarily removing the outer layers, dissolving the wall, and allowing the innermost heart to glow in the open, as if you share the innermost heart with the universe and the whole of existence. Dwell in this unique energy field and allow it almost to move out of your chest and to become fully present and visible. In this way, your heart reveals its true presence, which has no edge or boundary. Meditating on the heart's secret, ask yourself: what lies at the core of my heart?

4. Continue to rest in this wide, vibrating openness. If you choose to do so, you can remain in this state of unharmed open-heartedness even after you come out of the meditation.

· · · · · · · ·

Loving-Kindness Meditation

The popular and highly researched loving-kindness meditation—in Pali, *Metta Bhavana*—has its roots in early Buddhism, although the principle of loving-kindness can also be found in the early Hindu *Upanishads* and in early Jainism.

Historical Background

The earliest Buddhist scriptures, the Pali Canon, frequently recommend metta meditation to the Buddha's followers and elaborate on its benefits, such as improved sleep without bad dreams and a light waking, better concentration, and a sense of protection.[79]

However, the form of meditation that has been popularized in the West derives from a different set of instructions, found in the fifth-century systematization of the Buddha's teachings by Buddhaghosa, entitled *Visuddhimagga* ("The Path of Purification").[80] Ever since, additional variations on this traditional practice have been developed by modern teachers and applied in modern research settings.

The words *loving-kindness* describe an emotional state that is not a feeling of sentimental love. Rather, it can be described as an unconditional friendliness, benevolence, and goodwill. Generally speaking, there have been two approaches to the practice. The first focuses on loving-kindness itself: wishing a being happiness and sending out unconditional, inclusive love. The second approach focuses on compassion (*karuna*): wishing to relieve a being from suffering. Traditionally, metta and karuna have been practiced together. Both qualities belong to the four "divine abodes" (*brahma-vihāra*), which are the four main virtues taught in Buddhism: loving-kindness (metta), compassion (karuna), sympathetic joy (*mudita*), and equanimity (*upekkha*). It is considered impossible to become a bodhisattva (one who has attained enlightenment) without achieving a high level of metta and karuna.

Purpose

This meditation aspires to cultivate understanding, love, and compassion, first toward ourselves and then toward ever-widening circles of other sentient beings. The process helps to break down barriers that stand between us and ourselves, as well as those that we have erected to separate ourselves from others. Thus, the practice is a gradual softening of the mind and heart, an opening to increasingly deeper levels of the feeling of kindness or pure love.

---

79. Gunaratana, "11 Benefits of Loving-Friendliness Meditation."
80. Bramble, "The Six Stages of Metta-Bhavana."

Metta is not a sentimental feeling of goodwill or a moral obligation, but a quality that emerges from within our "Buddha nature." It is unconditional, inclusive love. It is not restricted to friends and family; it extends out from personal categories to include all living beings. It does not depend on how the other person feels about us; it is without any desire to possess another; and it does not depend on whether one "deserves" it or not. Moreover, the meditator is not supposed to expect anything in return. This is the ideal love, which everyone can potentially find within themselves. It is therefore a love unified with wisdom. In a deeper sense, it is designed to encourage us to develop the wish to liberate all sentient beings from the suffering of *samsara*, the perpetual cycle of life and death.

The proven benefits of the cultivation of loving-kindness and compassion range from increased well-being to relief from illness and improved relationships. However, as already mentioned, this meditation is ideally done in the spirit of expecting nothing in return.

Practice

Using visualization and phrases, we begin with loving ourselves, since unless we have a sufficient degree of this unconditional love and acceptance for ourselves, it is quite impossible to extend it to others. Then we include others who are special to us and, ultimately, all living things. In this way, the practice increases in difficulty with respect to the recipients of our loving-kindness: from ourselves to loved ones, neutral beings, difficult beings, and finally all beings. Gradually, both the visualization and the phrases blend into the actual experience, the feeling of loving-kindness.

The phrases of positive intention, which are repeated silently, are designed to invoke a desire for safety, happiness, health, and ease or peace for ourselves and for others. Classically, four phrases are used, such as "May I be safe," "May I be happy," "May I be healthy," and "May my life unfold with ease." Naturally, the phrases may be changed according to the recipient of your wishes. For instance, "May I be safe" becomes "May you be safe."

The participant is asked to notice the feelings and thoughts evoked by the phrases. It can take time to feel genuinely compassionate. At first, you may find yourself saying, "I love myself. I love all beings," without profound intention and feeling behind your words. Remember, however, that the practice is not mere autosuggestion—just repeating the words or striving after some ideal will not do the trick. Since the willingness to love is not yet the actual ability to love, you need to look deep inward, with all your being, in order to gain insight into the practice. If you look deep into your body, feelings, perceptions, mental formations, and consciousness, slowly your aspiration to love will become a deep intention.

Instructions

PREPARATION: This meditation requires between twenty and thirty minutes.[81]

1. Begin by focusing on your chest area, your heart center. Breathe in and out from that area, as if you are breathing from the heart center and as if all experience is happening from there. Anchor your mindfulness only on the sensations at your heart center.

2. Breathing in and out from the heart center, begin by generating this kind feeling toward yourself. Generate warm, gentle, loving, forgiving feelings for yourself. You can use an image, like golden light flooding your body. Feel any areas of mental blockage, numbness, self-judgment, or self-hatred. Then drop beneath them to the place where you do care for yourself, where you want strength and health and safety for yourself.

3. Continuing to breathe in and out, use three or four of the following traditional phrases, or use phrases that you have created yourself. Say or think them several times.

   May I be happy.

   May I be free of physical pain and suffering.

   May I be healthy and strong.

   May I be free from inner and outer harm and danger.

   May I be safe and protected.

   May I be free of mental suffering or distress.

   May I be able to live in this world happily, peacefully, joyfully, and with ease.

   May I be peaceful, happy, and light in body and spirit.

   May I be free from anger, afflictions, fear, and anxiety.

   May I learn to look at myself with the eyes of understanding and love.

   May I be able to recognize and touch the seeds of joy and happiness in myself.

   May I know how to nourish the seeds of joy in myself every day.

   May I learn to identify and see the sources of anger, craving, and delusion in myself.

   May I be free from attachment and aversion, but not be indifferent.

81. The instructions derive from Bramble, "The Six Stages of Metta-Bhavana."

4. Move to the person in your life who most easily evokes the feeling of pure, unconditional loving-kindness—the love that does not depend on getting anything back. This is usually someone you consider a mentor, a benefactor, or an elder. It might be a parent, grandparent, or teacher—someone toward whom it takes no effort to feel respect and reverence and who immediately arouses a feeling of care in you. Repeat the phrases you chose in step three for this person, changing pronouns as needed.

5. Move to a person you regard as a dear friend and repeat your chosen phrases again, breathing in and out of your heart center. Bring them to mind as vividly as you can, and think of their good qualities. Feel your connection with your friend, and your sympathy for them, and encourage these to grow. You can also use an image, such as light shining from your heart into theirs.

6. Move to a neutral person, someone for whom you feel neither strong like nor dislike. As you repeat your chosen phrases, allow yourself to feel tenderness and care for their welfare.

7. Move to someone you have difficulty with, including hostile feelings and resentment. Repeat your chosen phrases for this person. If you have difficulty doing this, you can say, prior to the phrases, "To the best of my ability, I wish that you be…" If you begin to feel ill will toward this person, return to the benefactor and let the loving-kindness arise again. Then return to this person. Let the phrases spread throughout your whole body, mind, and heart.

8. Move out spaciously to your immediate surroundings. Include every living being within this circle:

   May all beings in the air, on land, and in the water be safe, happy, healthy, and free from suffering.

9. As you feel your immediate surroundings fill with the power of loving-kindness, move on, expanding the surroundings in concentric circles until you envelop the entire planet. Radiate loving-kindness out to all beings. Stay in touch with the ember of warm, tender loving-kindness at the center of your being, and begin to visualize and engender a felt sense of all living beings. Have a sense of waves of loving-kindness spreading from your heart to everyone, to all beings everywhere. The traditional phrases are these:

   May all beings be safe, happy, healthy, live joyously…

   May all living beings be safe, happy, healthy, live joyously…

• • • • • • • •

May all breathing beings be safe, happy, healthy, live joyously...

May all individuals be safe, happy, healthy, live joyously...

May all beings in existence be safe, happy, healthy, live joyously...

Allow the phrases to simply be a conduit for the force of loving-kindness. Through these five phrases, empower your imagination to touch the hearts of all forms of life in the universe, unconditionally and inclusively. Stay with all beings until you feel a personal sense of the profound interconnectedness of all life.

10. You may move on to specific categories of beings:

    All females of all species (or the feminine principle of the universe within us all).

    All males of all species (or the masculine principle of the universe within us all).

    All awakened ones.

    All seekers.

    All celestial beings.

    All humans.

    All animals and other beings in difficult places.

    These are simply more ways of including every being in the universe within your heart.

11. Expand your loving-kindness until you are able to visualize Earth spinning within the vast, mysterious universe. If you like, continue expanding the sense of your loving-kindness, filling the endless emptiness of the universe:

    May all living beings everywhere, on all planes of existence, known and unknown, be happy, be peaceful, and be free from suffering.

NOTE: If you wish, you may add, with time, the aspect of karuna or compassion by bringing to mind people who have been unfortunate and wishing them freedom from their suffering.

Tonglen

Tonglen strives to achieve *bodhicitta*: union of compassion and wisdom. As such, its clearest goal is to enhance a person's capacity for universal compassion. However, as a provocative practice that intensely challenges the limits of what the heart is willing to contain, it achieves even more than this.

· · · · · · ·

Historical Background

Tonglen has traditionally been taught as one of many practices in the tradition of Tibetan Lojong (mind-training), which is often attributed to the famous Bengali teacher Atisha (980–1054 CE), who brought the second dissemination of Buddhism to Tibet. The seeds of the Lojong teachings, and thus Tonglen, were planted by classical Indian Buddhist treatises, particularly Nagarjuna's *Precious Garland* and Shantideva's *Guide to the Bodhisattva's Way of Life*. The various Lojong practices were initially considered secret and highly advanced teachings, but they have eventually become a shared heritage of all of the major schools of Tibetan Buddhism.[82]

As a result, Tonglen is considered a compassion practice common to all Tibetan Buddhist traditions, a step further beyond the loving-kindness (metta) meditation that also appears in this chapter. The word *Tonglen* is Tibetan for "giving and taking" (or "sending and receiving").

Purpose

Tonglen is said to have the capacity to reduce fear and ego-clinging. By learning to engage deeply with the suffering of others, we confront our own fear of suffering and liberate ourselves from age-old patterns of selfishness. In this way, it ultimately leads us to a realization of our enlightened nature, which transcends our pursuit of pleasure and avoidance of pain.

In the words of the American Tibetan Buddhist teacher Pema Chödrön, who has helped to disseminate Tonglen in the West: "Tonglen is a method for overcoming our fear of suffering and for dissolving the tightness of our hearts. Primarily it is a method for awakening the compassion that is inherent in all of us, no matter how cruel or cold we might seem to be."[83]

Practice

The meditation involves the use of breathing and visualization to awaken compassion; on the in-breath, you visualize yourself taking in the suffering of others, and on the out-breath, you send out relief. This implies that you breathe in feelings you would generally hope to get rid of (fear, frustration, pain, anger, guilt, bitterness, doubt, and rage) and breathe out that which you find pleasurable (happiness and well-being, peace of mind, healing, and fulfillment). Be aware that the essence of the practice is not about feeling "compassion for others," but experiencing a deep "exchange of oneself for others."[84]

The process opens with the realization that there are millions of others just like you, who at this very moment feel the same pain or sadness. You breathe in the pain and suffering of all those people who deal with these same emotions, and you breathe out relief or "space" so that

---

82. McKnight, "Tonglen Meditation's Effect on Levels of Compassion and Self-Compassion," 11–12.

83. Chödrön, *Welcoming the Unwelcome*, 154.

84. McKnight, "Tonglen Meditation's Effect on Levels of Compassion and Self-Compassion," 16.

the sufferers' hearts and minds can live with their discomfort. This helps you realize that the "individual me" and the "individual you" are mistaken ideas, since suffering is universal. At the peak of the practice, you breathe all the miseries of all the people in the world—all the darkness and negativity that exists anywhere, past, present, and future—and let them become absorbed into your expansive heart.

By reversing the logic of avoiding suffering and seeking pleasure, we begin to break down the habitual pattern of selfishness. This introduces us to a far larger view of reality: we learn to move from judgment, isolation, and ignorance to caring, connection, and understanding.

Naturally, this technique goes against the concept of positive thinking, which recommends throwing out misery and negativity and breathing in joy and happiness. Here, you breathe out all the joy and blissfulness that you have. You pour yourself into existence, so to speak—you drink in all the suffering and pour out all the blessings. This is the other face of oneness with the universe.

It is common for people to worry that they might absorb the suffering or negative energy of others, but this is not the case. You simply use your breath to *acknowledge* their dark emotional states, and you *visualize* their suffering transforming into love and compassion. More deeply, Tonglen activates the heart as a transformer, thus showing us the great power that the heart has in responding to this suffering.

One of the heart's powers is to alchemize darkness and to bring everything to its original state of pure love. When we are afraid of absorbing darkness, it is only because we are not aware of this power of the heart. On the other hand, when we are no longer afraid, this power becomes activated and we come to recognize love as the one true invincible power in the universe. As the twentieth-century spiritual teacher Osho said, "Once you have learned that your heart can do this magic, this miracle, you would like to do it again and again."[85]

Instructions

PREPARATION: This meditation requires between twenty and thirty minutes. But it may also be done quickly, "on the spot," whenever you experience yourself or another being suffering.[86]

1. Sit quietly and bring your mind home. Then, meditate deeply on compassion. Invoke the presence of all the Buddhas, bodhisattvas, and enlightened beings so that, through their inspiration and blessing, compassion may be born in your heart.

---

85. Osho, *Meditation*, 115.

86. The instructions derive from McKnight, "Tonglen Meditation," 14–16, and Chödrön, "How to Practice Tonglen."

2. Begin by setting your intention to invite suffering in and to remain present with it. Envision yourself in a safe space. You will be taking in feelings such as grief, anger, and anxiety, so it is important that you feel comfortable where you are. Remember, if anything comes up that you don't feel able to handle at that moment, you may simply return to your breath and take a more relaxed approach to the practice.

3. Bring your awareness to your breath, and as you inhale, begin visualizing pollution entering your body—smoke, dark clouds, or just a general feeling of obstruction and darkness. In a state of open awareness, this negativity will have nowhere to "stick" in your body (you can imagine your body as not really solid, but made of a light substance), therefore allowing it to be processed and transformed.

4. As you exhale, imagine that you are breathing out bright, pure, nourishing air, as if your body were a plant, receiving pollution and sending out clean energy. If your mind wanders, come back to your breath and the textural rhythm of giving and taking.

5. Now, imagine in front of you, as vividly and poignantly as possible, someone you care for who is experiencing emotional discomfort or suffering. Try to imagine every aspect of the person's pain and distress. Allow their suffering to open your heart to compassion. Feel the wish to relieve the person of all suffering: physical, mental, emotional, and situational. You may make a wish, such as "May you be free of suffering and the causes of suffering." Then, imagine that all of their suffering manifests together and gathers into a great mass of hot, black, grimy smoke or a dark, heavy cloud surrounding them.

6. Move your awareness to your heart area and breathe in deeply, imagining yourself inhaling those dark, heavy, uncomfortable, cloudy feelings directly into your heart. Visualize that this mass of black smoke dissolves, with your in-breath, into the very core of your heart. There, it destroys completely all traces of self-centeredness, thereby purifying all your negative karma. It is as if in an instant, both that cloud of misery and your self-centeredness mutually extinguish each other, leaving no trace of either behind.

7. Imagine now that your self-centeredness has been destroyed, that the heart of your enlightened mind, your bodhicitta, is fully revealed. As you breathe out from the heart area, imagine that your heart is a source of bright, warm, compassionate light, and that you are breathing that light into the person who is suffering. The dark feelings are disappearing without a trace into the light of your heart; the dark clouds are transforming into a bright, warm light at the center

• • • • • • • •

of your heart, alleviating the person's suffering. You may add a compassionate wish, such as "May you have happiness and the causes of happiness," along with visualizations of anything that might bring the person relative happiness and transcendent joy. Visualize that this person in front of you becomes happier and healthier with each breath.

8. The rays of this brilliant, cooling light of peace, joy, happiness, and ultimate well-being, which you've sent to your friend in pain, are also purifying all of their negative karma. At the moment the light of your bodhicitta streams out to touch your friend in pain, it is essential to feel a firm conviction that all of their negative karma has been purified and a deep, lasting joy that they have been totally freed of suffering and pain.

9. Next, try extending your compassion to a stranger or a general population, such as a particular community or an impoverished country, that may be experiencing dark, heavy feelings at this moment. As you did for your loved one, imagine inhaling cloudy, dark feelings away from those people and into your own heart. As the dark feelings settle into your heart, imagine that they are disappearing without a trace into the light of your compassionate heart. You can imagine this person or people being enveloped by the calm and comforting light that you are breathing out from your heart.

10. Continue the above process of sending and receiving, but this time, extend your compassion to someone you find it difficult to associate with, or even a so-called enemy.

11. Now, as you continue with this cycle of inhaling and exhaling suffering and relief, begin to visualize suffering beyond any individual person. You might expand spatially, outward from your body: people who live on your block, in your neighborhood, in your city, and so on.

12. Allow the size of the group to gradually expand until you are taking in suffering from all directions. Breathe in the miseries of all humans, animals, and plants on this planet—all the darkness and negativity that exists anywhere, past, present, and future. Breathe out healing and relief in all directions.

13. Now you may return to resting in open awareness for several minutes or as long as you wish. Follow the breath, and on the exhale, release any tension that may have arisen during the meditation. Continue with a few deep breaths, or even sighs if it feels good to do so. Relax and let go, arriving in the present moment.

· · · · · · · ·

Prayer of the Heart

The Christian Prayer of the Heart or "Jesus Prayer" was transmitted from the early Desert Fathers to Byzantine monks, and it has been preserved to this day by Russian, Romanian, and Greek hermits and pilgrims.

Historical Background

This unique prayer meditation began to spread with the birth of *hesychasm* (from *Hesychia*, "inner stillness" in Greek), an early form of Christian mysticism in the fourteenth-century Byzantine empire, which later became absorbed into the Eastern Orthodox Church.[87] Hesychasm is a type of monastic life in which practitioners seek divine quietness through an uninterrupted internal recitation along with each breath. The recitation is either Jesus's name or the Jesus prayer: "Lord Jesus Christ, Son of God, have mercy on me." This form of prayer is followed by a special psychophysical technique that began to be practiced by monks on the Holy Mountain of Athos. The technique involves specific bodily postures and deliberate breathing patterns meant to support the main purpose of the prayer: attaining a union of the mind with the heart so that eventually the prayer will become a "prayer of the heart." Due to its dimension of bodily awareness, the Prayer of the Heart is sometimes called "Christian yoga."[88]

The Prayer of the Heart is essentially an oral tradition, and the written accounts we have don't tend to provide full instructions on how to carry it out. Although these reports do share some of the experience, they emphasize the need for sincere personal practice. In addition, the practice is considered among those spiritual exercises that are esoteric and complex and require caution. Here I will present a simplified form of the practice.

Purpose

In some respects, this meditation can be considered a continuation of the Inner Cave of the Heart (discussed earlier in this chapter). It makes it possible for you to access your inner cave as the physical seat of your truest, innermost Self.

The principle is simple: by engaging in an uninterrupted repetition of the name of the deity along with your breathing, you are able to focus your attention on the sense of self within your chest. As the practice matures over the years, meditators go through major inner shifts. First, they progress from the verbal prayer to internal and silent prayer. Later, they experience an inward deepening of the focus in the chest. With time, they are able to leap from a volitional

---

87. Louchakova, "The Essence of the Prayer of the Heart," 1.
88. Louchakova, "The Essence of the Prayer of the Heart," 1.

repetition of the name to a state in which the name spontaneously emerges from within their very being. Advanced practitioners of the Prayer of the Heart experience a dissolution of the name into wordless prayer of sustained presence and states of inner union. Since their concentration is increasingly absorbed inward, they can directly know their essential Self.

Just like with any other prayer-based approach, you will start by contemplating your supreme self in the form of someone who appears to be outside of yourself. The focus on a deity helps release you from the constraints of your individual ego. Instead of meditating on a formless and inconceivable supreme self, you have a name as an intermediate support. Thus, Jesus's name is a symbol of the unity between the human and the divine. Although the Christian practice centers on Jesus, remember that this practice can be used by meditators of any orientation. Instead of Jesus, you can attach any other divine name to your heart and breath.

As the practice deepens, the form drops away by itself. Since this is, after all, a mystical meditation, Jesus's name (or that of any other deity) is only meant to lead you to the living divinity within you—so at a certain point, the duality of you and Jesus dissolves in the depths of your heart. The researcher Olga Louchakova calls this a "non-dual prayer":[89] it is a form both of worship and of self-inquiry, a dialogue and a sense of unity. Ultimately, the individual self disappears and only the divine self remains.

Practice

The simplest form of the technique consists of the repeated invocation of the name of Jesus, tied to a physical concentration of attention in the region of the heart. Two accounts of Christian monks provide a description of this basic process. First, you should enter a secluded room, sit, and bring yourself to a state of deep calm, without worrying about worldly affairs. If you wish, you can relax yourself by focusing your gaze and awareness on your navel for a while. Then, you should concentrate your mind and "lead it into the respiratory passage through which your breath passes into your heart."[90] Follow every in-breath to enter the depths of the heart with your mind.

After your awareness descends into your heart with your inhaled breath, you will find only darkness there at first. Later, however, you will feel united with your soul and will be filled with indescribable joy and luminosity. The second step is to repeat and meditate on the prayer "Lord Jesus Christ, Son of God, have mercy on me" deep within your heart. This invocation, which enables the presence of Jesus to inhabit your heart, will instantly destroy any distractive thoughts.[91]

---

89. Louchakova, "The Essence of the Prayer of the Heart," 6.
90. Hisamatsu and Pattni, "Yoga and the Jesus Prayer," 65.
91. Hisamatsu and Pattni, "Yoga and the Jesus Prayer," 7.

So, prior to your recitation, you need to look for the physical seat of your innermost self within your chest, using your in-breath to move deeper into its depths. After you have settled there, you should begin to associate the breath-paced repetition of the divine name with this sense of self in the chest. As you move inward with every breath, the name flows through the sense of self and back into the spiritual heart, the birthplace of your self-awareness.

Getting in touch with the unknown regions of yourself may lead you through unconscious layers, such as hidden desires, emotions, motivations, and past memories. Acknowledge them and embrace them through your spiritual heart. This will eventually contribute to an increased sense of inner completeness and wholeness. You may also face mental chatter, emotional states, and other states like silence or darkness. Whatever you face, focus your attention on the name, and this will counteract these passing states. Repetition of the name continuously removes distracting thoughts, suspends preconceived ideas, and purifies your experience. Similarly, you can direct your emotions to the unknown god within your heart so that they become transmuted and refined. Be aware of the fact that while your mind is in constant flux, your heart awareness is unchanging.

At the same time, strengthen your intention to access the core of your divine heart. This will indirectly weaken the power of thoughts and emotions. Aspire to center your entire attention on the secret chambers of your interior space, where the prayer is no longer, since you become one with what you meditate on.

This entire meditative process doesn't necessarily happen only to those who have practiced the prayer for several decades—in fact, it can unfold within a single session of introspection.

Instructions

PREPARATION: The meditation usually lasts twenty minutes.

1. Make yourself as calm as possible by leaving behind your worries about the transient world. You can become more peaceful by focusing your gaze and awareness on your navel for a long moment.

2. Bring your attention into the area of the heart through sensation (rather than visualization or emotional prompts). Grow aware of its volume, aliveness, and subtle movement within your chest. Remember, the heart is not simply a metaphor, but the physical anchor of the divine presence within you. Feel how with every in-breath you are pushed further into the depths of your chest. To settle in the heart's true location, place your attention midway between the breasts (right at the bottom of your sternum) and, using your inner vision and feeling, pierce deep into the chest and move into the frontal part of the spine. Just before

• • • • • • • •

this part of the spine, and facing inward as if toward the spine, you find the heart, deep within the central channel of the subtle body. Merge your awareness with your heart.

3. With your attention so anchored, on your in-breath silently and inwardly utter the words "Lord Jesus Christ," allowing the presence of this living master to fill your entire being. On the out-breath, silently "utter" the words "Have mercy on me," remembering that mercy actually means the lifeblood of divine love flowing within you and within the world.[92] Continue to recite in this way for twenty or thirty minutes.

4. As you progress with the recitation, use it to move deeper and deeper into your spiritual heart. Strive to reach a state in which the prayer transforms from a volitional verbal repetition into the heart's wordless prayer and internal presence.

Dhikr

Dhikr (Arabic: also spelled *Zikr*, literally "remembrance") is a form of Islamic mantra meditation in which sacred phrases or brief prayer sentences are chanted repeatedly to help the chanter remember God.

Historical Background

The practice of dhikr is central in Sufism, a form of mystical Islam. Each Sufi order has its own adopted dhikr, which is accompanied by a specific posture, breathing, and movement (see also Sufi Whirling, a physical form of dhikr, in chapter 6).

Repetitive prayer meditations are not a unique Sufi practice. The same principle can be identified in the Prayer of the Heart in the Eastern Orthodox Church, Nembutsu in Japanese Buddhism, or Japa in Hinduism. Sufis use mantras such as *La ilaha illa 'llah* ("There is no God but God") or one of the ninety-nine names or attributes of God, but primarily the name of Allah, which is said to contain all of God's divine attributes.

Numerous verses in the Koran refer to the need to remember God. Above all, the Koranic basis for this practice, which is often referred to by famous Sufi authors, is this urging sentence: "Mention thy Lord, when thou forgettest."[93] The Koran, however, doesn't mention how Allah

---

92. Bourgeault, "Prayer of the Heart."
93. Surah 18:24.

is to be remembered. For the Sufis, this verse and many others are read in a mystical sense: remembering the divine means a direct experience of God's presence; a state in which you forget all about yourself and are only aware of the existence of the divine. This is, in a sense, the most essential aim of meditation!

Dhikr is generally divided into two types of practice: recollection with the tongue and recollection in the heart. Spoken dhikr is often performed collectively, while the dhikr of the heart, which is regarded as the superior way, takes place in solitude. You can also think of these as stages. First, there is dhikr of the tongue; this should be performed with intention of the heart, and not as a routine repetition of a divine name. The second stage is dhikr of the heart, which starts as voluntary internal recitation and slowly becomes a natural flow. Finally, the third stage is the dhikr of the inmost being, a part of us that is more subtle than the spirit, in which we get to experience unification.[94]

Purpose

Dhikr is a meditative journey through a phrase that leads you to ecstatic mystical union. If you hear it with the ear alone, nothing can happen. But, as Sufi masters write, for those who hear it with their souls, imprint it on their souls, and repeat it until it penetrates their hearts and souls, their whole being becomes this word.[95]

In this sense, the repetition of the phrase or the prayer is not done for the purpose of mental focusing, but for attaining an experience in which every cell of your body repeats the dhikr. One well-known Sufi statement about this practice captures this point: "First you do the *dhikr* and then the *dhikr* does you." If you follow it all the way, the name becomes a part of your subconscious and sings in your bloodstream.[96] This is why Sufi masters recommend uttering your dhikr both during your practice and throughout the rest of the day, until it takes root in you to a degree that you continue to repeat it even during your sleep. Eventually, there is no longer a sense of separation between meditation, God, and daily life.

The first purpose of dhikr is to concentrate all your energy and attention in just one thought. Instead of remaining stuck in the grooves of your mental habits, the dhikr uses the same tendency of mental repetition for a higher purpose: getting stuck in the single groove of a holy name. In this way, your automatic thinking process becomes a useful tool for positive spiritual conditioning.

However, the dhikr doesn't work only as a mental mantra, since you connect it with love of the divine and awareness of the location of your innermost heart, the seat of the knowledge of

94. Geels, "A Note on the Psychology of Dhikr," 231.
95. Vaughan-Lee, "Dhikr as an Archetype of Transformation."
96. Vaughan-Lee, "Dhikr as an Archetype of Transformation."

divine things. This implies becoming both single-minded and single-hearted. When the dhikr takes firm root deep inside your heart, your worldly concerns naturally diminish and you feel effortlessly drawn to the source of life. Through the dhikr of the heart, the "beloved" becomes your constant companion.

According to the Sufi mystic Llewellyn Vaughan-Lee, the effect of the dhikr is even more subtle and powerful. In the sacred language of a dhikr, the vibrations of the word resonate with what it names, so the word is able to directly connect you with the divine. The dhikr is not only a process of mentally reminding yourself of divine reality—it is an echo of reality that infuses your unconscious remembrance with the light of consciousness. In Vaughan-Lee's words, "The name which we repeat is the name by which we knew Him before we were born. It is the name engraven into our hearts."[97] The dormant memory inside your cells responds to the call of this continual prayer, and your body begins to reverberate at a higher frequency. Eventually, the name grabs hold of you and illuminates your whole being.

Practice

Dhikr of the heart is performed silently and without moving the body. There is also no particular posture that should be followed. An obvious advantage of such a practice is what Sufis termed "solitude within society": it could be done in the midst of other activities rather than being limited to specific times when one was free from other chores of life. Additionally, a silent dhikr allows you to practice the Sufi path without other people knowing about it and reacting to it in any way.

The silent dhikr requires the meditator to direct awareness into different parts of the body while repeating the mantra, concentrating the mind and regulating the breath. These additional techniques make the mantra much more than an "incantation" because they engage your entire body and mind.

There are different ways to do silent dhikr; feel free to follow your own inclination. For example, you may direct the dhikr into the center of your chest or allow it to emerge from there. Or you can repeat the mantra while keeping your heart absolutely still. You can also visualize yourself imprinting the mantra on your spiritual heart and then gazing at it. Another option is synchronizing the dhikr with your breath. For example, on the in-breath you utter within your heart "Aal" and on the out-breath, "Laah." One form of practice carries the words from one body part to another. If, for instance, your dhikr is *La ilaha illa 'llah*, the word *La* begins at the navel and ends in the right side of your lower chest; the second word (*ilaha*) starts in the right side of your chest and ends in the left side of your lower chest; and the remainder

---

97. Vaughan-Lee, "Dhikr as an Archetype of Transformation."

of the mantra (*illallah*) is imprinted deep in the heart.[98] I have focused here on a practice that is one of the two central practices of the Naqshbandi Sufi; it is called *Zikr-e-Sir* or *Wakoof Kulbi* ("awareness of the heart").

In Arabic, the word for meditation is *muraqabah*, which literally means "to watch over," "to wait," or "to protect." The essence of Sufi meditation is thus keeping your attention focused on the divine and awakening love in your heart, and at the same time constantly guarding your heart—watching your mind so that no other thought except that of God enters the heart. While meditating, your work as the "lover" is to be silent, to wait, and to always listen with the "inner ear of the heart" and be attentive to "divine hints."

Instructions

PREPARATION: The practice itself can be done seated or lying down, and the recommended length is at least half an hour. Select one of these mantras for your practice of continual remembrance of the divine:

- *La ilaha illa 'llah* ("There is no God but God"): Consider starting with this mantra—it may help you negate the concerns of the material world and affirm complete concentration on the divine

- *La ilaha illa hu* ("There is no God but He")

- *Allah* ("God")

- *Allah hu* ("God, just He")

- *Allāhu akbar* ("God is greatest")

- *Al-ḥamdu lī'llāh* ("Praise be to God")

Although your goal is to inscribe the name of the divine in your heart, you can initiate contact with your chosen mantra by repeating it vocally, gazing at its written form, or even writing it repeatedly on paper.

1. Start by collecting your dispersed energies, as if you were gathering them from the outside world back into yourself. Still your mind and senses so that you can directly experience the inner reality of the heart. Feel that you are guarding your heart and that your awareness prevents any other thoughts from entering it.

---

98. Bashir, "Movement and Stillness," 203–4.

· · · · · · ·

2. Focus your attention intensely on the place where the physical heart is located until you forget all about yourself. This state of self-abandonment is considered the straight path to divine reality. Keep your attention focused on the heart center, while simultaneously cultivating feelings of love for the beloved.

3. Softly begin practicing your dhikr. Strive to experience the dhikr as a natural inner flow rather than a repeated mantra. You can even connect your heartbeat with your dhikr, as if the dhikr were the pulsating of your heart.

AFTER THE MEDITATION: Your dhikr can be followed throughout the entire day. As much as possible, keep the dhikr going on within your heart at all times.

Meditate on This: Meditation and Self-Love

At the beginning of this chapter, I briefly mentioned that one of the purposes of meditation is the aspect of healing. Meditation can ultimately act as a powerful healer.

We often tend to separate the spiritual from the therapeutic. There are some forms of spiritual therapy that introduce meditative principles into the world of therapy, but we also need to consider meditation itself as a form of therapy. As a matter of fact, a daily meditative practice can spare you the need to go through at least some dimensions of your therapeutic processes. But why is this so?

Remember that meditation develops your mind's ability to achieve a state of pure attention, while dissociating itself from any other element. This, in itself, has great therapeutic benefits. The implication is that you temporarily disconnect from your memories and patterns, and you come into contact with a fundamental state of mental and emotional balance. By doing this on a daily basis, you repeatedly remind yourself that your true being has nothing to do with any of those other elements.

A second potentially therapeutic aspect is the way that meditation heals our sense of loneliness and separation. In the world of meditation, separation is the first mental distress: the sense that we are disconnected or even expelled from the universe and that we are completely isolated. This sense causes a deep wound of separation that no communication with other people can heal. In meditation, we rectify our connection with life. When we sit and meditate, we feel that we are connected again, not only through our consciousness but also through our heart. We can quickly regain the sense of thread that connects us to others and to the universe, feel part of a greater whole, and rest in it. This state of resting in wholeness is a form of therapy! If you meditate deeply enough, you will never feel lonely again, even if you're on a deserted island.

These are two aspects of healing. But my main attention will turn now to a third point: the issue of self-acceptance. This is an important aspect of our relationship with ourselves, a relationship that is too often broken and conflicted. The good news is that meditation can help alter this predicament.

Meditation Means Resting within Oneself

Meditation as an aid for self-acceptance is a perspective that isn't usually considered. We mostly try to accept ourselves using forms of self-analysis and techniques of positive thinking. Meditation, however, includes an insight that can radically uproot the problem of self-acceptance: it reveals to us an essential misunderstanding.

Before discussing this misunderstanding, I want to introduce a quotation from the twentieth-century yogi Paramahansa Yogananda that illustrates the way in which meditation is connected to self-acceptance: "Meditation is like giving a hug to ourselves: getting in touch with the awesome reality in us. While meditating we feel a deep sense of intimacy with God, a love that is inexplicable."[99]

Let's start with the first part of this quotation: "Meditation is like giving a hug to ourselves." First of all, perceiving meditation in this way can make your practice so much sweeter. You start recognizing that meditation is not an effort, but more like giving yourself a hug. Imagine if, prior to your daily practice, you thought, *Now I'm going to give myself a hug.* Wouldn't that be much more appealing? Then, as soon as you close your eyes, you are already attuned to the sweetness of this intention.

It is vital to understand that the journey of acceptance would be over if we could genuinely give ourselves a hug. Others may hug you with all their heart, but as long as you cannot give this hug to yourself, the embrace will not penetrate deeply enough. Some mistrust will remain; there will be a part of you that thinks, *Wonderful, but in my heart of hearts, I know that something is wrong with me. They just don't know it, or they pretend not to know it.*

So, what does meditation as self-embrace really mean? Let's first take a look at the issue of self-acceptance through a meditative lens, then explore the way that meditation resolves the issue. The issue can be summarized by the common statement "I can't accept myself" and the very opposite of this statement—since thought always works in pairs of opposites and contradictions—"I (finally) accept myself."

What hides behind these statements is the imagined notion that if I tried really hard, going through all sorts of self-analysis and therapy, I could improve myself and eventually become likeable to myself. Then, one day, I would reach the point when I could actually declare, "That's

99. Gupta, *Two Great Masters*, 126.

it! Now I accept myself." But the big problem with self-acceptance, and the reason that it is so lasting and persistent, is that *you* cannot accept *yourself*.

Take a look at this sentence: I cannot accept myself. It means that of these two, "I" and "myself," one is a false me and doesn't even really exist. If we don't understand that one of the two doesn't exist, we are doomed to try to accept ourselves while finding it hard to do so. We will keep fantasizing that one day, we will reach a point when "I" will accept "myself." But which of the two doesn't really exist?

Since the core of the problem is that some element cannot accept "myself," obviously the element that creates this constant conflict is the "I" at the beginning of the sentence. The "I" doesn't exist, because it is not an actual self. On the other hand, when I speak of "myself," I intuitively know that there is a self there, that there is an actual being that can be either accepted or not. This being is myself, as I am right now: my actual body, smile, personality, reactions, patterns, passions, and desires. These are the contents of myself.

What is "I"? Who is the "I" in me that doesn't accept myself, while it is not a self? When you begin to look at the element that detests, compares, judges, and condemns, you realize that it is not you at all. These are internalized voices that we have assimilated from society—from others who have compared us to others still, until we have taken on the mission and started doing it ourselves.

So what we see here is nothing more than a bundle of social voices, pretending to be an actual "I," which then says, "I cannot accept myself." These are just voices, and voices cannot be a self; they can only be a cluster of thoughts. Perhaps someone once told you, "You should be more like this. Why aren't you like your brother or sister?" Through commercials, television, and cinema, society conveys similar messages. Consequently, we assimilate the feeling that "myself" is not enough.

This is the birth of "I." The fundamental activity of the "I" is comparison: internalized voices that compare obsessively, unrealistically expecting us to somehow become not-ourselves—a completely different self. Given the fact that our selves were handed to us as products of the genius of the universe, trying to become a different self makes very little sense, and that's the source of our pain.

What the "I" wants me to become is what I call a "should-be me." Thus, there is me and next to it there is a should-be me, who is the "right" me, the one I should become someday. Since this me exists in a parallel universe, it is impossible for me to reach it. In the parallel universe, this should-be me does everything right. It works exactly as the "I" wants it to be. It behaves magnificently. It doesn't have patterns. It is always peaceful. It is beautiful. It is everything that you—you!—could ever hope for, the fulfillment of the fantasy of the "I." Never forget, this is not even *your* fantasy!

• • • • • • •

This means that there are two entities that don't exist: "I" and its perfect creation, the "should-be me." Comparing me to the should-be me is agonizing because we always feel the unbridgeable gap, and the more we feel the gap, the more the "I" condemns and judges: *Look at yourself, you're not becoming the should-be me! But one day, when you do become the should-be me, I'm going to accept you, and then everything will be at peace.* This is the big, false promise. This is why self-acceptance is always in the future—but because this future is a product of imagination, it can never truly come.

This entire mess exists only in our thinking. Our thinking is split into these two entities and is therefore in a state of constant fighting, comparing, and fantasizing. It engages us in the big project of self-improvement, of being always "almost there": *I will read this book, I will practice that, I will change this pattern, and then...* That's the should-be me—always almost there.

This project hinders the reality that the "myself" is really God-given, or cosmos-given. It has been made by the greatest genius ever. It may not be perfect, but what does *perfect* mean? Perfect only exists in comparison to the should-be me. In any other way, it doesn't make sense. "Myself" is whole and complete. It is simply what it is.

Since the mind can only continue to create the false hope that we can one day attain self-acceptance, what could resolve the problem? The only part of us that can genuinely put an end to this conflict is the heart. When you move into the heart and settle in heart-perception, you realize that the heart is not divided, since the very way it perceives is unity. So your heart cannot have an "I"—it can only know "myself." Thus, when you rest in the heart, you rest in yourself.

This is the reason that meditation is a powerful remedy for the problem of self-acceptance: in meditation, you rest inside your heart, which also means that you finally get to rest within yourself.

In Meditation, There Can Only Be One Self

Even without meditation, you can start to be suspicious of this "I" that cannot accept "myself." Ask it, "Who are you?" Realize that it doesn't really exist. This was the way that the spiritual teacher and author Eckhart Tolle awakened. This very realization happened to him intuitively and unintentionally. One night he woke up in the early hours with absolute dread and the feeling of self-loathing. He repeatedly thought, *I cannot live with myself any longer.* But then, all of a sudden, he became aware of an unfamiliar thought arising from his innermost being: *Am I one or two? If I cannot live with myself, there must be two of me: the "I" and the "self" that "I" cannot live with. Maybe,* he concluded, *only one of them is real.* This razor-sharp realization stopped his mind.[100]

100. Tolle, *The Power of Now*, 4.

This intensity of self-loathing is a point that many of us have reached at least once: hating ourselves so much that we wanted to die. When the "I" begins to cause such a torment due to its ceaseless judgments and comparison, we may feel we cannot live up to its demands. This seems like the only solution: that "I" will strangle myself to death. But the "I" has always been nothing more than a thought. Therefore, the only part of us that needs to die is this thought.

When you close your eyes and delve into the realm of meditation, you move away from the mind's split. That's why meditation is characterized by a sense of harmony, which is an expression of unity. You are in a state of unity within yourself. There is only one being, and this brings about an immediate peace of heart and mind.

Meditation is the most powerful and immediate way to experience this inner unity. As soon as you begin to rest inside yourself in meditation, the "I" simply collapses and dissolves into your being. Thus, the first thing that takes place is that you finally experience the ability to be as you are. This is a tremendous therapeutic power: *you can be as you are.* And you are because you are; there is no need for justification, addition, or modification. You are already complete.

So, first the "I" collapses into "myself." I realize that I can only be myself, and that as myself, I am whole. My mind no longer divides because I fall into the heart. I can finally relax into my being. In fact, all I have is my very being. But then, there are two even deeper stages. Another quotation from Yogananda manages to express the first advanced stage perfectly: "When, by meditation, we withdraw restless thoughts from the lake of the mind, we behold our soul, a perfect reflection of spirit."[101]

When I go more deeply in my meditation, I move from "myself" to the pure self. Because if I am only aware of myself, it is not even myself—it is just pure awareness of my very own being. I am only aware of my "soul." Prior to meditation, we tend to assume that our innermost is our thoughts, emotions, and feelings, but when our meditation deepens, it is easy to recognize that our innermost is our pure being.

This is the point at which your meditation affords you an inner space of profound intimacy. You may have known all sorts of intimacy with people, animals, plants, and the cosmos. But this is when you learn to experience intimacy with yourself: feeling the closest to what you are, to your original being, without dividing layers of concepts and emotions.

Remember our discussion of unity consciousness: returning to original unity, losing this gap that separates me and others. The first break, however, is between me and myself. When this heals, you can feel and declare, "I am what I am; I am just aware, with nothing to be aware of, aware of my own being." This endows us with an extraordinary sense of self-embrace. There is only self-love. Now that you have moved from loving yourself to a love of self, how can you not love this pure reflection, this beautiful and natural being?

101. Prafullananda, "Paramahansa Yogananda."

• • • • • • •

And then we move to the last stage in our meditation. We move from loving ourselves to the love of self, and then our small self is absorbed into the big Self. Our small self becomes absorbed because in the depths of meditation, we come to realize that ultimately, there is only one Self in the universe—only one "I am."

When you begin to be aware only of yourself, you reach a lucid state, a perfect reflection of spirit. It is like a drop that is uncontaminated by anything. But the drop is so similar to the ocean that there is absolutely no point in it remaining a drop. Finally, your meditation opens up, and you leap from self to Self.

This is a natural meditative journey, and it begins with hugging yourself. Instead of pointlessly trying to end this split in the mind, sink into the heart and experience inner wholeness. Then go even deeper. Pay no attention to the mind's refusal to believe that this inner split could possibly end without becoming perfect. The only true resolution lies at the heart of meditation.

CHAPTER 8

Throat Chakra Meditations:
Use the Hidden Powers of Sound

The throat chakra is a door. Behind this door is your inner world, and beyond it is the outer world. It is where your inner world begins and ends, and where the outer world begins and ends. This door either allows or inhibits the flow from the inner world to the outer world, and vice versa. How much do we allow our door to be open? Is it slightly open? Half open? Fully open? Completely shut? How much do we allow ourselves to be revealed through this door, which means allowing our innermost to become a visible reality? This door determines and regulates the level of our expression and of our receptivity—the measure of how open we are to fully receive. Obviously, the meditations we are going to encounter in this chapter experiment with both directions.

But how does the throat chakra enable or inhibit the flow? This is done through language. Language should be understood here in a much deeper sense than the common definition. It is not just the words that we speak; it is the very way we translate communications from one world to another, the way we give voice to a certain thing from one world such that it becomes comprehensible in another.

Let's take feelings as an example. I may have very deep feelings, and hopefully I understand the language of my own feelings. But we don't always understand this language—feelings belong to the sacral chakra and are therefore too far away from the brain, which understands verbally. (At least in the limited sense of the brain as the center of mental activity.) So when I want to express my feelings so that they can become comprehensible to the listener, I need to let them come out through the door; I must be willing to open the door. Perhaps I do so hesitantly at first,

• • • • • • • •

but when I finally allow this expression, I also need to ensure that I have translated the language of my feelings in a way that can be understood and shared verbally and emotionally. So there is a process of translation, but also a process of editing, because I need to decide how much information I am going to share and what I would rather retain in my inner being. To what extent do I allow the information of my inner world to pass through the door? Obviously, this process doesn't always work: sometimes I express my feelings and the listener doesn't understand what I am talking about. This means that I haven't managed to translate my feelings or make use of the throat chakra's door in a way that we can actually share. This can be a challenge sometimes.

The greatest expression of this function of letting things come through the door and back again is sound. We sometimes say "I want to find my voice." This actually means "I want to find the right language to express, in an ideal way, my deepest perceptions, truth, and fulfillment in the world." So the voice is, both literally and metaphorically, the major way through which we enable information to flow. The voice is also that which enters me: voices of others. Sometimes these are actual voices and other times they are sounds. Thus, voice, sound, and expression are all one and the same.

If we think more deeply about the principle of sound, we can think of sound in our context as a bridge that connects the unmanifest world and the manifest world, potential and actualization, inner and outer, and also inner vision and its fulfillment; even more deeply, it is the bridge that connects the source of life with creation.

Think of the biblical story of Genesis. The first statement of the biblical God was "There shall be light." The usual translation is "Let there be light," but I translated this statement directly from the Hebrew version, which I feel touches on something even more accurately: "Let there be light" might still sound like a suggestion, whereas "There shall be light" means that these words determine what is going to be, and then it so becomes. As soon as the statement was uttered, light came into being. This means that in God's fortunate case, there is no distance between intention, statement, declaration, and manifestation; the door is wide open, and, in a sense, there is not even a door at all. But the appearance of light is born through sound. This utterance is a sound, an echo, a vibration that makes creation come into being.

So it is all about the sound that we let out and the sound that we receive. This is exactly what the throat chakra group of meditations is concerned with: the sound that we let out, the sound that we receive, and the artful way of letting it out and receiving it. The sound that we deal with in this group of techniques is a sound that uses the right languages: those that can heal our physical body, bring our subtle body into a state of resonance, lead us to our true selves, show us the sound of silence, and enable us to communicate with our souls. What this group of meditations does is enable us to release the flow from the inner to the outer—and from the outer to the inner—in a way that can heal, balance, and awaken us.

• • • • • • • •

You Are a Vibrational Being

Let's discuss the nature of sound and of meditations that revolve around sound—in short, let's explore sound. One good way to demonstrate the nature of sound is by looking at the example of a guided meditation. In guided meditation, the guide makes use of their voice. This sound flows toward the listeners, and following the sound of the guide's voice and the words they use, the listeners often enter a state of meditation. What actually takes place?

First, the use of words that can leave a powerful impact on the hearer's mind is obviously important. Words themselves are rather empty, but there is a power behind the word itself—an energetic charge—and this is what we respond to. When words are used properly, they can actually transport you to a different state. The second element is the voice itself. The voice is used in a meditative intonation: it is slow and deep, and there are gaps of silence between the words. The voice transmits not only verbal messages but also, as mentioned before, a certain energetic charge. Third is the hearer's own active participation, because by listening, they are tuning in, and this is not a passive state at all; they participate in and fertilize both the guide's words and voice in a way that makes them transformative and effective. So, these three elements—powerful words, the energy of the voice, and the level of receptivity and listening—create together the full experience of the guided meditation. Notice what a major role sound plays here. A guided meditation could be a sort of musical event, in which we receive a certain sound that can change us—but also, the way that we receive the sound changes us; guide and listeners play a symphony together.

Based on this example, we can say that sound is vibration. This word has a great deal of significance in our context. Of course, sound is vibration also in scientific terms: it is defined as vibration that propagates itself as an acoustic wave.[102] In human physiology and psychology, sound is the *reception* of such waves and their *perception* by the brain: the way we, the listeners, receive these waves and the way the waves are received by the brain. In this, both the meditative understanding of sound and the scientific understanding of sound are the same.

On the other hand, what may be scientifically disputable but meditatively meaningful is that aside from this vibration that reaches us and the reception of these waves by us, we should also consider ourselves to be vibrational beings. This is a deeper reality. The whole of creation is vibrational: it starts as vibration and then gradually, as the vibration slows down, it becomes a physical reality that we can actually perceive.[103] When the vibration is very quick, it is closer to the spiritual or invisible reality. This is what we could regard as high frequencies. Deep silence certainly seems to imply that everything slows down. However, if you are very attentive, you

102. Berg, "Sound."
103. Hunt, "The Hippies Were Right."

• • • • • • • •

realize that silence is, in fact, a very quick vibration: the space of silence vibrates quickly and powerfully, and that's why silence is not only calming but also immense. Creation as a whole is vibration, but a vibration that is slow enough that it can be perceived as something dense and fixed. At a deeper level, it is oscillating, eternally pulsating.

This means that sound is a vibration that speaks directly to this part of our being, which is deeper than our material being. This is why we respond so strongly and instantly to music: because we are vibrational beings. Words penetrate us rather slowly—they need to persuade us, to massage the brain first before we are willing to receive them. But music! Think how quickly we respond to music. It immediately changes something in us. What is it that changes? Since we are musical instruments ourselves, we are played by the right sounds. Certain sounds tune in to the instrument that we are. We intensely respond from parts of ourselves that our understanding cannot reach. When it comes to music, we don't understand what is happening, but we open to receive it. It stirs something in us. It goes beneath and bypasses our intellectual grasp. This is why it penetrates directly, without interference, into our vibrational beings.

Sound as Meditation

This is the power of this group of meditations and the reason they are so immediate. Generally speaking, there are seven types of meditations that use sound in a meditative way and, as a result, awaken and work on our vibrational being. You may think of more, but these are the central ones:

1. **Sacred Music:** This is the type of music that is designed to lead us to spiritual states. It silences our mind and evokes a longing to return to our spiritual home and feelings of spiritual humbleness and surrender. Sometimes we listen to music and immediately our heart jumps out, as if we are spoken to.

2. **Healing Sounds:** Sounds that can affect our physical imbalances by reminding our body and mind of an ideal and harmonious reality.

3. **Singing:** Using our own voices to create vibrations that alter our own being by awakening our vibrational being.

4. **Prayer:** Prayer can take place silently but also in an audible form. The difference is significant: making use of the voice and uttering the "right words" can engender both a vibration in our being and waves that ripple out from our mouths all the way to the edge of the universe.

5. **Chanting:** This is a blend of prayer and singing, and it refers specifically to the singing of repetitive mantras.

· · · · · · · ·

6. **Mantras:** Mantras are an extremely helpful form of sound that, unlike chanting, is uttered and allowed to resonate within our mind. We can say that chanting is an external mantra and that mantras are an internal chanting.

7. **Humming:** Vibrational sounds that we make, directed into our bodies rather than outward.

So sound as meditation is all about a quicker vibration: the quicker the vibration, the stronger the awakening of the vibrational being that we are and the closer we move to our original nature.

Of course, sound or vibration can never be the ultimate reality. The absolute reality or the source of life is the source of all vibrations. Therefore, we cannot say that we experience the divine through vibration, but we can definitely say that a quicker vibration can lead us back to divine reality, because to a certain degree, it is closer to the divine. Osho has a sound meditation called "Nadabrahma," based on Tibetan techniques. *Nada* is "sound" and *brahma* is "god," so this can be interestingly interpreted as "god of sound" or as "sound is god." Thus, to a certain degree, sound can be divine or it can be an echo of the divine. The vibrational world can act as an echo of reality.

Pay attention to the word *echo*. An echo is like a resonance that reverberates all the way from the source to us; when we use it, we can return all the way to the source. This is why the echoes of reality are sometimes so profound that they are said to be the basic sounds of creation. Mantras, for instance, are sounds that the sages and seers of ancient India and Tibet claimed to have heard from the absolute reality itself—it is as if they became attuned to the right radio station. All these sacred sounds are considered by these traditions to be vibrations that existed prior to the material world.

These kinds of basic sounds of reality have the power to take us back home, or at least to evoke in us the longing for our spiritual home. They are surely more powerful and immediate than words, since they are emotional and speak directly to our feelings. Feelings, as you may remember from the sacral chakra's group of meditations, are connected to the world of life force and prana. Feelings are much closer to vibration than words can ever be, and they are by nature far more immediate. In fact, the way we contact vibration is through feeling. When we feel the right vibration, our vibrational being becomes synchronized at once. We experience what can be called *vibrational alignment*.

When spiritual teachers teach, we may not necessarily understand what they say. Sometimes we cannot yet grasp the intellectual or experiential meanings, yet even the tone of the teacher's voice can put us in contact with these kinds of messages. Speech can have the right vibration that leads us to ourselves.

· · · · · · · ·

The Nine Purposes of the Throat Chakra Group of Meditations

We are going to experiment with five meditations that have the power to alter our vibrational density. These meditations aim to quicken our vibration for different reasons, from healing and enlivening our subtle body to spiritual awakening and soul-remembrance. Here are the nine roles and purposes of the throat chakra group of meditations.

1. **Offering hidden languages that can heal, balance, and awaken us.** All five meditations provide our throat chakra with subtle languages, from words to sounds, that enable us to communicate with our inner world.

2. **Providing sound as physical and emotional healing and balancing.** This includes chakra healing and balancing, since sound is vibration and vibration speaks so effectively to our chakras, which are vibrational centers. This is the reason that harmonious music immediately aligns and purifies our chakras.

3. **Connecting with primordial vibrations that lead to unity.** Primordial vibrations are expressions and representations of pre-creation and pre-material realities. We return to them by hearing their special tunes.

4. **Connecting with silence, the soundless sound.** This may sound off, because silence and sound appear to be opposites, two separate worlds, but meditation can reveal that they are actually one complete world.

5. **Learning the art of receptivity and listening.** We learn how to use the right sounds, and also how to receive. The way we receive sound is the art of listening.

6. **Connecting with nonhuman languages, like the language of the soul or the divine.** There are languages we don't know how to speak—at least as long as we rely on our conscious mind. These meditations offer us languages that can help us bridge and contact different worlds, such as our conscious mind and the hidden layers of our being.

7. **Expressing and fulfilling heartfelt devotion.** This is a form of Bhakti yoga, the path of love and deep emotion. We can fulfill an important aspect of devotion by devoting the sounds we produce to the higher realities.

8. **Removing the barrier between us and the world.** This can lead us to unity of the inner and outer worlds.

9. **Reaching vibrational harmonization.** This is most famously achieved through devotional songs and music.

· · · · · · · ·

Aum Meditation

Aum, the primordial mantra, has been with us since the dawn of meditation in ancient India.

Historical Background

Aum is first mentioned in the early *Upanishads*, which date back to the sixth or seventh centuries BCE. The *Mandukya Upanishad* considers Aum to be the representation of the supreme reality: "a symbol for what was, what is, and what shall be," the fourth state that transcends the waking, dreaming, and deep sleep states.[104] The *Katha Upanishad* praises Aum as the "greatest support to all seekers."[105]

Aum is described as the vibration of the cosmic motor, the divine mantra that keeps bringing the universe into existence. In this sense, it is close to the first sentence that the biblical God uttered ("Let there be light"). It is the mantra of manifestation and actualization, the first word, and for this reason, it is sometimes used to enhance one's power of manifestation. It is fascinating to realize that the Aramaic (and later, Christian) "Amen" is quite similar—especially if the sound is slowed down and made longer: "Aaaaa-mmmmm-ennnnn." It is the word that validates the prayer and enables its manifestation. "Ameen," the Arabic equivalent, is also similar in this sense.

In meditation, Aum is the direct representation of the Self (Atman), which is said to dwell in the inner cave of our heart (see chapter 7). This means that if we follow this sound all the way to its root, it leads us to Self-realization. Ultimately, Aum is not a mantra to be chanted, but an essential sound to be heard and discovered in the depths of meditative silence, when our mind has become an untainted mirror reflecting the true nature of the Self. In this way, we realize that Aum has always been there, and that it is not a human-made mantra. (Significantly, Aum exists not as a part of any alphabetical language, and it appears only as a symbol in Sanskrit, Pali, and Tibetan.) With that being said, this does not mean that chanting or meditating on this mantra—moving in the reverse direction—cannot be deeply beneficial.

Purpose

Aum is the most fundamental mantra meditation. The term "mantra" translates as "instrument of thought," and it can be thus considered the one thought that takes us beyond thought. Mantras make use of the principle that "what you focus on, you become": they are designed to unify our being by focusing our mind and heart on a single thought, drawing our attention from false

104. Easwaran, *The Upanishads*, 203–5.
105. Easwaran, *The Upanishads*, 78.

thoughts to the one thought that represents our true self. Of course, when the mantra fulfills its task by leading you to your true self, it vanishes into the silence of your meditation.

More deeply, mantras like Aum are not just mental tools, but are perceived as sounds that exist prior to human thought and outside the human mind. These are sounds that were gathered by the ancient seers, who seemed to pick up vibrations from nature and the cosmos. When we let these sounds reverberate within our minds and hearts, they communicate directly with our vibrational being, playing the musical instrument that we are. The purpose is clear: if we follow them all the way to the place from which they emerge, they lead us back to our original being, just like a mother's soft voice that calls us to return home.

Practice

Although Aum is the most widespread mantra in the world, it has been poorly used as a meditation practice in the West. This is because of misconceptions regarding the way we pronounce it and the way we use it.

The *Mandukya Upanishad* makes it clear that the mantra, though indivisible, consists of three basic sounds: A-U-M.[106] This means that it is not the flat "Om," as most people know and pronounce it. All sounds are said to be combinations of these three basic sounds or derived from them. They are like the subatomic particles that compose each atom in the universe. Interestingly, these are also the three sounds that someone who has no tongue would be able to utter.

The right pronunciation is as follows: open your mouth and say "A"; gently close your mouth and it becomes "U"; close it fully and it becomes "M." These are three consecutive sounds that are basically one long sound, uttered as one. All three sounds should be equally uttered. The utterance should be made with a deep, low voice, as if coming from the depths.

As for the ideal way of using the mantra, the *Katha Upanishad* puts it beautifully: "Aum should reverberate unceasingly within the heart."[107] Following this advice, we should start by intoning it loudly and outwardly—since it is, after all, a throat chakra meditation—and then internalizing it. Make sure that you intone it slowly and deeply. Be filled with it and forget everything else. Become the Aum; become the sound. Let it vibrate through your body, mind, and nervous system.

When you begin to feel harmonious with it, stop intoning it loudly and start doing so inwardly—but still "loudly" in the sense that the sound spreads all over your body and reaches every part of it. Feel vitalized by it, as if your body is a musical instrument and this is the harmonious melody it needs the most. Remember that we are musical beings, and that that is why we respond so strongly and instantly to harmonious sounds.

---

106. Easwaran, *The Upanishads*, 204.
107. Easwaran, *The Upanishads*, 78.

Remain alert. Don't allow yourself to fall asleep. Chanting can easily make you fall asleep because it is mechanically relaxing. Inwardly, let the sound be long and slow. Move the sound to the background and make it your eternal background—an essential sound that has been there since the beginning of time, prior to your existence, and that you only find inside yourself.

Instructions

PREPARATION: The complete process lasts twenty-five minutes.

Stage I (Ten Minutes)

Intone Aum loudly, deeply, and slowly. Be filled with it and forget everything else. Become the Aum; become the sound. Let it vibrate through your body, mind, and nervous system, and feel that your entire being is filled with it; every cell is vibrating with it.

Stage II (Five Minutes)

Continue to let Aum resonate inside your being, "loudly." Allow it to reverberate like a strong echo of your previous vocal chanting. Allow the sound to spread all over your body and to reach every part of it (not only the head). Feel vitalized by it, as if new life is entering you.

Stage III (Ten Minutes)

Let Aum move to the background, becoming like a distant echo. You are no longer chanting it. This is not your mantra—it is the universe's mantra, and you are just listening. It exists outside of you, outside of your mind. You are only experiencing its reflection in your mind. Imagine it as a sound that echoes from the beginning of time, vibrating at the far edges of the cosmos, calling you home. Follow each Aum as if you were holding it by the tail. It is like a magical creature that can take you where it came from: the origin of the universe. It emerges from this source and returns to it over and over again. With every appearance, it creates the universe and sustains it, then returns to emptiness. Thus, creation is flickering constantly. Whenever you follow Aum to its root, let it lead you to the unfathomable depths of the silence from which it emerged. At the end, remain in stillness for a long moment.

AFTER THE MEDITATION: You can walk around, allowing the Aum to resonate slowly in the background all the time. Now, whatever you look at has the eternal background of Aum. Whatever you do, you are connected to the cosmic unknown. Let the Aum be an underlying sound beneath your mundane thoughts and emotions. In this way, even mental activity has a broader cosmic context.

• • • • • • •

The Center of Sound

This meditation covers a different aspect of throat chakra meditations: the passive aspect of learning how to receive a sound and let it fully enter our being. In other words, learning how to listen.

Historical Background

This meditation is an adaptation of a technique presented by Osho (see also chapter 5, "Mystic Rose") in his book *Meditation: The First and Last Freedom*. It also indirectly communicates with the currently widespread meditative practice called Sound Bath, in which the sound healing practitioner "bathes" the participants in sound waves produced by various sources, including healing instruments such as gongs, singing bowls, percussion, chimes, rattles, tuning forks, and even the human voice itself.

Purpose

Naturally, this type of meditation is concerned with the ear's energy and the essence of the hearing process. The ear, Osho suggests, is more meditative than the eye, since it is inherently passive and nonaggressive.[108] It is like a door: it lets in and allows. So, the main purpose of this meditation is to reveal the truly receptive ear as a gateway to spiritual awakening.

Learning to listen, however, goes even deeper; in Osho's view, sounds are not received only by our ears.[109] While the ears do the transmission work, they also actively cut out what is useless to us. Since our ears make choices, only specific sounds are permitted to enter. Our ears are therefore the selectors of sounds, but not the real center of hearing. Moreover, the center of hearing cannot be found in the head at all. The full act of hearing takes place deep inside our body and mind, from every point in our being. Since sounds are received as a totality, listening is a complete experience of the whole body. When you recognize this, you will also realize that in true listening, there is no "I" that listens: you *are* the listening.

Practice

In this meditation, Osho makes use of a rarely acknowledged energetic principle of the ear–sound relationship: whenever a sound streams toward us, we are actually at its center. All sounds come to us from all directions. According to Osho, this is different from our experience with

108. Osho, *Meditation*, 146.
109. Osho, *Meditation*, 153.

sight because sight is linear, as if there is a line extending from the seer toward the object.[110] Sounds, on the other hand, come in circles: they encircle and envelop us, while we are in the center. Osho says, "For sounds, you are always 'God,' the center of the whole universe."[111]

After establishing this realization experientially, we move deeper and deeper into this center of soundlessness in the midst of all sounds. We use the sound as a finger pointing at the sound-less center that we are.

The principle of this meditation can be practiced wherever there is sound (not only music), and especially when the sounds are overwhelming, since the contrast is much sharper. Sit in the midst of the sound, without categorizing it as beautiful or disturbing; experience the encircling of the sound around you, and then, just like in Sufi Whirling (see chapter 6), fall into the middle. If you realize that the sound can encircle you but cannot penetrate your silent center, you can no longer be disturbed by it.

Instructions

PREPARATION: The meditation usually lasts thirty minutes. Prepare a twenty-minute track of elevating music, preferably sacred chanting or spiritual music from any tradition or religion. Use this track for the first two stages and play the music loudly enough to have it encompass your entire being.

Stage I: Receive the Sound (Fifteen Minutes)

1. Sit comfortably with your eyes closed. As the music begins, notice its different layers. Make yourself sensitive and open to receive the gift of the music.

2. Realize that you are not receiving the music only through the ears, but from all directions and through every point in your body. Become the listening itself, as if every point in you is penetrable. As you listen with totality, feel the whole universe filled with sound, as if the sound is everywhere.

3. Gradually, instead of just listening to the sound, recognize that it is not linear; it moves in circles around you, streaming around you and enveloping you. Bathe in the center of sound.

4. Feel as if every sound is moving toward you while you remain in the center. Feel the deep peace that results from the feeling that you are the center: the whole universe becomes the circumference, and everything is moving toward you, falling toward your silent, mountainlike being. It is penetrating your body

110. Osho, *Meditation*, 151.
111. Osho, *Meditation*, 151.

• • • • • • •

and mind, but it cannot affect your core. The sound is actually helping create a center in you by emphasizing even more the still being that is at its center.

5. Slowly realize that at the center, there is no sound. That is why you can hear sounds—a sound cannot hear another sound. Because you are soundless at your center, you can hear sounds. The center is absolute silence.

Stage II: Jump into Soundlessness (Five Minutes)

1. While the music is still playing, focus only on the center, the point in your field to which every sound is coming. Enter so deep into this point that all sounds seem to fade away and you tap into soundlessness. From a world full of sounds, jump into soundlessness. Start listening instead to the soundlessness, the center of life around which all sounds revolve.

2. Realize that you are now undisturbed. Any sound can come to you, but they can never reach you. This point where no sound enters is you. Where are you? Where is your center?

Stage III: Beyond Sound and Soundlessness (Ten Minutes)

1. Now that the music has faded, remain in silence. You can still feel the negative sounds of the music, the echoes. Feel their absence and continue to listen to the new sound that is the absence of sound, the gap that appears when the intense sound is gone, like the vibration that remains after the sound of a gong has faded.

2. When even this negative sound has dissolved, fall back upon yourself. Now that the sounds that pointed at you are gone, soundlessness allows you to fully move into yourself. Fall down into your own abyss; find yourself standing within. Break all bridges of communication with the outer world and stand within as if you are in the midst of the most silent desert. Let the soundless center expand to include all space—what does it feel like?

Kirtan Kriya

In Sanskrit, *Kirtan* is a devotional chant, while *Kriya* refers to any set of movements designed to produce a certain outcome in one's body and mind. Kirtan Kriya, sometimes called a singing exercise, blends singing specific mantric sounds—SA TA NA MA—with repetitive finger movements known as mudras.

Historical Background

Any form of kundalini yoga is designed to evoke the kundalini energy that lies dormant at the base of the spine and to channel it through the chakras and the subtle channels. Yogi Bhajan's (1929–2004) particular form of kundalini yoga is a vigorous combination of active and passive asana-based (posture) kriyas, rhythmic movement, chanting, intense breathing exercises (pranayama), and meditations that target the whole body system, including the nervous system, glands, mental faculties, and chakras. As part of his system, Yogi Bhajan taught nearly five thousand different meditation techniques and employed ancient yogic knowledge to relate many of them to distinct psychological disorders.[112] Interestingly, the Kirtan Kriya meditation, introduced here, has been found to enhance cognition in memory-impaired older adults.[113]

Yogi Bhajan's Kirtan Kriya (pronounced KEER-tun KREE-a), which originated in the ancient kundalini yoga tradition, was one of the first meditations taught by Yogi Bhajan and has remained a foundational meditation that is recommended for every student. Yogi Bhajan said that if you could practice only one meditation, this should be the one.[114]

Purpose

During his lifetime, Yogi Bhajan transmitted two essential mantras that were closely related. The first was SAT NAM and the second, which derived from the first, was SA TA NA MA. According to Yogi Bhajan, these two mantras were designed to reorient the mind and to open it up to the possibility of transformational change.

SAT NAM is the main mantra that appears in the Sikh sacred scripture called the *Guru Granth Sahib*. In Sanskrit, the word *sat* means "true" or "everlasting," and *nam* means "name." Thus, the mantra means "[The one] whose name is truth." Being a foundational mantra (also known as a *beej mantra*), it seeds the truth in our consciousness and prompts us to awaken to our divine identity.

SA TA NA MA incorporates the nuclear sounds of SAT NAM. Since it adds the fifth elementary sound of "A," this mantra is referred to as the *panch shabd*, a mantra with five sound currents. It utilizes these primal sounds to connect our psyche with the evolutionary impulses and forces of the cosmos itself. Deeply speaking, it reshapes the substratum of our psyche to align it with the forces of creative change.

---

112. Shannahoff-Khalsa, "An Introduction to Kundalini Yoga Meditation Techniques," 91.
113. Gard, Hölzel, and Lazar, "The Potential Effects of Meditation on Age-Related Cognitive Decline," 94.
114. Rattana, "Lesson 15."

. . . .

The meanings of the individual words in this vocal meditation reflect the mantra's motivation:

- **SA:** The beginning, infinity, the totality of everything that ever was, is, or will be

- **TA:** Life, existence, and creativity that manifests from infinity

- **NA:** Death, change, and the transformation of consciousness

- **MA:** Rebirth, regeneration, and resurrection that allows us to consciously experience the joy of the infinite

Yogi Bhajan believed that because the mantra was able to radically rearrange the subconscious mind, it had the power to break habits, addictions, and repetitive thought patterns by accessing the level of the mind where habits are formed. Moreover, he claimed that the reason we have great difficulty breaking our habits is an unbalanced state of mind that results from insufficient activity of the pineal gland.[115] By activating this gland through the mantra, the mind's balance would be restored, and consequently, we would have the freedom to discard unwelcome patterns.

Additionally, the ancient yogis who developed this technique believed that by uttering this mantra, eighty-four acupuncture points on the tongue and the upper palate are stimulated. In modern terms, this results in a biochemical transformation in the brain. So far, Western research seems to find support for these claims. Journals have reported improved cognitive capacities and an activation of parts of the brain that are central to memory, including an enhanced blood flow to particular areas in the motor-sensory cortex.[116]

Practice

Kirtan Kriya is easy to learn because it doesn't require an intense form of concentration or complex visualizations. In addition, your practice can be adapted to a brief process of just twelve minutes, a more extensive thirty-one minutes (traditionally the most recommended version), or even sixty-two minutes. Impressively, however, even the brief twelve-minute program has been scientifically proven to reduce stress and increase activity in areas of the brain that are central to memory when practiced for at least eight weeks.[117]

During your practice, the way that you chant the sounds should progress gradually. In the twelve-minute version, after one minute of silently focusing inward on your mind and body in the present moment, you begin by chanting aloud for two minutes (the voice of humans, which

---

115. Rattana, "Lesson 15."
116. "Practice the 12-Minute Yoga Meditation Exercise."
117. "Practice the 12-Minute Yoga Meditation Exercise."

represents awareness of the things in the world), gradually softening your voice into an audible whisper for two minutes (the voice of lovers, expressing the longing to belong), and then chanting silently for three more minutes (the voice of the divine that mentally vibrates within and meditates on infinity). Later, you do the reverse: you return to whisper-chanting for two minutes, and finally you chant aloud again for two minutes. The meditation practice is completed with deep breathing and visualization of light.

Mudras, or hand gestures, are highly important in Kirtan Kriya. While chanting, you alternately press the thumb with one of the four fingers. Press hard enough to keep yourself aware of the pressure. Keep repeating in a stable rhythm and maintain the hand motion throughout the entire meditation.

- When you utter SA, press the thumb and the first finger together with pressure. The first finger is also known as the Jupiter finger. The Jupiter finger brings in knowledge, expands our field of possibilities, and releases us from limitations.

- On each TA, press the thumb and the middle finger together. The middle finger is also known as the Saturn finger. The Saturn finger brings us patience, wisdom, and purity.

- Chanting the NA, press the thumb and the ring finger together. The ring finger is also known as the Sun finger. The Sun finger gives us vitality and aliveness.

- On each MA, press the thumb and the little finger together. The little finger is also known as the Mercury finger. The Mercury finger aids clear communication.

In addition to the progression of your chanting and hand gestures, visualize and feel how each individual sound flows into and through the crown chakra at the top of your head, down through the middle of the head, and out to infinity through the third eye. Thus, you visualize a sort of L form as you chant each syllable. This energy pathway forms the *golden chord*, the connection between the pituitary and pineal glands. Traditionally, maintaining this energy flow throughout the entire practice is considered vital for the cleansing function of the sound; it was even said that if this element of the meditation was not kept, the meditator may experience a headache.

Because Kirtan Kriya restructures the subconscious mind, you may be revisited by memories while meditating. Allow the memories to dance before your mind's eye for a moment and then release them with the mantra. If emotions come up, chant them out. Do not try to avoid or control any of your experiences.

- - - - - - - -

Instructions

PREPARATION: The meditation usually lasts either twelve or thirty-one minutes. Sit in a comfortable position with a straight spine. Apply neck lock—that is, lift the chest and sternum up while lengthening the back of the neck by pulling the chin toward it. Keep the neck, throat, and face muscles relaxed. Relax your arms and rest your wrists on the knees or thighs, keeping the elbows straight. Begin in gyan mudra (connecting the tips of your thumbs with the tips of your index fingers while relaxing all your other fingers) with a firm but gentle pressure. Close your eyes and bring your mental focus to the brow point.

Twelve-Minute Version

1. For two minutes, chant SA TA NA MA out loud, changing your mudra with each syllable.

2. For two minutes, chant in an audible whisper.

3. For three minutes, chant silently. Remember to keep the mudra, the visualization of the L shape in the head, and the tongue moving in tandem.

4. Then, whisper for two minutes.

5. Finally, chant for two minutes out loud.

6. During the last minute, listen inwardly, hear the mantra, and visualize the L shape in the head. Do not apply any finger movements.

Thirty-One-Minute Version

1. For the first five minutes, chant SA TA NA MA out loud, changing your mudra with each syllable.

2. For the next five minutes, chant in an audible whisper.

3. For ten minutes, chant silently. Remember to keep the mudra, the visualization of the L shape in the head, and the tongue moving in tandem.

4. Then, whisper for five more minutes.

5. End with five minutes of chanting out loud.

6. During the last minute, listen inwardly, hear the mantra, and visualize the L shape in the head. Do not apply any finger movements.

AT THE END OF BOTH VERSIONS: Inhale deeply, raise your arms up in the air, and vigorously shake the arms and fingers. Involve the whole body and the spine. Exhale and bring your arms down

. . . .

slowly in a sweeping motion. Repeat this once or twice if you feel the need to do so. This is an important part of the meditation because it helps move and release the energy gathered in your body.

Take a few minutes before going about your day, or make some time to relax, lying on your back. If the practice is done before bedtime, go directly to sleep.

Meditation on the Inner Sound

In Sanskrit, *nad* means sound, thunder, howl, cry, or roar. The additional A makes it a *nada*, a sound or tone. *Nada* also means river or stream. When these two meanings of "stream" and "sound" are combined, the object of meditation in nada yoga becomes clear: identifying an internal "sound stream."

Historical Background

The practice of nada yoga originates in the *Rig-Veda*, India's ancient collection of sacred hymns, which is three and a half millennia old. The *Rig-Veda* includes a group of minor mystical scriptures called the *Yoga Upanishads*, and among them we find the *Nada Bindu Upanishad*. This far less ancient text (100 BCE–300 CE) teaches meditation on the *nada*, or the inner sacred sound. Later, much of this text was incorporated into the *Hatha Yoga Pradipika*, a classic fifteenth-century Sanskrit manual on Hatha yoga written by Svātmārāma.

At the foundation of the practice of nada yoga, we find the notion that the entire universe is continuously vibrating, and that this vibration connects and binds everything in it. Since vibration is sound, everything is sound. This universal vibration is everywhere and also without beginning or end. Thus, in the deepest sense, nada is the first vibration out of which all creation manifests.

Consequently, we can say that each of us vibrates on many levels, but that among these various vibrations there is an internal sound that connects us with the cosmic sound stream. The nada that vibrates in our depths is constant and ever-present. Therefore, all we have to do is listen and wait patiently. As soon as this subtle sound has arisen in our awareness, we should fix our attention on it and strive to become one with it. In the succinct words of the *Hatha Yoga Pradipika*, "One who desires true union of yoga should leave all thinking behind and concentrate with single-pointed attention on the nada."[118]

---

118. Muktibodhananda, *Hatha Yoga Pradipika*, 584.

According to the system of nada yoga, there are different levels of sounds, all of which require our attention and practice if we ever hope to attain the inner sound. There is the external world of sounds around us; sounds of the mind, like sound memories, internal dialogue, and sound imaginings; and the sound beyond sound, called *para* ("beyond"). If we follow the latter, it will lead us beyond both sensory sounds and mental sounds to higher realms of consciousness.

Some traditions, such as the Surat Shabd Yoga lineage, recommend practicing the inner sound in conjunction with meditation on the inner light. The form of practice that is presented here derives from the same principle.[119]

Purpose

The scriptures consider the inner sound meditation to be a technique that can only be fully practiced by advanced yogis. The reason is that inner sound only becomes accessible after the yogi has purified all their subtle channels (nadis), especially the central channel (sushumna nadi). When this has been accomplished, the yogi can use sound meditation as an incomparable technique for the profound state of self-absorption.[120]

Nevertheless, the practice of nada yoga is not really complicated or inaccessible. In the end, all it requires is the act of listening, first externally and later internally. The more you cultivate a listening mind and heart, the more you are capable of going beyond ear-based sounds and piercing the hidden sounds of your being.

We search for this type of sound in this meditation because it is a manifestation of our own divine voice that calls us back home. By following this voice, we see what direction we should take in order to return to our natural state. If you manage to hear this sound, it will fill you with an indescribable, blissful vibration in both body and mind, which is your indication that you are closer than ever to your authentic being. Another effective metaphor is that of the nada as a river of sound that carries us to the ocean of bliss—by focusing our mind on it, we reunite our essential self with the infinite and the eternal.

Remember that this sound is unstruck (*anahata*); it is not engendered by any trigger and it cannot fade away. This implies that you don't need to make it happen or struggle to preserve it. It is just there, self-sustained and continuous. In this sense, it is the unchanging constant of your universal consciousness. Thus, by perceiving and relaxing into it, you can easily drop into deeper levels of meditation.

119. Hersey, *The Practice of Nada Yoga*, 105–7.
120. "Siva Samhita."

Practice

The goal of this practice is to come into contact with the inner light, and on the basis of this revelation, to penetrate the sacred sounds. Even when you turn your attention toward the inner sacred sound, you do so while maintaining the open space in which your mind and the divine light in you are one. For this reason, the practice is divided into two parts, the second of which entirely depends on the first as a firm foundation.

In the early stages of your practice, it may take some effort to concentrate on seeing the light and hearing the sound. This is not the effort of trying to make something happen, but the need to sustain a state of active looking and focused listening. Since the sound is internal and subtle, don't expect to hear it right away. While maintaining your connection with the light, wait attentively with a loving heart, and simply allow the possibility that in time, you will hear it.

Trust that after practicing for a while, your effortful attention will be replaced by quiet awareness of light and sound that are already there. You will gradually learn to differentiate between sights and sounds that your mind creates and those that you witness and reveal. Ultimately, the light and sound should be experienced as being as real as what you perceive through your external senses of vision and hearing.

This practice draws your attention to one specific nadi (a subtle nerve channel) that starts under the right eye. This nadi runs down your cheek to the jawbone, along the jawline to its hinge, and onto the neck, and there it runs back up behind your right ear. To gain a more tangible sense of this nadi, trace its path using your right index finger. Being aware of this channel can help you connect with both the light and the sound.

In the early phase of your practice, you should physically block both ears. This can be achieved using your fingers. However, the best way to seal the ears and to turn your perception of sound inward is by using foam earplugs. After a period of practice, you will be able to concentrate on the internal sound and exclude external sounds around you without plugging your ears.

In the process, strive to discern all aspects and frequencies of the internal sound and to identify its subtlest dimension. It is like looking for the sound that is behind, above, within, and beyond the sound. Of course, you may hear several sounds at once, either pronounced or subtle. Additionally, the sound may take various forms, like buzzing, a resonant ringing, a low rumble, a shimmering vibration, or a high, sustained tone. The *Hatha Yoga Pradipika* describes external sounds that resemble those that may be experienced internally: "The ocean, thunder, a large waterfall, low drums, [a] large bell, conch shell, horn, flute, tinkling chimes, bees or crickets."[121] Since the sounds may change from meditation to meditation, don't get attached to one particular sound. What matters is the concentration on these internal sounds, not which sound you hear

121. Muktibodhananda, *Hatha Yoga Pradipika*, 256.

on any given day. After regular practice, however, the highest, most luminous sound (similar to overtone singing) will focus your attention.

If hearing the inner sound is interrupted by your talkative mind, notice that you are no longer listening and gently return to focused attentiveness. Your task is to cultivate longer periods of unbroken listening. With time, the presence of the inner light and the inner sound will naturally quiet your mind, and this stillness will open the way for deeper levels of meditation. Remember that the light and the sound are mutually enhancing; if the sound grows louder, your absorption into the light deepens, and vice versa. Simply dissolve into them and the resulting blissful feeling will consume any mental activity.

According to the *Hatha Yoga Pradipika*, we should "listen with one-pointedness to the sound of the nada within the right ear."[122] After focusing your listening so that you hear nothing except for the nada, allow the sound to pour from your right ear into your head and entire body until you have become the sound. Feel how this inner vibration connects you directly with the vibration of the greater universe, since they are, in reality, one and the same.

Instructions

PREPARATION: This meditation requires between twenty and thirty minutes. If possible, sit with your legs crossed with one of your heels pressing into your perineum. Alternatively, you may sit on a rolled-up blanket or pillow placed between your legs to create pressure on your perineum. Find a position that allows you to remain in a state of perfect stillness. Then, block the sound entering your ears with earplugs. Place your hands on your knees and keep your spine straight. Finally, close your eyes.[123]

Stage I: Invite the Inner Light

1. Recall a past experience of unconditional love and let your heart be filled with that feeling. For a moment, rest in the heart center permeated with that love.

2. Then, direct your internal gaze between your eyebrows. While your gaze is inward, your focus is as if you were looking outward into the distance. Try to do this active looking as effortlessly as possible. Imbued with the sense of unconditional love, invite the inner light to arise. Trust that the light already shines within you. If thoughts appear, let them pass like clouds in the sky and bring your focus back to looking between your eyebrows.

122. Muktibodhananda, *Hatha Yoga Pradipika*, 561.
123. The instructions derive from Hersey, *The Practice of Nada Yoga*, 110–11.

· · · · · · · ·

3. At first you may see only darkness, but sooner or later you will begin to see flickering, clouds or rays of color, or lights. Don't doubt this internal perception. If light arises, let it be without controlling it, and be grateful for its arising. Over time, the lights may eventually become a single focused point of light. It may be a very small, intense dot or fleck of light, a bright ball of white light, or other forms of brilliant radiance.

4. Realize that you are not separate from the light. Move the light into the center of your head while also drawing your eyes back in, toward the center of your head. Let the light blissfully cover your head. Then, let that blissful feeling spread throughout your entire body. Maintain a feeling of moving forward into the light as you are drawn into one another. Remain totally still to maintain that blissful physical comfort.

Stage II: Dissolve into the Inner Sound

1. Mentally trace the subtle nerve channel that runs from below the right eye to behind the right ear. Connecting with this nadi will now lead you from the light to the sound. With an open and surrendered heart, invite the inner sound to arise. Trust that the sound already vibrates within you.

2. Listen through the right ear for an internal sound. The sound may take many forms. If you don't hear any particular sound, be patient until it naturally arises. Then let it be without controlling it, and be grateful for its arising.

3. Fix your attention on the subtlest part of the sound. When you do this, it will increase in volume and intensity.

4. Pull the sound from your ear into your head and entire body. Follow it and let it pour into you. Realize that the light and the sound are indistinguishable, and furthermore, you are inseparable from both of them. Allow yourself, the light, and the sound to merge. Remain utterly still in your body and mind.

· · · · · · ·

Hitbodedut

Hitbodedut is a form of prayer meditation that originates in Judaism, specifically Hasidic Judaism.

Historical Background

Hasidism is an important Jewish religious group that arose as a spiritual revival movement during the eighteenth century in Eastern Europe and has quickly spread ever since. The movement was founded by Israel Ben Eliezer, commonly known as the "Baal Shem Tov," and it was primarily inspired by Lurianic Kabbalah. Hasidic teachings strongly emphasize God's all-pervading presence in the universe, the need to become one with God (*devekut*), the devotional dimension of Jewish religious practice, and the spiritual dimension of earthly life and mundane acts.

The practice of Hitbodedut (in Hebrew, "self-solitude," or making time for oneself) was not exclusively Hasidic; secluded meditation practices had been encouraged by many medieval rabbis. However, Rebbe Nachman of Breslov (1772–1810), a great-grandson of the Baal Shem Tov, revived the Hasidic movement. He wrote extensively about this type of practice and gave it a unique and accessible dimension. Here I will present his version of the technique.

In Hasidic circles, this practice has other names, such as *sicha* (conversation) and *yishuv haDa'at* (settling the mind). Author Ariel Burger even suggests calling it simply "speaking meditation."[124] The simplicity of the names reflects the nature of the practice: Nachman of Breslov, whose religious philosophy revolved around closeness to God, recommended speaking to God in a form of normal conversation, as you would with a best friend. This requires nothing more than a heart and a mouth, a set amount of time, and space to be alone. There are no other rules, and for this reason, this form of meditation represents an unscripted approach that strongly deviates from formal synagogue prayers. Put simply, Hitbodedut is your personal conversation with God.

Nachman of Breslov claimed that his type of Hitbodedut had been the main mode of spiritual activity from the earliest days and had in fact been practiced by the forefathers of Judaism, including Abraham, Moses, David, and the biblical prophets. He even suggested that Adam and Eve engaged in Hitbodedut. His idea was that spontaneous prayer had been the original practice—what began as spontaneous expression gradually became, due to our increasing loss of ease and comfort with spontaneity, a series of fixed prayers composed by rabbis for the people.[125]

124. Burger, "On Hitbodedut."
125. Burger, "On Hitbodedut."

If you are worried that conversation with God might not suit you because you are agnostic or atheist, feel free to speak to the universe, the unknown, your heart, yourself as a child, or even to parts of your body. (The latter was actually suggested by Nachman to one of his students.[126])

Purpose

This meditative practice is designed to lead to a sense of closeness to the divine source of life in a way that formal prayers can rarely achieve. It instantly bypasses dogma and intellect and initiates an I-God connection at the soul level. By enabling straightforward and unfiltered communication, this technique can dissolve the barriers that stand between your heart and the great mystery of life.

To accomplish this intense sense of intimacy, Rebbe Nachman emphasized speaking simply and openly—again, as if you were conversing with a close friend. When we openly speak to a friend about a problem we have, we see no reason to hold back, so our words flow spontaneously and even uncontrollably; we often start saying something that soon leads to something else until, before we know it, we find ourselves revealing the innermost secrets of our heart to them, and also to ourselves.

Another metaphor for the experience of Hitbodedut, which derives from the biblical statement that we are children to God, is that of a child pleading before their father. We are meant to pour out our thoughts, feelings, and troubles. Even though we might find it strange and somewhat uncomfortable to speak so candidly and childishly to the divine reality, Nachman of Breslov was adamant that we mustn't draw distinctions between higher and lower. Your talk may center on your wish to develop closeness to God, or it may be about your needs, large and small.[127] Your practice of Hitbodedut should encompass the entire spectrum of your life, from the most trivial daily affairs to the lofty spiritual heights you may aspire to. Transcend your sense of guilt and embarrassment; speak about your material needs concerning good health, success in business and livelihood, or help raising your children, and allow your conversation to clear away burdens and unspoken issues from your heart.

According to Nachman of Breslov, if you consistently set time aside to speak freely to God, you can eventually nullify all your desires and negative character traits. This may lead to the final mystical fulfillment of your Hitbodedut, which is called *bitul* (nullification): you concentrate your meditation on God's presence to a degree that your concentration nullifies your sense of physicality and you become absorbed in the divine.[128]

---

126. Burger, "On Hitbodedut."
127. Kramer, "Hitbodedut & Jewish Meditation."
128. Shulman, "Awake at Night."

Practice

Traditionally, Hitbodedut was a consistent practice that should take place every day for at least one hour. However, this doesn't imply that you cannot attain profound insights as a result of only a few experiences or occasional practice. Similarly, the traditional ideal time for Hitbodedut is at night, when the world is at rest. In this way, you can easily connect with the feeling that time and space have dissolved and that only your open heart and the divine have remained. If you can't get up in the middle of the night for your practice, you may try to find the time to converse with God in the early morning, before getting caught up in the rush of yet another busy day. However, if early morning doesn't work either, any other time can be just as effective. The essential guideline to follow is that the quieter, the better.

Nachman of Breslov used to recommend practicing Hitbodedut in forests or fields, claiming that "when a person meditates in the fields, all the grasses join in his prayer and increase its effectiveness and power."[129] But the underlying principle is to look for a location that is conducive to meditation and can allow you to concentrate on your words undisturbed—the more secluded the place is, the more ideal it is for Hitbodedut. Thus, a private room would be ideal for your secluded meditation and conversation with God.

Speak out whatever is in your heart, in the language that you usually speak, preferably your native language. When you entreat the divine in the language you are used to, the words are closer to your heart and will therefore flow more fluently. In addition, make sure you speak out loud. Remember, this is not a silent prayer, but a conversation with your closest friend. Speaking out loud enables you to connect your inside—your preverbal thoughts, feelings, and intuitions— with your outside: expression in the space that you are in. This interface keeps the conversation from being amorphous and forces you to articulate your thoughts and feelings. Since you are able to listen to yourself, you become a witness to your own words. Thus, you form a powerful dialogue not only between you and the divine, but also between you and yourself. It is natural to feel awkward at first. Simply incorporate this embarrassment and any other subtle impediments into your spontaneous conversation and keep talking. Over time, the practice of audible self-conversation will feel more natural to you.

Instructions

PREPARATION: The meditation usually lasts sixty minutes. After settling in a secluded and quiet spot, sit, stand, or walk quietly and tune in to yourself. Clarify your intention to come closer to the divine (or to the universe, your heart, or higher self).[130]

129. Monaghan and Viereck, *Meditation*, 164.
130. The instructions derive from Burger, "On Hitbodedut."

1. Begin by speaking slowly. Notice what you feel and how your feelings and words develop during the time you have set aside. Be aware of the internal and subtle movements of your thoughts and feelings. You can speak loudly—shouting, jumping, freely expressing—or softly.

2. If you feel you have nothing to say, you can begin with something you are grateful for. Keep your attention on this and try to speak about how and why you are grateful. Or try to list as many things as you can that you appreciate about yourself. Be specific. (If it helps, you can write these down first, then read them and reflect out loud.) Then shift to someone close to you and talk about what you appreciate about them. The main thing is to go slowly so that you have a chance to feel the gratitude permeating your being.

   When you feel ready, you can move to yearning: what do you deeply want or wish for? You can begin with "I wish" as a prompt. Notice how you feel as you express a desire. You could also talk about where you find joy and where you struggle with it, and express your desire for more. You can borrow joy from the future too: what are you looking forward to, and can you feel the happiness waiting for you there, now?

3. Choose whatever topic you feel close to at the time. You may focus on an area you want to work on. By slowing down and feeling how important this aspiration is to you, you can begin to awaken real longing for it. This may give you deeper focus as you go about the rest of your day.

4. Dance, sway, or jump while you speak so that your body joins the conversation too. Let your body lead you. Listen to what it has to say and translate that into words.

5. Don't be afraid to use humor. The religious imperative to cultivate awe should be balanced with feeling at home in your spiritual life, so find a balance between reverence and casualness.

6. Repeat a word or phrase over and over as a mantra. Rebbe Nachman of Breslov invited his students to say "Ribono shel Olam," which is Hebrew for "Lord of the Universe." Finding a phrase can be helpful for those moments when the words seem to dry up. The phrase needs to resonate with you and feel like something that can open your heart.

· · · · · · · ·

7. Talk to parts of your body. Express support for each limb and ask for its cooperation in leading a meditative life. For example, you can tell your ears, "Ears, let's learn to listen openly and receptively to other people."

8. Feel free to come up with any practice that feels more authentic to you. Although practices are not required, they can help you build momentum until you feel comfortable with a perfectly spontaneous conversation.

NOTE: Although Hitbodedut is by definition a solitary practice, it can be engaged in with a community. Go somewhere as a group, separate so that each person has privacy, and then come back together later to share your experiences and insights.

Meditate on This: Meditation as Listening

The throat chakra is traditionally linked to the sense of hearing. This indicates that the way we listen is no less important than the sound we make. But do we know how to listen?

In meditation, much depends on our level of listening and receptivity. Too often we rely on the power of the technique itself, as if the power exists outside of the one who receives and responds to the technique. But even if you are given an extremely powerful mantra, this will not be enough to transform you. How deeply you listen determines the level of your transformation—one person can listen to a mantra and be completely affected, while for another, nothing will happen. In a sense, the mantra in itself is quite powerless.

In the deepest sense, we rarely listen. It is important to admit this, because listening is not something to be taken for granted. Listening has depth, and it is an art that one needs to develop. Even if you have some basic understanding of this art, there is so much more to it.

When we say that someone is a good listener, what do we mean? What qualities are involved? Probably, we mean that when we tell them something, they don't immediately react. They don't rush to intervene. Instead, they contain us. They allow us to complete a statement. They hold our statement. And they are fully there. A good listener is someone who must be fully awake and present. If somebody allows us to speak fluently and uninterruptedly, but they are half asleep, they can't be a good listener.

A good listener is someone who is completely there, but at the same time doesn't react and has the ability to contain. They don't have to constantly push themselves into the picture by adding something of their own. They don't have to involve you in their own story. They don't say "Oh yes, this reminds me of…" or "Yes, that is exactly what I experienced. Let me tell you about that." They are just there, fully present, fully containing, and we feel that we are held in

· · · · · · · ·

a sort of space. A good listener doesn't stand in the way of a conversation. Their ego isn't constantly demanding to be recognized.

Now, are you a good listener?

Beyond Agreeing and Disagreeing

The first thing that most of us do when we receive a certain message, either by word or sound, is respond to it from the past. This response indicates that what we have heard is something we already know; we might think *That reminds me of a story I once heard* or *This is like that experience I had*. Therefore, we compare what we hear to our experiences.

The other thing we do when we receive a message is instinctively agree or disagree. Agreeing is when we compare something to our previous knowledge and the new transmission matches it. Disagreeing is when we compare something to our previous knowledge and they don't match so we believe this new information can't be true or right. But this is obviously not listening—it is more like hearing. Hearing is technical. Most of us are able to hear, more or less, depending on our capacities. But very few of us are actually able to *listen*.

This is often evident on social media. On social media, I have the option to "Like" and sometimes to "Dislike" as well. Now, what do I convey by clicking "Like"? Often this means "I agree." But if I agree, what is the value of agreeing? Both agreeing and disagreeing mean confirming something that you already know. Essentially, this means very little; what you agree with is aligned with your previous knowledge to a degree that it is nothing more than an echo of it. Your mind has not been irritated or stopped; instead, it is in a comfortable state in which it can immediately and automatically think *Yes, I agree. I like it*. Of course, if by liking I mean "Thank you, this is a new perspective that I haven't considered," that is a very different case.

The question is, then, can we listen without agreeing or disagreeing? Even what I just wrote about social media culture—you may agree or disagree with that. But can you simply listen? Can we listen to something without reacting immediately and without classifying it as "good" or "bad," that is, according to the perspective that I already have and merely wish to validate?

We hear from the past and we compare. But we also label everything. This is even more subtle. For example, we behold an astonishingly colorful sunset and instantly exclaim, "What a beautiful sunset!" In my mind, it is already classified as a sunset, and then as a beautiful sunset. There is a verbal description that already summarizes the experience. This means that I experience very little of it when I tag it because I already have a picture in my mind. This is why we need stronger stimulation to shock our senses. Once we label something, we get used to it, which means that we no longer listen.

To a certain degree, what we call the listener—ourselves—is actually the one who reacts. After all, if you remove the reaction and the labeling, where are you? What we consider the listener right now stands in the way of true listening. In the deeper sense, listening cannot have a listener,

• • • • • • • •

at least not the listener as we usually know it: the one who reacts, labels, compares, agrees, disagrees, and judges.

Now, how is this all related to meditation?

To Meditate Means to Listen

In so many respects, learning meditation is learning the art of listening. Meditation is all about listening, and it helps us develop this form of intelligence.

I don't know if you have ever thought of listening as a form of intelligence. Listening can be considered an intelligence in its own right, like the passive aspect of spiritual intelligence. However, it is not really passive—it is tremendously awake and full of presence.

This is a meaningful perspective because deeply speaking, meditation is listening more than it is watching. Meditation teachers always repeat instructions like "Watch" and "Observe," but these are problematic terms. Watching and observing make it sound like this should happen in the brain. Being an observer is a somewhat mental or intellectual position. Even more, this sounds like a neutral point of view.

What we call awareness in meditation is actually a state of listening. This is, fundamentally, a matter of the inner ear, not of the eye. Feel for a moment what it means to listen. Of course, in meditation there is no difference between watching and listening; no difference between the ear and the eye. The two organs become one and the same. Watching takes place through listening, and listening takes place through watching. However, following an instruction like "Listen" may shape your meditative experience differently.

Try to feel the difference between listening to your thoughts or emotions and watching them. Don't you feel that immediately, you have assumed a more empathetic position? This is because the ear is much more passive and significantly less reactive and intellectual. It is more about receiving sound rather than interpreting. The ear is far less quick to interpret.

So try to play with this new perspective on meditation—listen. Even in mindfulness, instead of observing your breathing, try to listen to the in-breath and the out-breath. If you try to follow this instruction, you will quickly realize that this is exactly what we do when we are aware of something: we are actually listening. This part of us that is awareness, the so-called observer or all-witnessing eye, is actually an all-listening ear.

In meditation, we train ourselves to be good listeners. We sit with closed eyes, practice awareness, and retract our judgmental reactions. Second, we stop labeling and refrain from our compulsive need for words that must describe everything. Third, we do our best to be like a container, a space that holds. These are all qualities of good listening: we learn to just listen to thoughts, emotions, feelings, and sensations. We begin with our inner world so that later, we will be able to enter the outer world and listen to it.

• • • • • • • •

Only Pure Awareness Can Truly Listen

Meditation means separating the essence of awareness from all the things it is identified with. By disengaging our awareness from thoughts, emotions, sensations, body, gender, and personal history, we leave it as pure as possible. Doing this is also the beginning of a fresh and innocent state of listening. In this state of pure awareness, we can actually listen.

Developing the art of listening in meditation is a long journey. Generally, we can say that this journey consists of three major stages. Our starting point is the stage of *reacting*. In this stage, we are not aware of any state other than our automatic reactions: we agree, disagree, compare, and label. We stand in our own way, hardly listening, mainly hearing. Then we move to an important stage of *reflecting*, which will soon be explained. Transitioning to this stage may require a long time, depending on how much we cling to our reactions. Last, from reflecting we eventually move to the stage of *oneness*, when our listening and what we listen to become one and the same.

Let's try to understand what the stage of reflecting is. When you truly listen, you only reflect what you listen to; you are like a mirror that doesn't distort or interfere with whatever it reflects. You don't add yourself via your perspective and interpretation. You can start practicing this by listening to a piece of music. That's an easy start: for the first time, don't label the music in any way. Instead of thinking *I like this music* or *It reminds me of…*, just listen to the music and reflect it through your ear without separating yourself from it. Listen as if your ear has become transparent.

When your ear is transparent, you realize that the listening itself is no different from silence. This is why it is so important to practice listening: listening leads to silence because in real listening, there can be no activity or movement in the mind. If you want to truly listen to something, there has to be complete silence on your part. This is the thing: as long as you are there, with the noise of thought, you cannot listen to another sound. Sound cannot listen to sound. But *silence* can listen to sound. In other words, only silence can listen.

If you learn to listen to a piece of music with a transparent ear, you can move on to reflecting your inner world. You can try to reflect any pain or anger that rushes through you. Listen to it as you would listen transparently to a piece of music: there is pain, but listen to it without attempting to change it.

A good listener never tries to change what they listen to. Try it once. This is a very extraordinary experience. You listen without prejudice, and you are then able to listen to yourself without distortion. You begin to listen even to your own responses and reactions—not only to the way others speak, but to the way you speak. When the listening is transparent and has no center, it reflects what it listens to without any distortion.

If this ability to reflect goes deep, you find yourself moving to the third stage: oneness with what is listened to. It is like one flow, one movement. You cannot really separate the listener and

· · · · · · · ·

what they listen to. When you listen to music, you become the music. Why is that? It is because when it comes to pure awareness, the separation is quite artificial. If there is complete silence as listening, then this is the complementary half of the sound. Silence and sound come together. They are like two halves that form a perfect circle.

In such deep listening, there is no past and there is no listener, at least not in the sense of reaction and labeling. As a result, listening becomes as fresh as the morning dew. It has nothing to compare its object to, for listening knows nothing. In this state, listening no longer takes place only through the ear. It is not located in a specific part of the body. It involves the whole body, from head to toe. Every part of your body participates in the act of listening.

There is an idiom that says, "I'm all ears." If you go all the way with this idiom, it means that your first identity, what you are before anything else, is that of a listener. This is your core identity in your relationship with all that is, and everything else springs from it. In this way, you listen to people and to situations. Positioning yourself as a listener does not imply that you cannot respond to people and situations; it is only that your first identity is that of a receiver and a reflector, and from that, a response arises—not from memory, but from the here and now.

If you can meditate in this way—if, for example, you can truly listen to a mantra—what happens is that your listening becomes more transformative than the mantra itself. The implication is that listening is your most important meditative work. It is not the sound that you receive, but the way you listen that really matters in meditation. Listening, after all, is not passive. It is a state of complete participation that gives meaning, significance, and depth to what is listened to. And when you master this art in your meditation, you begin to practice listening in real life, and your life as a whole becomes meditation.

CHAPTER 9

Brow Chakra Meditations: Open Your Inner Vision

As we are climbing the chakra ladder, we are getting closer to the peak of our being. This doesn't mean that the third eye group of meditations is necessarily more important. Each group is a gateway: if you open the gate, walk through it, and follow the path all the way, you will find reality waiting at the end of the road. However, by the time we have reached the brow chakra meditations, we have grown our meditative capacity based on previous experiences and insight. This is also the way that the meditative journey works in general—your advanced meditation, associated with the higher chakras, builds on the previous accumulated awakenings of the five lower chakras.

In so many ways, the third eye group of meditations is the complementary half of the throat chakra group: the throat chakra is all about sound, vibration, and listening, whereas the third eye is all about seeing and vision. The way we see and the way we hear are the foremost ways we interact with the world. Even more deeply, the two groups also correlate with the Hindu distinction between yantra and mantra: mantra is all about sound, the vocal and vibratory element, and yantra is the visual element, the shape and form. Yantra embodies the same energy that the mantra vocalizes. Thus, together they create a perfect form of sound and shape.

Of course, since this is the world of meditation, when we speak of the ear in the throat chakra group, we refer to the inner ear and to our inner listening. Similarly, the brow chakra group is concerned with inner seeing, which is enabled by the third eye.

· · · · · · ·

Looking into Yourself

The brow chakra—or *ajna*, to use its Sanskrit name—is often referred to as the third eye. We need a third eye to be able to look inward. Our two physical eyes cannot be used for inward perception and realization. Since they are designed to perceive the world, they are turned outward, facing the world. To perceive the inner world, we use our third eye, which is like a projector, throwing light on inner images and visions. This includes our dreams, which appear visually within our minds. If you want to turn your gaze inward, you need to withdraw from external vision. Thus, to be able to open the third eye, you first need to close the two physical eyes. As soon as you turn off your external vision, you begin to activate the third eye.

Meditation often begins with instructions to close our eyes. This is because we are meant to start communicating with our inner world—in other words, we start seeing through the third eye. This is not only the reason for the invention of eyes-closed meditation, but it is why eyes-closed meditation has been classically recommended at the beginning stages of the meditative journey.

The easiest way to stimulate the dormant "eye of Shiva," as it is sometimes called in Hindu literature, is to close your eyes and concentrate both of them on the middle point between the two eyebrows. Another traditional way is to leave your eyes half open and gaze at the tip of your nose; this is also a quick third eye-opener. Using either of these techniques is a fast way to become attentive; with the exception of the heart chakra, no other chakra responds so quickly to this kind of concentrated attention. You can easily feel the third eye beginning to be stimulated. When you pay attention to the third eye, it absorbs the attention immediately because it is a magnet for attention. After all, the third eye is attention itself. In tantric scriptures, it is said that attention is food for the third eye.[131] If you give it attention, your attention is immediately drawn to it and becomes absorbed in it. It's as if both your eyes become hooked on and hypnotized by the third eye.

In the same way, you can try to look at the world from your third eye with your eyes open. Imagine that you have only one eye and that the two physical eyes are secondary. Notice what the world looks like. You can also place yourself at a deeper point, as if you are looking at everything from the eye behind the eyes. Realize that two things happen immediately: your mind is silenced without any difficulty, and you come into contact with the pure awareness that you are. Concentrating the energy of the two eyes in this midpoint silences the mind, and moving deeper into the brain awakens pure awareness.

Let's discuss the meaning of the third eye in relation to what third eye meditations are all about. The very term *third eye* is a popular use of a principle that comes from the East. This

---

131. Osho, *Meditation*, 169.

concept is a tremendous contribution that we have been given by South Asian seers: the understanding that there is a third eye that ordinarily remains dormant, but once awakened, it can radically alter our sense of identity, the way we perceive the world, the way we perceive our inner world, and our relationship with everything.

Curiously, you can also find a clear description of third eye awakening in the New Testament. This is how Jesus himself is quoted in Matthew 6:22: "The light of the body is the eye: If therefore thine eye be single, Thy whole body shall be full of light."[132] This is a perfect third eye teaching, though in a more encoded form. It states that the eye is the "light of the body." There is a source of light within the body, and this source is not the eyes, but the *eye*, singular. The eyes through which you look at the world throw light on the visible world, but this single eye is the source of inner illumination. If you are able to move to single-eye vision, then "the whole body shall be full of light." Even Jesus seems to indicate that there is a single eye with which we look inside ourselves and reveal the light within. This should be understood both metaphorically, since the third eye is like the light of consciousness—the light that makes everything known and revealed—and also literally, because in third eye awakening, we become flooded with light from within. The third eye sometimes radiates literally. When, for instance, you enter darkness meditation and remain with your eyes open, sooner or later you will realize that the third eye is shining in the darkness.

Interestingly, by leaving behind the duality of the two eyes in favor of a single, cyclops-like eye, the third eye also seems to nourish and clear the vision of the physical eyes. To a certain degree, you can see better when you are washed by the light of awareness.

The Master Is Home

Physically speaking, the third eye is associated with the pituitary gland, which resides behind the eyes. Interestingly, the pituitary gland is known to be the master gland. This is also a perfect description for the third eye since traditionally, it is the master chakra, or in Hindu terms, the chakra of the inner guru.[133]

If the third eye is not open, our mind and our being as a whole are extremely fragmented and scattered. It is as if our being consists of many, often contradictory voices. These contradictory voices even emerge from the different perspectives of the seven chakras, each layer pulling in its own direction. Thus, everything is split, including the mind itself. One very clear expression of this is the split between the thinker and the thought: there is the part that observes thoughts and tries to change and improve them, and there are the thoughts themselves. For example, when there is anger, there is also anger *about* the anger, a voice that tries to correct the anger. This

132. King James Version.
133. Saraswati, *Kundalini Tantra*, 129.

battle within the mind can only be solved through the emergence of awareness that is beyond both parts. You move beyond the thinker and the thought, and behind both, you find supreme awareness, which has no conflict with anything.

So when the third eye opens, it brings order and unity. Thanks to its luminous clarity, it brings light into the system. Accordingly, it is the chakra of seeing things clearly. With this clear perception, it brings one voice that can govern our being as a whole and guide its evolution. This chakra harmonizes the different forces and puts each in its right place. In the end, all other parts obey the third eye's vision and follow what the third eye sees and understands.

Certain Zen parables refer to the third eye. These parables speak of a master who needs to return to their home because the house is empty and burglars can freely enter. In this metaphor, the burglars are the contradictory voices, and the master of the house is the third eye. When attention is fixed on the third eye, it immediately commands all the energy of the mind to return to it. This is why it is admired as the guru chakra—finally, the master is home!

Ordinarily, the mind's energy is extremely scattered, but once focused on the third eye, this energy can no longer be wasted, and awareness becomes separate from thought. This is what meditation is all about: thoughts will pass in front of you, but they pass like clouds in the sky; you are simply unable to identify with them, even if you try really hard. Next time your mind is scattered, instead of attempting to silence your thoughts, shift your attention and place it on the third eye. You will probably discover that when your mind's energy is concentrated, no thought can take over—not without the permission of the brow chakra.

Usually, there is no separation between attention and thought. We rarely experience being aware of our thoughts. Instead, we immediately become our thoughts. Here, however, we must return to the first aspect of the law of attention (see chapter 6): in reality, there is a gap between awareness and thought. But when we don't realize this, identification takes place so quickly that we simply find ourselves in the form of the thought. If sexual desire emerges, we become the sexual desire. Likewise, if anger or jealousy arises, we become angry or jealous, often without even realizing we have made that choice.

In this sense, the third eye is meditation itself. The third eye is where we detach awareness from thoughts and objects. It is for this reason that in some traditions, the process of the chakras starts with the third eye rather than the root chakra. This makes sense: you start by activating the third eye, thus bringing the master home, and then descend to work on the root chakra.[134] This is also why in all traditions, the first meditative phase is learning how to concentrate. Concentration, in this context, means taming the mind's energy to return to the third eye and not to leave that point—attaining the ability to be one-pointed, or single-minded. Before you move to awareness, you first gather the scattered and wasted energy of the mind.

134. Saraswati, *Kundalini Tantra*, 127.

• • • • • • • •

Now, then, we understand that third eye activation can happen in two ways. You can practice being purely aware, and as a result the third eye awakens. Or you can achieve this almost physically: you can practice focusing on the third eye and looking both inward and outward from it. As a result you will find yourself purely aware. Both methods can work. The latter, the physical way, is obviously the quickest. If you center yourself in the third eye, the witnessing self will naturally and effortlessly appear.

In the introduction to the heart chakra techniques (chapter 8), you were encouraged to practice headlessness. You might be wondering why we are moving our attention back to the head. But centering yourself in the third eye has nothing to do with the head. The third eye is not the head! It is the observer of thoughts, and thus it can be regarded as existing behind and beyond the head. For this reason, when you have found this precious point and it responds to you, your entire subtle being will awaken too, and you will feel how the essence of breathing, the prana, begins to travel all the way from the lower parts of your body toward the third eye. So, the third eye is a point of concentration that leads you to awareness behind and beyond the head.

When this point of concentration grows in power, the ratio between awareness and physical existence changes dramatically. You become more awareness than body. In the case of advanced meditators, this could be 90 percent awareness and 10 percent physical existence. That may sound extreme, but 10 percent is more than enough—you can do a lot with 10 percent!

This is perhaps the greatest message of the third eye group of meditations: your mind is not just confused thoughts. Thoughts are actually a peripheral activity of the mind, its lowest activity. With the aid of the five meditations in this chapter, we can tap into higher activities of the mind and realize what an extraordinary tool for transformation it can be.

Eight Roles and Purposes for the Third Eye Meditations

1. **Opening the third eye for spiritual intelligence, vision, and intuition.** This means placing the guru chakra back in its rightful position in order to bring the master back home.

2. **Using the mind to go beyond the mind.** The mind is like a springboard that can take you far beyond itself. But this is only if you first realize that it is not synonymous with the head.

3. **Revealing the true spacelike, expanded nature of the mind.** The mind has different layers: the superficial layer of sense-related thoughts, the finer layer of the conceptual and abstract mind that conceives ideas, and the pure mind.[135]

135. Yeshe, *The Bliss of Inner Fire*, 87.

The pure mind actually constitutes most of the mind, and it is as vast and all-inclusive as outer space.

4. **Creating the ideal conditions for insight.** These meditations prepare our mind for a shift in brain activity, which leads to a nonlinear, total understanding that can shatter the boundaries of ordinary thinking.

5. **Acquiring the transformative power of inquiry.** Some of these meditations are based on the art of spiritual inquiry. Although this may seem intellectual and philosophical, it is a demonstration of our ability to use the mind in order to go beyond the mind.

6. **Cutting through illusions.** Some of these techniques make use of the third eye as the sword of truth, a destroyer of illusion. The third eye in its sharpest form has the power to cut through illusions, confusions, dreams, and emotional projections of the mind.

7. **Achieving mental purification.** This means getting rid of as many thoughts, memories, and concepts as possible, in order to replace them with fresh awareness.

8. **Using sacred geometry, letters, and other shapes as vehicles of transformation.** Seeing is not only an internal activity. Sometimes, gazing at the proper image can activate the third eye and lead to spiritual transformation. For example, in Jewish mysticism, the meditator contemplates letters and words as shapes that contain transformative potency.

Koan

Koans appear, at first glance, as nonsensical riddles, but they are, in fact, brief pronouncements, exchanges, and anecdotes that derive from discourse records and biographies of antecedent Zen masters. Each koan is an encapsulation of a certain spontaneous expression of the master's awakened mind in response to his disciples' queries.

Historical Background

Between the years 960 and 1279, a new form of Buddhism was developing in China.[136] In order to flourish, it needed a new kind of practice. That practice was koan, paradoxical anecdotes or riddles used in Zen Buddhism to provoke spiritual enlightenment.

The word *koan*, or *gongan* in the original Chinese, means a public case or precedent: looking back to the precedent, to the understanding of the masters, as a starting point. Initially, koans were simply stories about things that had happened. They were a record of a conversation, usually between teacher and student, and more rarely between two students or other people. Over time, additional elements such as poetry and references to popular culture were folded into the developing body of koan texts. Later, Japanese Zen, both Rinzai and Sōtō, took over the use of koan study and practice.

Koan is a problem to be solved through meditation. While there are some ways to bring the richness of the koan tradition to people who can't have a one-on-one relationship with a teacher, traditionally koan is a part of student-teacher interaction. A nonrational riddle, which often takes the form of a question, is introduced to the student by the master, who assumes the position of the questioner. As a part of the master's efforts to guide the pupil toward a final realization of the koan, they may engage the student in a rapid series of questions, called *mondo*, to compel them to supply spontaneous and intuitive answers.

After the student is given a koan, they keep constant company with it, even in the sleeping and dreaming states. They look for the through line underneath the koan while sitting, walking around, and sleeping. The day-and-night, strenuous concentration on the koan takes place in tandem with occasional sessions where the student offers the master answers, which are mostly rejected. However, with time, senior students develop a much stronger nonconceptual mind. While a great breakthrough is rare, there are varying degrees of openings. Students learn to see through words and concepts and to realize their empty nature, and also not to take their own reactions too seriously. They understand that their wrong answers reflect their own limitations and life lessons, as well as their tendency to conceptualize rather than transform. Similarly, the rejection of answers by the master reflects conditioned reactions such as frustration, self-doubt, and anger.

Purpose

The role of the koan is not to develop intellectual agility, but to transcend the intellect altogether. In the words of the renowned Buddhist philosopher D. T. Suzuki, the koan is designed

---

136. Schlütter, *How Zen Became Zen*, 1.

to "let the intellect see by itself how far it can go, and also that there is a realm into which it as such can never enter."[137]

One of the striking things about working with koans is that we use language to cut through language. Through koans, you begin to develop the ability to rise above ordinary preconceptions and ways of thinking. Responses don't come from intellect or emotion, but from a more fundamental place.

Every koan, in its own way, points to our original nature. The ultimate purpose of the koan is to lead to *satori*, a form of ultimate answer and the fulfillment of the Zen experience. Suzuki explains that the teacher's demand that the koan be brought to a resolution generates increasing psychic pressure to such a degree that finally, "the entire personality, mind and body, is thrown into the solution."[138]

Practice

Koans are a living tradition by nature. They are not words on a page or a particular story or question, but an interaction between that story and anyone who takes it up.

When facing the koan, you don't look for an "answer." Rather, you use the question to cut through conceptual thoughts like a hot knife through butter. In the process, you attain your true nature. You let the koan emerge in your mind naturally, not holding on to it but looking at it when it arises; not trying to intellectualize and analyze, but just looking at it from different angles.

Koans don't really explain things. They are not intended to describe something to you or to teach you anything. Instead, they show you something by opening a gate, and you decide to walk through it. As you keep company with the koan, it draws your attention to something you already have, but might not have valued.

Accept a koan into your life so you can experience the same state of consciousness as the characters in the story. In a sense, you step into the story and try on someone else's realization. Zen Master Su Bong once said that to work with koans, you have to be a great actor.[139] This means that you completely *become* the koan. So if someone is hanging from a tree branch by their teeth, it is you hanging from that branch, and you are hanging there completely. Although you bring your life to the koan, you become the situation and are not limited to your own life in any way. By inhabiting the various roles in a koan, you are called upon to investigate your true nature through the specifics of that koan.

---

137. Suzuki, *The Zen Koan as a Means of Attaining Enlightenment*, 70.
138. Suzuki, *The Zen Koan*, 70.
139. Blacker, "The Wonder and Mystery of Zen Koan Practice."

Instructions

Preparation: The meditation usually lasts thirty minutes.

1. Intuitively choose one of the sample koans below (or look for other examples elsewhere; hundreds of translated koans are easily available online):

   • The coin lost in the river is found in the river.[140]

   • A Zen master asks, "Show me your Original Face, the face you had before your parents were born."[141]

   • A monk asked Kegon, "How does an enlightened one return to the ordinary world?" Kegon replied, "A broken mirror never reflects again; fallen flowers never go back to the old branches."[142]

   • The master holds up a stick and dares his disciples, "If you call this a stick you will be clinging; if you do not call this a stick you are ignoring the obvious. So, now, tell me, what do you call it?"[143]

   • When you can do nothing, what can you do?[144]

   • What is the sound of one hand clapping?[145]

   • When Chao-chou came to study Zen under Nan-ch'üan, he asked, "What is the Tao (or the Way)?" Nan-ch'üan replied, "Your everyday mind, that is the Tao."[146]

   • A monk asked Master Haryo, "What is the way?" Haryo said, "An open-eyed man falling into the well."[147]

   • When questioned about whether a dog has Buddha nature or not, Joshu shouts "No!"[148]

---

140. Tarrant, "How to Practice Zen Koans."
141. Strand, "Green Koans Case 12."
142. "Zen Koan."
143. Hake, "How and Why to Analogize Socratic Questioning," 39.
144. "Zen Koan."
145. "Zen Koan."
146. Suzuki, *The Zen Koan*, 69.
147. "Zen Koan."
148. Hooper, "Koan Zen and Wittgenstein's Only Correct Method in Philosophy," 284.

• • • • • • • •

- A monk asked Zhao Zhou to teach him. Zhao Zhou asked, "Have you eaten your meal?" The monk replied, "Yes, I have." "Then go wash your bowl," said Zhao Zhou. At that moment, the monk was enlightened.[149]

2. With this koan, you are joining a timeless conversation. Feel as if you are standing at a gate, just about to enter. You are going to form a deep relationship with the koan, one that could lead to a total merging. Contact this wish to merge with it so that its deeper secret will be revealed. Trust that there is a very profound secret awaiting you.

3. Repeat the words of the koan to yourself several times. Let them sink into your deepest core, into the deepest space inside your mind and being. Don't be forceful—simply let it in. Open your being to receive it as it is. Don't work on the koan, let it work on you.

4. Observe your surface reactions and the ways that your thoughts cope with the koan. Throughout the meditation, answers will arise. Reject easy and smart answers and remember that your past is not relevant. This is a meeting in the Now. Don't bother searching your memory for an insight. At the same time, don't judge, criticize, assess, or find fault with anything that arises in your mind.

5. Although your past is not relevant, it is personal; something in your life will rise to meet this koan, but it will not be what you expect.

6. Become the koan. Enter into it more and more. Feel it from within. Be truly inside it, as you are entering its world, as if it is the only world in this moment. Apply true listening and become one with what you hear.

7. Become all the different components of the koan, one after the other—see and feel from their perspective. See yourself doing or being these actions.

8. Focus on each part or component separately—any part of the koan is all of the koan. Then combine all components into one total experience.

9. You can play and experiment with the koan: change the sentence, reverse it, feel where the ending leads, ask yourself questions, doubt it, fall into it, make mistakes, try to misunderstand it, find its virtues. Don't worry, you can't break a koan!

149. "Zen Koan."

. . . .

10. Enter a state of enlightenment, even if you don't understand. Remember that it is not about understanding—a koan is a matter of being. Examine what takes place at the level of your being and what quality of mind emerges from this. Move even deeper behind this and see what you find there.

11. Invite the koan to enter your life and revisit it frequently in meditation or while engaged in daily actions. Don't be content with your current insight into it.

"Who Am I?"

This inquiry-based meditation is designed to lead you directly and rapidly to self-realization, far quicker than traditional meditations. Turning the question "Who am I?" onto yourself is like turning a powerful flashlight on a dark room: the light instantly reveals all of your false identities and attachments, and everything that has become associated with your pure sense of "I." (First and foremost, the thought that *I am this body*.) Aided by this illuminating question, you can then discard these identities and remain only with the reality of "I am."

Historical Background

The Indian yogi Ramana Maharshi (1879–1950) experienced a spontaneous inner awakening, without prior effort or desire, at the very early age of sixteen, when he was only a schoolboy called Venkataraman. While alone in a room, he suddenly felt that he was going to die, although he was perfectly healthy. Strangely, he knew that he had to solve the problem himself, there and then. He asked himself, *Now death has come; what does it mean? What is it that is dying?* and the answer came, "This body dies." To give greater reality to his inquiry, the boy lay down and imitated a corpse. He visualized how his dead body would be burned and reduced to ashes and continued to question himself. *But with the death of this body, am I dead? Is the body I?* The young Ramana could feel the silent presence of the "I" within him, apart from the body. He realized directly that his "I" was a deathless spirit, and his fear of death ended.[150]

While many people have reported similar insightful moments in meditation, these insights tend to fade away with time. But in Ramana's case, this experience led to a continuous absorption in the sense of Self, a state in which his attention became fixed on this "I." After six weeks, he left his family behind and went directly to the holy mountain of Arunachala in South India. After a few years of living on the mountain's slopes, Ramana began to attract disciples.

150. Maharshi, "Ramana Maharshi Enlightenment Story," and Godman, *Be As You Are*, 4.

As a teacher, Ramana Maharshi remained silent most of the time. But he did impart lucid teachings, which have mainly been compiled in David Godman's classic work *Be As You Are*. Clearly inspired by his own spontaneous self-inquiry at the age of sixteen, Ramana encouraged his students to adopt a method of active meditation based on the question "Who am I?" This method has become widespread among spiritual circles in the West as a result of the teachings of Maharshi's student, H. W. L. Poonja.

Purpose

Maharshi explains that the feeling "I exist" is the only permanent, self-evident experience that everyone has. But while the "I am" is reality, "I am this or that" is unreal.[151] We constantly adopt identities, like "I am a man" or "I am a European," but when we meditate on this question, we can gradually return to a state of original and untainted awareness. In Hindu yogic terms, we move from a personal "I" to our true "Self."

In Ramana's view, the personal "I" (*aham-vritti*) was nothing but a thought that could only exist by identifying with something. This personal "I" only appears to exist because of the incessant flow of identifications—remove all these identities and it is gone forever. On the other hand, there is the Self that cannot be modified and that remains as is, regardless of thoughts and actions. Thus, the question "Who am I?" eventually causes the personal "I" to subside back into the true Self.

Practice

Self-inquiry is paying constant attention to the pure awareness of "I" instead of "I am this." Repeating "I" mentally will help at first, but in the end, it is not about being *aware* of an "I" as an object, but about *being* the "I." So while in the beginning stages, your attention to the feeling "I" is a mental activity, as your practice deepens, the thought "I" will give way to a profoundly felt experience of "I."

This technique can be compared somewhat to the Hindu *neti neti* ("not this, not that") approach: instead of looking for what is real, you focus on removing unrealities, until all that remains is reality itself. In other words, you become aware of what you really are by withdrawing your attention from what you are not.

Don't expect any intellectual answers. "Who am I?" is not about finding a final "answer," but about eliminating all your familiar and conditioned answers on your way to deep silence. It takes away the answers and leaves you with an experience.

This technique is gentle, since it doesn't require any method of controlling the mind. It also has nothing to do with concentration. Instead, awareness is directed to the source from which

---

151. Godman, *Be As You Are*, 28.

all thoughts spring. Rather than removing one thought after another, this form of inquiry turns immediately to the first thought and uproots it. It is like cutting the roots of the tree of illusion instead of removing each branch and leaf. When the first thought is gone, all other thoughts follow it.

Instructions

PREPARATION: This meditation requires between twenty and thirty minutes. Note: You may write down the answers and thoughts that appear in response to this inquiry.

1. Close your eyes and turn the question "Who am I?" to yourself. Feel how the question can unveil all of your identities and attachments—all of your "I am this" and "I am that." Begin to scrutinize the answers that arise. Be as thorough as possible.

2. Notice how with each identification with a thought or object, the "I" changes into "I am this" or "I am that." But can the "I" remain after you have removed all these associated identities?

3. Continue to look into the very sense of "I," the root of all identities, using the question "Who am I?" Be aware of whether subtler identities and attachments arise.

4. Now, put your attention on the innermost feeling of "I" and hold that feeling for as long as possible.

5. If your attention is distracted by other thoughts, revert to awareness of the "I" as soon as you become aware that your attention has wandered. This should feel like choosing to look beneath the thoughts rather than at them. You may also ask yourself, *To whom did these thoughts arise?* If the answer is "To me," inquire *Who am I?* and feel how your mind turns back to its source, and the thought also subsides.

6. Inquire: *What is the personal "I" when all identities are removed? Where does this "I" come from? Does it originate in the body? If not, what is it?* Realize that if you seek it with full attention, it vanishes like a ghost. All that remains is a pure sense of "I."

7. Continue to ask "Who am I?" and use the question to look behind any particular thought for the fundamental thought of "I." Constantly look for this first thought. Stick to it and question it to find out what it is.

· · · · · · · ·

8. How do you feel the "I" now? Realize that the more you ask this question, the more you become your original Self. Reside in this pure consciousness that is the true "I."

9. Just like the pearl diver who finds a pearl at the bottom of the sea, feel how you are diving deep within yourself to attain the pearl of Self. Keep the mind fixed in this sense of true Self. Even if you experience deep peace, continue to ask yourself, *Who is having this experience? Who is experiencing this stillness?*

AFTER THE MEDITATION: Asking "Who am I?" is not a limited practice—it is a question to live with. Self-inquiry can easily take place while you are fully engaged in daily activities.

Sri Yantra

The Sri Yantra diagram is one of the most sacred symbols of tantric Hinduism, and it is traditionally used in yogic meditation practices.

Historical Background

In general, geometrical diagrams based on the yantra principle have been used throughout India for the worship of deities both in temples and at home, and representations of the yantra in India arguably date back to 11,000–10,000 BCE.[152] Based on the principles of sacred geometry, each yantra design contains a center point or "dot" from which geometric shapes and designs radiate. They are often composed of a small dot surrounded by circles, triangles, and squares, each of which is symbolic.

However, Sri Yantra ("holy instrument")—also known as Sri Chakra—is considered to be the supreme yantra from which all other yantras derive. In their book *The Tantric Way*, Ajit Mookerjee and Madhu Khanna claim that "Sri Yantra, in its formal content, is a visual masterpiece of abstraction, and must have been created through revelation rather than by human ingenuity and craft."[153] Some writers say that this yantra contains all forms of sacred geometry and the golden ratio. The golden ratio is a special irrational number, approximately equal to 1.618, that provides the most aesthetically pleasing proportion of sides of a rectangle, according to the ancient

---

152. Dokras, *How to Build a Sri Yantra Temple*, 39.

153. Huet, "Śrī Yantra Geometry," 622.

Greeks and many artists and architects.[154] Researchers who have attempted to grasp and imitate this yantra have been impressed with its complexity and mathematical precision.[155]

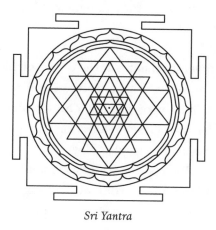

Sri Yantra

Considered to be the "queen of yantras" (*rajayantra*), Sri Yantra is the symbol of the great divine mother principle: the source of all energy, power, and creativity. Vedic traditions, specifically the Shri Vidya school of tantra, regard the design as the representation of the universe, as well as the body of the goddess related to the feminine principle of shakti, or energy. Every line, triangle, and lotus petal symbolizes a specific type of shakti.

Purpose

In tantric Hinduism, the purpose of yantras in meditation is twofold. The first is merging with a deity through their corresponding yantra. The yantra itself is a symbolic composition of the energy pattern of the deity as seen by tantric seers. A yantra is the body or form of the deity (*devata*), whereas a mantra is the deity's mind, consciousness, spirit, or name. Thus, yantra is the external, visual expression through which the deity receives devotion. However, if the meditator transcends their analytical attitude and succeeds in invoking the deity through the yantra, the latter becomes not only a symbolic representation but the deity itself. In this sense, every yantra can become the dwelling place of the deity it represents, and therefore, no idol or picture of a deity is as powerful as a yantra in meditation.

The second and more universal purpose of the yantra is as a centering device. It is used to withdraw our consciousness from the outer world so that we can go beyond the ordinary frame of mind to the altered state of consciousness known as *turiya*: the fourth state beyond the waking, dreaming, and deep sleep states. This process releases the deepest spiritual awareness of the

154. "The Golden Ratio Triangles."
155. Huet, "Śrī Yantra Geometry," 610, 622.

· · · · · · · ·

third eye chakra. Interestingly, the word *yantra* comes from the root *yam*, which means support-ing or holding the essence of an object or concept; the syllable *tra* comes from *trana*, or libera-tion from bondage. This implies that a yantra is designed to lead you to self-liberation.

Practice

The meditation starts with gazing into the dot at the center of the Sri Yantra diagram, which is called *bindu*. The dot is the link between finite and infinite reality, and between individual aware-ness and pure consciousness. Meditation on this point brings your mind toward abstract concen-tration, which is used as a means to attain self-realization and pure consciousness. It is the visual expression of resting your awareness on a single point.

Then, you will slowly broaden the scope of your vision until you have encompassed the total-ity of the design. This process symbolizes evolution and expansion—the universe that erupts from singularity. A circle is an extension of the point: the point draws a circle around itself and expands. However, the circle also creates an individual consciousness out of cosmic conscious-ness. After the point and the circle, the triangle is the simplest yantra form. The three points forming the angles of the triangle stand for any number of trinities, such as beginning, middle, and end; subject, object, and means of knowing; Brahma, Vishnu, and Shiva; past, present, and future; earth, sky, and heaven; or doer, action, and means of performing action. Upward tri-angles draw the attention up and away from the world, indicating rising energy and upward movement in the human body. Triangles that point downward represent divine grace. More-over, the vision of the upward triangles meeting the downward triangles represents the union of the divine masculine and feminine.

After gazing at this structure as a whole, you will do the reverse and return from the whole all the way to the dot, a process that represents involution, or a return to the source of all. After completing this back-and-forth movement, you will internalize the yantra and merge with it.

Instructions

PREPARATION: The meditation usually lasts between thirty and forty-five minutes.

1. Position the yantra so that its center is at eye level and a comfortable distance away. Sit with your spine straight. Breathe in and out slowly until your breath flows naturally.

2. Begin with your eyes open, simply gazing at the yantra. Focus on its center, the "dot" that represents the unity that underlies all the diversity of the physical world. The key is to maintain a receptive, alert frame of mind, free of concepts,

without drawing any conclusions. As you feel yourself gathering consciousness, allow yourself to flow with the momentum of this consciousness.

3. Now allow your eyes to see the triangle that encloses the bindu. The downward-pointing triangle represents the feminine creative power, the womb of all creation, while the upward-facing triangle represents male energy, movement, and transformation.

4. Allow your vision to expand to include the circles outside of the triangles. They represent the cycles of cosmic rhythms. The image of the circle embodies the notion that time has no beginning and no end. The farthest region of space and the innermost nucleus of an atom both pulsate with the same rhythmic energy of creation. That rhythm is within you and without you.

5. Now bring your awareness to the lotus petals outside the circle—they are pointing outward, as if opening. They illustrate the unfolding of our understanding. The lotus also represents the heart, the seat of the Self. When the heart opens, understanding comes.

6. The square at the outside of the yantra represents the world of form, the material world that our senses show us: the illusion of separateness, well-defined edges, and boundaries. At the periphery of the figure are four T-shaped portals, or gateways. Notice that they point toward the interior of the yantra, the inner spaces of life. They represent our earthly passage from the external and material to the internal and sacred.

7. Now take a moment to gaze into the yantra, and as if in slow motion, let the different shapes and patterns emerge naturally, allowing your eyes to be held loosely in focus. Gaze at the center of the yantra. You are gazing at perfection— pure balance and equilibrium. Imbibe it. Without moving your eyes, gradually and very slowly begin to expand your field of vision, lingering over each layer as you do so. Continue slowly expanding your vision until you are taking in information from more than 180 degrees.

8. Now, slowly reverse the process by gently drawing your attention back in. Move gradually from taking in everything around you, and begin to narrow your gaze. Move your awareness slowly back to the yantra's four gates, and stay there for a long moment. Then, ever so gently, move deeper into the yantra. Drift your soft gaze slowly back through each circular channel of lotus petals and triangles and ultimately back to the bindu—back to the source. Take a few minutes to do

• • • • • • • •

this. This process of moving back to the bindu is called *involution*, moving from multiplicity, our multidimensionality, to oneness as you drift your awareness back into the center of the yantra, layer by layer. Become one with the bindu. Now see the seer of the bindu by looking back at your third eye. (You don't need to stare at the yantra beyond a comfortable amount of time; up to fifteen minutes is perfect.)

9. After you have gazed at the yantra for a long moment, gently close your eyes for between five and twenty-five minutes. Let the yantra unfold in your mind's eye. Watch the yantra, imprinted in your mind's eye, and allow it to gradually guide you within. This practice of letting the yantra unfold within you is a powerful part of the meditation, as the stored geometric images allow you to drift back and forth between doing and being. The patterns of creativity represented by these primordial shapes express the fundamental forces of nature that flow through existence and through you. Do nothing, and you will find yourself participating in pure consciousness, without the mind defining it. You may even feel that your body itself is the embodiment of the yantra.

10. When you are done with both parts of the meditation, simply sit and let the subtle nature of what you have experienced ripple through your thoughts, being, and breath. Notice how you feel. Notice the volume and activity levels of the world around you and then become aware of the world within you. Witness yourself throughout the whole process.

11. When you are ready, take a deep breath, begin to move your toes and fingers, open your eyes, and become aware of your surroundings once again. The trance-like effect of the meditation may carry over into the next few hours of your day.

Deity Yoga

Deity yoga is the most fundamental method of Vajrayana Buddhism. Among the highest yoga tantra practices, it is considered the initial "generation stage," or the "stage of imagination," which is like a rehearsal for the "stage of completion."

Historical Background

The principle of this technique is simple: the yogi or yogini learns to think, speak, and act as if they were already a fully enlightened Buddha. Deity yoga is practiced not only in meditation, but all day long, so it can be more broadly thought of as embracing a different way of being. The practitioner needs to cultivate an intense awareness of their body as the deity's body, their speech as the deity's mantra, and their mind as the blissful wisdom of the deity. This involves an ongoing contemplation: How does a deity look at the world? How does a deity make decisions? How does a deity love?

It is easy to confuse the deities of deity yoga with conventional deities that function as objects of worship. The former, however, are really archetypes and manifestations of our true nature, the most profound level of our consciousness. By identifying with these forms, we are quickly led to a fully realized state of bliss, emptiness, and nonduality. For this purpose, the Buddhist tantrics regard them as *meditational deities*, all of which represent essential qualities of the fully awakened experience latent within you. Each tantric practice regime focuses on a particular meditational deity who embodies a certain aspect of the fully evolved, enlightened mind (accordingly, each tantric deity has its own unbroken lineage of practitioners). When you focus your attention on such an archetypal image and identify with it, you arouse the deepest aspects of your being and bring them into your present reality. Thus, you *find* the deity inside you as your own natural being. In Vajrayana, this is put elegantly: "Only a deity can (truly) worship a deity."[156]

Purpose

Deity yoga is considered the swiftest path to Buddhahood, for the simple reason that it encourages you to think of yourself as a god or a goddess right now. You are not in the process of becoming a divine being—you are one already. By embracing this practice, you reject the assumption that perfection is something that awaits you in the future. While most meditative paths encourage you to start off as a seeker, slowly progressing and longing to merge with the higher reality someday, deity yoga focuses on eliminating the self-image of the seeker altogether. It brings full awakening to the present moment of your spiritual practice. (This is why it is called the *resultant* vehicle to enlightenment.)

From this surprising perspective, your present experience and image of yourself is a false appearance, whereas your divine identity is who you really are at this moment. However, since it is not easy to come into contact with your fundamental, pure nature, the purpose of deity yoga is to supply you with an alternative self-image, a clear vision of your enlightened being. This resembles the visualization approach that helps disease-ridden people heal by seeing themselves

156. Yedor, "So What's Deity-Yoga?"

· · · · · · · ·

as whole and healthy; the image of being diseased is released from the mind and replaced by an image of radiance and vitality.

Deity yoga relies on the power of visualization and also points out that we visualize all day long anyway—specifically, we visualize a constricting image of ourselves that manifests. In essence, our consciousness is free to assume any form. It is a simple fact that the anger, jealousy, loving-kindness, compassion, or great wisdom that we choose to manifest don't derive from our face or body, but from the power of our mind. So, if you can convincingly picture yourself as beautiful and divine, you will become the manifestation of your own profound qualities.

Practice

The great Lama Yeshe, a twentieth-century Tibetan teacher who chose to disseminate deity yoga in the West, believed that the practice didn't have to focus on traditional Tibetan deities.[157] Seeing yourself as a deity has nothing to do with Tibetan culture. Even within Vajrayana Buddhism, *deity* does not mean "god," but a fully enlightened being. So, choose to manifest your true nature in accordance with your cultural upbringing or personal inclinations.

The first step is to look for a clear, large, and radiant image of the deity, saint, or enlightened being that feels most suitable to you. Your choice should be deeply personal: remember, the reason you pick an image is because you recognize something of yourself in it. For instance, you may choose to identify with Jesus, Saint Francis, Kwan Yin, or any other holy being. However, while each deity and saint arouses different feelings and activates different qualities within us, ultimately they all lead to the same realization of transcendent bliss.

Having selected the ideal representation of yourself, become familiar with the attributes of the deity or saint and what they stand for. If your choice was purely intuitive, without prior knowledge, read a little about this being. This knowledge, combined with the image, helps you gradually stimulate the growth of this being's qualities in your own mind. Pay attention to their physical appearance and also to the details surrounding them: just as the ordinary mind creates its own limited environment, the deity's fully realized mind creates its pure environment. This combination of deity and its surroundings is known as a *mandala*.

In the early stages, the practice is largely artificial, partly because we may be overwhelmed with doubt. But as we persevere, we will be able to perceive this self-generated deity with more clarity than our present self-image, and we will transcend our mundane appearance. Gradually, the second and third phases of the technique convince us that the presence of the deity in us is, indeed, closer to us than our own personality.

157. Yeshe, *Introduction to Tantra*, 55.

• • • • • • •

Instructions

PREPARATION: The practice should ideally be divided into three stages. When you feel, after days or weeks, that you have realized the potential experience of each stage, feel free to move to the next level of meditation. However, you may also go through these three stages as a complete practice; the complete process lasts thirty minutes.

Stage I: Meditate on the Deity or Guru

1. Sit in a meditation posture, either in front of an image of your chosen deity or saint or, if that is not possible, without any image, relying solely on your visualization.

2. With your eyes open, start by looking at the external image. First, look at the image as a complete, total vision, including both the deity's form and its surroundings.

3. Narrow your gaze and focus your attention at the top of the deity's body; slowly move downward, contemplating one area at a time. Become aware of details and qualities (the face, the eyes, the posture, the aura, the presence, the qualities emanating from the deity's being). If you wish, you can briefly write down some of these qualities.

4. Then move from the bottom to the top, slowly moving upward. Again, contemplate one area at a time. Become aware not only of details, but also qualities. If you wish, you can briefly write down some of these.

5. Once again, look at the image as a complete, total vision, including both the deity's form and its surroundings. Feel the image deeply, and make sure that you capture it clearly and vividly. Become familiar with the entire manifestation and every detail in it as precisely as you can.

6. Now close your eyes and do the same inwardly: Hold in your mind the complete image of the deity and its surroundings, focusing neither too tightly nor too loosely. Capture it as a total unit…Then focus your attention on the top of the deity's body, moving downward, then upward…Again, become aware of the complete vision, while including every detail as precisely as you can. (You may open your eyes now and then, until the image has been deeply internalized.)

7. Now that the image has been stabilized in your mind, allow it to become saturated in bliss. Visualize how the deity or guru does not have a solid body, but rather a radiant light body, which could be either white or blue. Add to this visualization

• • • • • • • •

the mandala—the surroundings, which are also illuminated and in fact cover the entire universe. This visualization is inseparable from emptiness, like a rainbow or a reflection in a mirror. It is just between existent and nonexistent.

8. For a moment, focus so intensely that it feels as if only the deity exists and you do not. The deity covers the entirety of space, including the space that was previously your physical body.

9. Open your heart's center to the deity and begin to feel the magnetic force of attraction that flows from both sides. Feel the love and respect that you have toward this being. Feel the desire to surrender and to merge into the deity: any admiration is the wish to become that which you admire. You can add the thought *I give myself to you.* Feel what this presence does to your being, your subtle body, your central column, and your chakras. Let it flow into your being and penetrate into your subtle body and chakras.

Stage II: Share the Essence of the Deity

If you have chosen to practice the second stage as a complete meditation, start by quickly going through the first stage.

1. For a moment, allow the vivid image of the deity to disappear until only its energy or essence remains. What is behind the form that you were meditating on? Feel this essential energy pulsating powerfully in front of you. Recognize that in essence, this energy is an expression of your shared Self—the deity's innermost and your innermost are one and the same.

2. Now imagine that the deity comes to the top of your head, dissolves into light, and descends through the central column into your heart. As the deity sinks into you in this way, visualize yourself experiencing the dawning of the very subtle, clear light consciousness. Meditate on the unification of the deity's blissful wisdom with your own subtle mind. As all ordinary appearances dissolve into the empty space of nondual wisdom and bliss, concentrate single-mindedly on this dissolution, thinking, *This is the enlightened truth body, and this is who I really am.*

3. Feel how the energy and you become so intermixed that there is no differentiation. Feel how your own dormant qualities have been enkindled by the qualities of this presence. As you merge with one another, recognize that you are the presence on which you were meditating all along—you have projected this

image as a way to return to your Self. Drop all conceptual effort to feel a natural state of nonduality between you and the deity.

Stage III: Meditate on Yourself as the Deity

1. Sit in a meditation posture, this time relying solely on your visualization. Hold in your mind the complete image of the deity, focusing neither too tightly nor too loosely.

2. Now imagine that the deity comes to the top of your head, dissolves into light, and descends through the central column into your heart.

3. Then, let the deity's form begin to spread from your heart until it manifests fully as your own complete form. Shed the familiar body and instead, wear this illusory body. Remember, you don't create the deity—you find them inside you, as your natural being.

4. Start looking at your deity's form. First, feel it from within as a complete, total vision.

5. Slowly narrow your gaze and focus your attention on the top of your deity's body; slowly move downward, contemplating one area at a time. Become aware of details and qualities (the face, the eyes, the posture, the aura, the presence, the qualities emanating from your being). Then move from the bottom to the top, slowly moving upward. Again, contemplate one area at a time.

6. Once again, look at your form as a complete, total vision. Arise as the deity themselves. Have a clear and vivid appearance of yourself as the deity. Think, *I am...*

7. Now that the form has been stabilized in your mind, allow it to become saturated in bliss. Visualize how the deity's form is not a solid body, but rather a radiant light body, which could be either white or blue. Add to this visualization the mandala—the surroundings, which are also illuminated and in fact cover the entire universe. This visualization is inseparable from emptiness, like a rainbow or a reflection in a mirror. It is just between existent and nonexistent.

8. Allow your deity's form to disappear into the emptiness and to reappear in flashes.

9. Now meditate as the deity for a while. Feel the quality of the meditation when the meditator is you as the deity.

10. Slowly stand, and walk and move in the room as the deity. Drop your mental and conceptual effort and allow yourself to be the deity naturally.

. . . .

Darkness Meditation

Darkness meditation—also known as *dark yoga* or *dark retreat*—has been used by a variety of spiritual traditions throughout the centuries as an advanced practice for self-realization and peak spiritual experiences. In this process, the aspirant meditates in a perfectly darkened room and spends a number of days, weeks, or even months under conditions of sensory deprivation in order to leave the manifest world behind and to evoke profound insight.

Historical Background

Some historians suggest that ancient Egyptians and Mayans practiced a form of dark retreat, which traditionally lasted ten days: holy men would go to the center of their respective pyramids, completely removed from light and sound.[158] The catacombs and the underground network of tunnels of the first Christians in Rome, as well as other places such as the caves of the Essenes near the Dead Sea in Israel, might have been used as places for dark retreats as well. Even among the Shipibo tribe of the Amazon rainforest, such practices have taken place in conjunction with plant medicine (Ayahuasca) as a way to heal and transform. Reportedly, some shamans have spent up to a year and a half in complete darkness, with the intention of receiving the healing wisdom of the plant in order to heal others.[159]

In the ancient Indian system of Ayurvedic medicine, immersing oneself in darkness is a form of *Kaya Kalpa*: "ageless" or "immortal" (*kalpa*) "body" (*kaya*). This Ayurvedic treatment aims to maintain youthful vitality so that one can delay death long enough to achieve final liberation of the soul (*Jivamukti*). In Tibet, dark retreats have been practiced in mountainside caves. Traditionally, these retreats were done by advanced practitioners in the Dzogchen lineages of Tibetan Buddhism, and the period varied from a few hours to decades. Some Tibetan monks recommend a forty-nine-day dark retreat.[160] A retreat of this length, however, is recommended only to experienced meditators, since such a retreat requires psychic and meditative stability.

In Taoism, the dark was the final journey of spiritual work, in which one could return to the primordial state and reunite with the true self and divinity within. According to Taoist master Mantak Chia, author of *Darkness Technology*, "In the Taoist tradition, the cave, the Immortal Mountain, the Wu San, represents the Perfect Inner Alchemy Chamber. The Tao says: 'When you go into the dark and this becomes total, the darkness soon turns into light.'"[161]

---

158. "Darkness Retreat."
159. "The Brain Science Behind Dark Room Therapy."
160. "The Tradition."
161. Chia, *Darkness Technology*, 2.

Purpose

This ancient practice has primarily been done for the sake of obtaining extraordinary states of consciousness. While most meditations require closing the eyes to cut off awareness of the visible world, settings of complete darkness literally make the world disappear even while the aspirant keeps their eyes wide open. There is nothing to grasp at in terms of objective reality, not even one's own physical existence, and so, immersion in space becomes far more effortless and immediate.

The more you befriend the inner and outer darkness, the more you can penetrate into hidden regions of your subconscious, as well as the true nature of your consciousness. Moreover, all the traditions that advocate darkness meditation speak of an intense opening of the third eye chakra, which involves the experience of inner light, flashes of insight, and visions, intuition, and psychic abilities.

This meditation, some suggest, can also be thought of as entering into the state that is ordinarily only experienced in deep sleep. At first, we may see nothing and feel that we are surrounded by nothingness since our consciousness is still directly associated with the objective world. But the more we remain with this apparent nothingness, the more we realize that it is actually saturated in consciousness and bliss.

According to Mantak Chia, extended periods of darkness cause the pineal gland to respond by producing a psychedelic substance called dimethyltryptamine, or DMT.[162] This substance is typically only released at birth and at death. Nicknamed "the spirit molecule," it seems to be related to states of altered consciousness and feelings of universal compassion.

The second purpose of darkness meditation is healing. Not only the ancient Indian Ayurvedic system and Amazonian healers have employed this practice for healing purposes; there are also contemporary westerners who have adopted dark yoga to invite the lost power of darkness into their lives. According to this perspective, night has become day in modern times, since artificial sources of light pierce the darkness outside and inside our homes. As a result, millions of people suffer from sleep disorders. When our body clock receives signals that it is not time to sleep, it sends signals *not* to produce melatonin, which is a highly crucial hormone released when light dissipates. For this reason, the practice of darkness meditation may be rejuvenating.

Practice

The twentieth-century spiritual teacher Osho writes: "First a deep friendship with darkness is needed…So do one thing as a preliminary step: sit in darkness, turn off the lights, feel darkness. Have a loving attitude towards it; allow the darkness to touch you. Look at it. Open your eyes in

162. Chia, *Darkness Technology*, 28.

· · · · · · · ·

a dark room or in a dark night; have a communion, be together, imbibe a relationship."[163] However, according to Osho, the first step toward this communion is to uncover your unconscious fear of the dark. Darkness is perceived as negative, the "dark part of our being," but our task is to learn to associate it with relaxation and meditation.

After making yourself more comfortable in the dark, try to surrender to it and to allow your body and mind to dissolve into it. Allow this flow to be mutual: let the darkness pour into you, and at the same time, let your body and mind disappear into the darkness. Since in sheer blackness there can be no awareness of distinct boundaries and everything merges into space, enjoy this state of no-time, no-space, and no-body.

The duration and intensity of your meditation are completely up to you. Don't push it—progress slowly. You may start by following only the first stage, which centers on healing and relaxation. Meditate with either open or closed eyes (at a certain point, you will realize that there is no real difference). You can sit, stand, or lie down.

Develop the capacity to witness any thought, sensation, or emotion that may appear. This capacity can actually be stronger in the dark, since darkness reveals the content of your mind more clearly. You can enhance the witnessing consciousness by asking the question "Who am I?"

During the meditation, different images and visions may appear. Even if they seem fascinating or scary, do not let yourself be taken over by this imagery. Perceive the stories as unreal and impermanent, and gently shift your focus when your mind starts wandering. Keep your attention focused on your awareness itself. You can even ask yourself, *Who is the witness of all these visions?*

It is possible that your subconscious will be unloaded, similar to the way impressions are unloaded in the form of dreams. Let the darkness absorb this psychological "darkness"—just as black holes absorb enormous quantities of matter, trust that the darkness can absorb your limiting personal emotions and psychic residues.

Make sure that you have had sufficient sleep before entering this practice to avoid falling asleep during your session. On the other hand, there is nothing wrong with occasionally falling asleep as a result of profound relaxation. Free yourself from the idea of having a strict plan for this process. Your awareness will grow naturally and overcome potential boredom. The state of deep relaxation and awareness gradually eliminates the constant need for stimulation.

Instructions

PREPARATION: The meditation usually lasts between thirty and sixty minutes. Choose the room in your home that is the easiest to darken. Making the room utterly dark may require some

---

163. Marion, "Osho Speaks on Darkness."

technical solutions, but the darker it is, the better. After finding the right position for your meditation, keep your eyes open as much as possible.

Stage I: Healing

1. Start immersing your being in the darkness, slowly making yourself comfortable in it. Delve into the world of darkness and let it heal, nourish, and relax your body and mind. Realize that darkness can be a friend.

2. Look around you, above you, and below you—what do you see? Of course, nothing. It is as if the horizon is filled with nothing, and even your body seems to be nonexistent, dissolved in the nothing. This means that for the time being, space and time have ended for you.

3. You don't need to think about anything, because you are not part of the world at this moment. You are a part of spacious, silent, and vast darkness.

4. Breathe into this darkness. Feel how it gradually calms your nerves, soothing tension and relaxing every tense muscle, every bit of your being that is worried, agitated, and troubled. Feel how your body is slowly melting away, as if its boundaries have become very thin, until they finally cease to exist.

5. Nothing needs to happen. There is nowhere you should go and nothing you should become. You are just as you are at this very moment, enjoying this sweet, soft dissolution of the boundaries of your body—becoming spacelike, and at the same time allowing the darkness to fill and penetrate every point of your being.

6. Feel how your brain is relaxing, as if it were a clenched fist that has now become open and available. Lose the sense of gravity; let all inner and outer heaviness be absorbed in this endless space.

7. It is as if you have entered the unknown territory of deep sleep, only you are awake now and your senses are wide open. Enjoy this wakeful sleep. You are now becoming aware of the subtle processes that take place when your body is asleep: how darkness envelopes, nourishes, and renews it.

8. Keep breathing into the darkness, into this timeless and spaceless zone, and observe whatever takes place during the remainder of your practice joyously, silently, and curiously.

* * * * * * *

Stage II: Transformation

1. Enter a deep meditation on the nature of darkness and the nature of your very being.

2. As you look around you, above you, and below you, you will slowly realize that right now, you are immersed in space without edges. It is as if there is no ground beneath your feet and no limit above your head; there are no measures and no outlines. Perhaps you already feel at home in this limitless open space. This is because it reminds you of your very nature, the nature of your own consciousness, the immeasurable depth of your being.

3. Realize how easy it is to dissolve thanks to this darkness. The outlines and the density of your body disappeared in no time, and so did your very sense of self and the outlines of your personality—the person that you become as soon as the world of objects becomes visible. Here, you are effortlessly nothing and no one; you are faceless and changeless. Feel how all memories, impressions, past knowledge, and ego-centered activity are consumed by the darkness.

4. Through your open eyes you perceive nothing, but the one that perceives nothing is also nothing. Be in this state in which nothing perceives nothing and there is only consciousness and space, completely interwoven. At the core of your being, you are this darkness: you are the vast space of the universe that contains all points of light, yet in itself is nothing. Feel how vast your being truly is. Can you identify any limits? Is there an edge to what you are?

5. Feel how you are spreading without end, while at the same time not spreading at all, but just being what you are. What was previously your head is now just an open space, flooded with the profound essence of the darkness. Allow yourself to not be, while also sensing the fullness of this space. You are this ancient dark space that has always been, since the beginning of the universe and even before it. Feel how right now you are standing at the beginning of time, before anything has ever happened, as consciousness and space without end.

Meditate on This: Meditation and the Art of Inquiry

In my experience, most meditators avoid adding active inquiry to their meditation practice. This is at least partly for two major reasons.

The Superstition about the Mind

The first reason is that we have a certain superstition regarding the mind and the intellect, a widespread belief that since spirituality is all about "silencing the mind," the mind must not be active. It certainly should not be troubled by too many questions and concepts. After all, all problems are resolved in silence, so as a rule, any form of mental activity needs to be quieted down. It seems as if we have to choose between intellect and experience.

This approach misses out on one of the strongest and fastest methods of spiritual transformation. Inquiry derives its power from the understanding that you can use your mind to transcend the mind. But doing this can only make your mind more silent, rather than heavier with thoughts and ideas. Nevertheless, this superstition has made most of us neglect this highly potent path.

By now, we understand that the mind is not just silly, redundant thought. It has an important capacity for intelligence. When this capacity is activated, this intelligence can effectively cut through illusion and support our inner liberation. For this reason, in every tradition of mystical enlightenment, from Buddhism to Hinduism, there has always been an emphasis on the cultivation of discriminating wisdom through methods of active inquiry. This path of wisdom has been cherished by traditions of meditation. In Hinduism, for instance, this is called Jnana yoga, the path of inquiry, which is not really different from Bhakti yoga, the path of love. In fact, love and wisdom can become one and the same so that we learn to develop a love of wisdom, as well as wisdom that comes from love.

In terms of chakras, inquiry activates the right side of the third eye. Every chakra has a right, active side, and a left, passive side. The third eye's right side is awakened, probing intelligence, whereas the left side is the silent mind, abiding in the spacelike nature of the mind. However, the right and left sides shouldn't be separated; they should work together and unite into one awakening.

One thing is for certain: if you silence the mind constantly, this will actually make you quite sleepy and dull, since you will have turned off your mind's fire. The right side of the third eye has a lot of fire, which is the energy of intelligence that is ignited by inquiry.

It is good to remember that the original English term *meditation* has never referred to the silencing of the mind; meditation means contemplation on something. Think of René Descartes's well-known *Meditations* or Nietzsche's book *Untimely Meditations*! Thus, meditation is not simply about letting your mind go. It also includes the act of engaging your whole being in contemplation on something.

· · · · · · ·

Mind in Ecstasy

When we begin to inquire, we realize that our mind is becoming more awake—and not in a bad way. Its higher faculties become activated, and when these faculties are activated, our awakened mind is no less blissful or enlightening than any other alive aspect of our being. On the contrary, sometimes this feels even more enlivening than any other form of meditative awakening.

Having an active mind is a state of true joy and ecstasy. While inquiring and turning on this form of higher intelligence, your mind goes beyond its occupation with trivialities, mundane concerns, petty thoughts, and tiny emotions. It is released from the domain of the personal and engages instead in universal questions. It feels expanded and looks broadly at the matters of life. It dares to think in a bigger way; in this way, it breathes in the fresh air of mental mountain peaks—this is what it actually feels like! As a result, your mind attains rare levels of lucidity.

Sometimes we experience this type of exhilaration of the mind when we philosophize, listen to or read the thoughts of bright minds, or have our intellectual curiosity enkindled by some new learning about the universe or the human soul. Your mind may be aroused, for example, by reading about the profound mystery of black holes or newly explored capacities of certain species. This may feel like a flame of interest that enlivens your mind. Why do we feel excited and fulfilled at these moments? Why do we like to know?

The reason is actually much deeper than you might think. We tend to reduce the source of our enjoyment to intellectual satisfaction, but let's consider a statement that several prominent cosmologists, philosophers, and mystics agree on, even if they express it differently. Here are two examples: philosopher and author Alan Watts writes, "You are the universe experiencing itself,"[164] while cosmologist Carl Sagan states, "We are a way for the cosmos to know itself."[165] Now, even looking into this idea is already enough to start an exciting inquiry!

Naturally, you tend to experience yourself in a personal and independent way, as if your growth and learning are for your own sake. So is it possible to experience a state of consciousness that makes you feel that right now, you are the universe experiencing and learning about itself? What does it feel like to have your mind as an extension of the universe? Just thinking about this can elevate your mind, pulling it out of its tendency to only consider things personally. Stopping personal thinking is an important step. This is exactly my point: the very act of inquiry is already the first step beyond the personal ego. You immediately come out of yourself—you must do so for your inquiry to blossom.

This is the deeper reason we become excited in inquiry: we are indeed a way for the cosmos to know itself. We possess self-consciousness because self-consciousness makes it possible for the cosmos to know itself. Of course, we tend to waste this self-consciousness on just thinking

164. Glattfelder, *Information—Consciousness—Reality*, 573.
165. Melina, "Are We Really All Made of Stars?"

about our own self-interest. And as a result of our excessive identification with our individual life, it often seems as if the cosmos is a way for us to know ourselves: "This entire, huge cosmos has been designed only for *me* to know myself." That is not a healthy and liberating perception, but rather a limiting illusion.

So why not experiment with the possibility that you are the intelligent extension of the cosmos? For a moment, consider how your ability to reflect on life is meant only to enable the universe to experience its own self-reflection. This also means that when you feel strongly, this is a way for the cosmos to feel itself; when you meditate, this is a way for the cosmos to meditate on itself; and when you gain an insight in your meditation, you are the universe understanding itself. If this makes you even a little ecstatic, as if your mind has been tickled, this means that you are already in touch with this path of meditative inquiry. When you allow this to happen, something bigger than you wakes up—it is the cosmos becoming excited about knowing itself. This is the deepest source of intellectual curiosity and excitement.

However, intellectual knowledge is limited. It makes little use of the capacity of your mind for higher intelligence. You may learn about black holes and become excited because this thrill of the universe takes place through your mind, but this knowledge doesn't necessarily change you. So this knowledge is different than the exhilarating and transformative experience of meditative inquiry. Meditative inquiry is a learning that transforms you: it is when you use your higher intelligence to achieve direct insight, a deeper experience of yourself and of life.

How Meditative Inquiry Can Transform You

I have already explained the first reason for the common tendency to avoid inquiry: the superstition about the mind. But here is the second reason: we simply don't know how to inquire. For this reason, whenever we try to think about things, we become confused or reach a dead end. This frustration leads us to conclude that we should simply stop and relax; we believe that these concepts can only agitate and trouble our minds, adding new and unnecessary ideas to our already thought-laden heads.

But first of all, it is good to be confused sometimes. In inquiry, confusion is a blessing. Confusion about silly things in life is not necessarily helpful, but it is perfectly fine to be confused, for example, by a Zen koan. This means that your mind is searching for a new way—it has come to realize that it cannot understand in an ordinary way, so it must go deeper.

Second, we mustn't let go too quickly. At the end of each real inquiry, a true insight awaits us. And insight is a tremendous thing. If you prefer only to feel and to have your mind silent because this is the easy and relaxing path, you will miss the advantage of wisdom. Wisdom is the absolute clarity that can illuminate and sustain your deep meditative experiences. Your experiences don't have to remain abstract and elusive—your third eye can make sense of them.

· · · · · · ·

So, let's discuss how to inquire. Generally speaking, there are four types of meditative inquiry:

1. **Contemplating a question or a riddle.** The Zen koan falls into this category.

2. **Contemplating an enlightened text.** The powerful thing about enlightened texts is that even one sentence is enough for your inquiry. You don't need to read a book; you can meditate on a certain spiritual idea that you encountered in written form, in a video, or in a spiritual gathering.

3. **Contemplating the nature of the self or the mind.** This is a direct form of inquiring into the root of your own consciousness. One good example is Ramana Maharshi's self-inquiry.

4. **Contemplating real-life problems.** For example, I can inquire into the nature of the thinking machine, my anger, human suffering, or conflicts in relationships.

In chapter 8, we explored listening as meditation. Inquiry is an active form of listening; based on deep listening, you begin to search for a direct insight into the reality of something, and as a result you begin to activate your intelligence. This is an extraordinary state.

For example, if you contemplate the meaning of just one sentence that you have found in a text written by a spiritual teacher, you need to experience for yourself what it actually means. Every sentence in such texts carries an energetic charge because it comes from the world of transformation. It is like a code; it contains the experience of reality itself. Every fragment of the text contains the whole. Our problem is not that we read too many or too few spiritual books, but whether we read them in a way that transforms us. Therefore, you contemplate until there comes a point when the energetic charge of the sentence is released, and it explodes like a tiny transformative bomb inside you. You mustn't let go until this happens. If you read it and think only *How beautiful!* or *What a remarkable idea!*, it will get you nowhere; it will be just another great quotation. Inquiry is about not letting go until your mind explodes together with the text.

We can do this with any meaningful and transcendental text. I will demonstrate this using the following koan-like statement from the *Gospel of Thomas*, which is considered by scholars to be a compilation of sayings and answers to students' questions by the historical Jesus:

· · · · · · ·

The followers said to Jesus, "Tell us how our end will be."
Jesus said: "Have you discovered the beginning, then, so that you are seeking the end? For where the beginning is, the end will be. Fortunate is the one who stands at the beginning. That one will know the end and will not taste death."[166]

This answer alone is enough for a lifetime of inquiry! The followers come to their master in the hope of hearing something about the end, which is either their future in the present lifetime or the afterlife. We all want to know what will happen at the end; our life's journey is propelled by a promised happiness, by the trust that everything that we do leads to something and that when we reach that goal, everything we have gone through will finally make sense. Here Jesus shatters this entire future. Instead, he throws us back to the beginning. But what does it mean to discover the beginning? We are in the middle of life, thinking about the end. But he says that it is neither about the end nor about the middle—it is about the beginning, since the beginning is somehow also the end.

Now, have I really tapped into the beginning, the source of everything, with my own mind, or am I satisfied with the brief inspiration of a beautiful quotation? If I take the instruction seriously, can I be in a state in which I only stand at the beginning? This means immersing my being in the state of meditation, where nothing evolves or becomes. This implies leaving behind the sense of time. If this is where you are, you will probably not even care about the end. You will get a taste of eternity, which means being free from death. So you see, going all the way with two sentences can lead you to freedom from death!

Only the Truth Remains

In meditative inquiry we are determined not to let go until we truly understand the object of our inquiry. Analytical understanding can never be enough. Of course, we need to use our analytical powers and to consider the components of the text or the riddle from different angles. But we know that analysis is only a helpful tool, and that it cannot lead us to complete understanding.

In the way that we approach our inquiry, we leave nothing for tomorrow (even if the full understanding may take years). If the object of inquiry is a text, a video, or a lecture, it is meant to transform you while you are reading or listening to it. This means that you open your being to allow the transmission to work on you right now. When you contemplate in this way, the text or riddle permeates your being and you recede into the background. Since your interest lies in seeing from the perspective of the text or the riddle, your ordinary perspective becomes secondary; what matters is how the riddle or text perceives reality and how you can see reality through

---

166. Meyer, *The Gospel of Thomas*, 31.

• • • • • • • •

its eyes. You therefore suspend your perspective and assume that you have understood nothing until this point. Everything you have believed to be true so far has been an illusion, and this is your precious opportunity to wake up. You are guided toward a reality that you have overlooked all along, and all you have to do is to pass through the text or riddle as if it were a gateway leading you directly into this reality.

In summary, here are six succinct guidelines on meditative inquiry:

- **Assume that the reality is what you find in the text or riddle.** The text or riddle represents the ultimate reality that you are looking for, so you gather all your being to penetrate into this reality, beyond the words. Perhaps at the moment, your experience of reality is completely different. This doesn't matter: you begin to align your mind with the quality you identify in the text or riddle, and for this, you are willing to leave your old person behind.

- **Don't let go until you have achieved a total perception.** Don't move to the next subject or jump to another inquiry. For instance, choose one subject to contemplate throughout an entire month: one sentence, koan, or question. Remember that if you become content too easily, or if you let go too quickly, you will never find the buried treasure.

- **Don't add new thoughts and concepts.** Sometimes, after reading many spiritual books, we think that we need to avoid reading altogether because we have accumulated too many good ideas. But this only means that we have read them wrong. Transformative books are designed to shatter your illusions, *take away* your existing concepts and thoughts, show you how your current perception is mistaken, and free your mind. Their function is to leave you naked in the here and now.

- **Don't analyze too much.** Use analysis, but don't assume that analysis will bring you to a truly satisfying understanding.

- **Disappear into the text or riddle.** When you contemplate deeply, you reach a state of concentration to a degree that you actually disappear, and only what you have contemplated (for example, a koan) remains. This is the ultimate purpose of any inquiry: dissolving the subject and object relationship. What you inquire into, you eventually disappear into, so we can say that in a sense, the inquirer disappears. This is when the secret is revealed. So, inquire until the inquirer disappears.

. . . .

• **The process of inquiry is the transformation.** It is not about getting an answer! It is about the way that the process changes you. If you really don't let go, by the end of your inquiry you will have stretched your mind's capacity to such a degree that eventually, your mind will simply crash into a state of total perception—an insight.

Crown Chakra Meditations: Connect to Universal Reality

When we know how to practice meditation and learn its different dimensions, it is capable of maturing us, perfecting us as human beings and as spiritual beings, and preparing us for the ultimate understanding. But what is the ultimate understanding?

It is only natural to conclude this book's journey with the crown chakra. This chakra, *sahasrara* in Sanskrit, is the endpoint of meditation. In essence, all meditations are designed to lead you to the crown chakra. Since the crown chakra is the supreme understanding, it is also the one true purpose of meditation. In a sense, this is why we meditate. Of course, you may stop wherever you want; you can climb the meditative ladder and decide to stop at step one or two, or choose to benefit from one specific level of meditation. Still, in the deepest sense, the reason we have meditation at all is to reach the crown and to rest in it.

This is also true in terms of the chakras: even if you go through the gateway of another chakra, just as we have done throughout the different chapters, the underlying idea is that by going fully through that chakra, its energy will be activated, refined, and released into the crown chakra. Every chakra's energy fulfills its purpose in the crown. Thus, only when all of your different energies have reached the crown can you say that your chakra journey is fulfilled.

To Infinity and Beyond

Although we technically call it a chakra, the crown is both a chakra and beyond the chakras. Like the other six chakras, it is definitely a major energy center, but this center—which is located deep inside the brain, just below the vertex, toward the back of the skull—is also a transcendent element. Geographically speaking, the crown chakra is like an opening; it is the boundary of our ego-consciousness, the upper edge of our existence as a separate unit of body and mind. Put simply, this is where "we" seem to end and where the universe seems to begin.

I use the words *seem to* to emphasize that the very distinction we make between us and the universe is the biggest joke in the universe. The crown chakra calls this distinction into question: What else can you be except for the universe? How can it be that there is suddenly a "you" and a "universe"? How is it possible that the universe doesn't include you in it?

Ultimately, there is only the universe, but as long as the crown chakra is closed (or largely closed), we experience that there is a universe "up there" and a self "down here"; therefore, we may come into contact with the universe, but we can never be fully at one with it. In this way, the crown chakra either connects us with our environment or separates us from it. Whether this chakra connects or separates us depends completely on our inner willingness to expand our being and meditative flowering.

When the crown chakra is largely closed, it is very much like a helmet that seals our boundaries and doesn't allow the cosmos to enter. On the other hand, when it is largely open, instead of a helmet it is like a transparent boundary that permits a free flow in both directions. The throat and heart chakra meditations already question this inside/outside division, but in the crown, this becomes the focus of our meditation.

When you keep this helmet tight, you think, *I am.* But if you remove it, even for a moment, you instantly become a part of the whole. In the deepest sense, however, you don't *become* a part of the whole, since you *are* the whole; there is no possibility of being anything else. Strangely enough, in order to realize this striking but simple truth, we sometimes need to meditate for twenty, thirty, forty, or even fifty years.

Sahasrara translates as "a thousand-petaled." This is not just a metaphor; when it is wide open, it is subtly experienced as a flower that has opened its one thousand petals to infinity. But even if you don't experience this directly, just visualizing it can bring about a sense of broadening. You can also think of this state as the experiential realization of the concept of having no mind of your own. This idea appears, for example, in the *Tao Te Ching*, where Lao-Tzu writes, "The sage has no mind of his own."[167] This may sound odd—does it mean losing your mind, going crazy? Fortunately, it implies a far more harmonious state: we are blissfully unable to identify clear edges of our mind. Where does our mind begin? Where does it end?

For you to possess a mind of your own, your mind must have definite borders; it must be a consciousness that has boundaries and belongs to someone. But what if it has no clear boundaries? This is what is more famously known as the state of no-mind. This doesn't mean that we should have absolutely no boundaries. If you lose the boundaries of the crown chakra, it will

167. Lao-Tzu, "Tao Te Ching."

enter a state of excess and hyperactivity. The crown chakra's healthy limits can be disrupted by psychoactive substances or overambitious meditation, especially kundalini practices. This can also happen when you prematurely participate in an intense spiritual retreat. So, as long as we are in human form, a certain limit must be maintained; that's why it is wiser to speak in terms of a "largely open" chakra.

Since the crown chakra is not part of our psyche, it is not a psychological chakra and doesn't contain any kind of psychological process. It is the part in us that is utterly transpersonal and has nothing to do with our humanness. We can even say that it is the part in us that is the most god-like. You may stumble across videos offering to heal the crown chakra—however, there is nothing to "heal" in the crown chakra, at least not in psychological terms. Spiritual issues related to the sense of belonging to the greater existence, crises of trust and faith, or feeling unworthy of being part of the divine reality are actually heart chakra concerns.

Think of the crown chakra as the point at which meditation has fulfilled its purpose and consumed itself. It is even beyond meditation itself, because in the crown chakra, the meditator and the object of meditation become one and the same and eventually dissolve. In this type of meditation, you often have no object to meditate on and also no mind to meditate *with*. This may also be imagined as a return to the point before creation. In general, all meditations aspire to take you back to your original nature, but the crown guides you all the way through the meditation line back to total formlessness. This primordial reality, which precedes all appearances, is what Gautama Buddha termed emptiness (*sunyata*); think of it as the reality that existed even before the idea of creation arose in the mind of the unknowable source of life. Of course, this is hard to contemplate—our minds cannot even meditate on it.

The crown chakra is like a leap from the chakra continuum toward a final transcendence of the journey itself. In the crown, there is no longer a journey. In the six other chakras, we feel that we are taking a path, making progress step by step, and that the more human and psychological aspects of our journey are accommodated. The crown, however, is a leap to a state that leaves behind the very sense of the journey. Moreover, this is also a leap from "I am" to the totality of existence. It is a total absorption of the drop into the ocean.

Chapters 4, 6, and 9 worked to establish a truly solid self, but in this chapter we discard this project altogether. Of course, we don't really get rid of it; we include it. But we move to an oceanic state, which the "I am" cannot survive. When a drop of water has been returned to the ocean, you can no longer identify and distinguish it. This is what the crown chakra is all about.

Secrets of the Subtle Body

The drop and the ocean are, in fact, more than a perfect metaphor. At the top and back of the head, the crown chakra contains a fluidlike kundalini substance, which in Hindu tantra is called

· · · · · · · ·

bindu. This kundalini drop contains within it the entire ocean—the substratum of the entire cosmos.[168] In kundalini practices, we aspire to stimulate this drop, because once this drop has melted, we can enter the oceanic state of expanded consciousness.

This drop is what has traditionally been considered the upper (or male) kundalini, whereas the kundalini substance of the root and sacral chakras is regarded as the lower (or female) kundalini. Some claim the source of kundalini is really in the crown and that what is commonly considered its seat is only a trigger point, like a button you hit to enable all your life-force energy to reach the actual kundalini. The beautiful and enticing imagery of the deity Shiva and his consort Shakti is often used to illustrate this subtle relationship; both Shiva, residing in the crown, and Shakti, residing in the lowest point of the spine, long to reunite. This is an irresistible love affair, the ultimate love story, which can be fulfilled through your own meditation.

All this makes it clear that the fulfillment of the meditative journey in the crown chakra has a strong physical and energetic aspect. This is because the crown chakra is also the fulfillment of the ultimate purpose of the subtle body; crown chakra meditations often work directly with the subtle body to fulfill what it was designed for.

Why do we have a subtle body? The answer is simple: to take us back home. Home is as close as it is very far, and it is as available and easy to reach as it is nearly unreachable. Therefore, for this special task, we require a means of transportation that can transcend ordinary time and space and enable us to cross through dimensions. That's why the subtle body becomes a major issue when we reach the crown chakra.

Even if you don't quite grasp the concepts of kundalini and the subtle body, these are still the energetic dynamics that take place beneath your meditative journey. The subtle body is the vehicle through which you experience all meditative states. So you can either reach your destination using a certain vehicle while not thinking about it at all, or you can study its mechanism and know how to activate it in order to reach your destination. Both methods work, and that is why some of the meditations in this chapter aren't explicitly concerned with your subtle body. However, many crown chakra meditations activate the hidden buttons of our subtle body.

Fortunately, while the subtle body is quite complex, there are only two major components that we are concerned with in this book: kundalini activation and the central channel, which in Hinduism is called the sushumna and in Vajrayana Buddhism is called *avadhuti.* This channel—which starts at the lowest point of the chakra column, pierces through the center of the body, and ends in the crown—is the core of our subtle being. Often, crown chakra meditations are designed to gather all our life force, especially from the two major side channels, and concentrate it deep inside the central channel.

---

168. Saraswati, *Kundalini Tantra,* 434.

. . . .

The central channel is the vehicle by which you achieve liberation. Imagine it like a highway that enables you to drive rapidly and smoothly and to be directly transported to the crown chakra. The central channel contains, deep within it, an even thinner and subtler tube, which is called *brahma nadi*. This extremely thin tube conducts the subtlest form of energy that flows all the way to the crown chakra and "hits" the secret button of the kundalini drop.

When it comes to kundalini activation, crown chakra meditations are deeply connected with some of the sacral chakra meditations. The sacral chakra is like the springboard of the lower kundalini; it is the point from which we shoot the energy up toward the source of kundalini in the crown. To return to my earlier example, just like in any other love affair, only in the arms of Shiva can Shakti's kundalini find its resting place.

Whenever we manage to travel all the way to the crown through the central channel, we experience bliss. Bliss is the unique feeling of the crown chakra, which will be explored in this chapter's last section. It is the ultimate form of happiness, the outcome of this energetic process of flow through the sushumna. This happiness includes a sense of total independence from the world along with an uninterrupted opening of the crown to infinity and beyond.

The energy flow doesn't end at the top of the central channel. It mysteriously continues to loop all the way up toward the source of life through yet another subtle element, which can be regarded as the eighth chakra. You may have noticed there are no eighth chakra meditations in this book. If you have reached the crown chakra, you don't need to be troubled by the eighth chakra—you will simply find it there. The opening of the crown means we are infinitely connected to the source of life through the central channel. It is not too difficult to experience this; this chapter's five meditations aim to help you do so.

Ten Roles and Purposes of Crown Chakra Meditations

1. **Dissolving the border between our upper skull and the rest of the universe.** This metaphorical and literal "breaking open" of the head is what crown chakra meditations are all about. Accordingly, we will identify this purpose in all five meditations.

2. **Absorption of mind and self into totality.** Some of these meditations are directly concerned with the dissolution of the sense of a separate self. Pay attention to the term *absorption*; this is meaningful, since these meditations don't aspire to extinguish your ego. The ego cannot be extinguished, but only purified, becoming a useful, healthy function of your mind. Thus, what these meditations hope to do is liberate you from the bondage of having the ego as your absolute identity.

3. **Fulfilling the purpose of the subtle body.** This includes moving away from the two side channels and awakening the central channel, and also activating the lower

• • • • • • • •

and upper kundalini. Essentially, all the meditations in the world aim to awaken kundalini, just as they all strive to reach the crown chakra. But in the crown chakra group, the major focus is to fulfill the union of the lower and upper kundalini.

4. **Unifying and absorbing all chakras.** While the crown chakra is a leap beyond the chakras, these meditations also unify the other six chakras: everything becomes just one line. Think of it as returning to the state of white light. If you break white light through a prism, you get seven different colors. Through the crown chakra, however, we move in the opposite direction, reunifying all the different chakra colors into the white light. For this reason, there are many crown chakra meditations that focus on all seven chakras, and any meditation that activates all seven chakras may be classified as a crown chakra meditation. The white light principle is also highly meaningful in this group of meditations, which calls attention to our nature as beings of pure light.

5. **Activating the microcosmic orbit.** Although I borrow this term from tantric Taoism, this will be practiced in our set of kriya yoga exercises, which derive from the world of Hindu tantra. The chakras have both a front and back part, and by activating both parts, we learn to unify these two lines, thus establishing a complete circle, which represents inner harmony and wholeness.

6. **Evoking bliss.** This will be discussed at length in the chapter's last section.

7. **Opening to, and being purified by, grace.** Meditations of the crown chakra often involve the action of grace. This mysterious descent of heavenly energy upon us, which penetrates the crown's opening, is deeply related to the possibility of final self-liberation in many traditions. So while the lower and upper kundalini are at play within our subtle body, there is a cosmic kundalini as well, which may sometimes intervene in our meditation. Preparing for the intervention of grace is another purpose of these techniques.

8. **The disappearance of the "doer."** The practice of Latihan arouses the realization that essentially, we are not the possessors of our lives—we don't "do" them. This is a liberating point of view.

9. **Forming the subtle body as a preparation for death.** Crown chakra meditations often deal with awareness of death. In Tibetan Buddhism, for instance, there is a series of meditations called Maranasati, which include visualizations of one's dying body and contemplation on the nature of death. Although none of the five meditations in this chapter confront this subject directly, some of them

· · · · · · · ·

are traditionally considered to prepare our being and subtle body for a conscious and liberating death. According to these traditions of meditation, if you possess a fully awakened and thus invincible subtle body, you can pass through death as if you are simply shedding a redundant layer of your being. More fundamentally, any kind of self-absorption is a preparation for death.

10. **Realization of reality as emptiness.** This is the endpoint of these meditations. Realizing reality's emptiness is like returning to the original state before creation. Although emptiness sounds negative, it is far from it. It doesn't mean that there is nothing, but only that there is just one thing. All that appears, including ourselves, arises from and disappears into this absolute ground of existence.

Empty Body and Subtle Body Visualizations

This pair of practices rapidly purifies the channels of your subtle nervous system, balances your chakras, and, in general, establishes a connection with your subtle body.

Historical Background

Just like vase breathing (see chapter 6), the empty body and subtle body visualizations are two preliminary techniques that have been adopted and developed by tantric (Vajrayana) Buddhism. Originally, these were designed to prepare the student's subtle body and chakras for the practice of Inner Fire meditation.[169] Inner Fire is classified as a completion-stage practice of the highest yoga tantra, in which the meditator focuses on the awakening of their subtle body in order to achieve the ultimate state of Buddhahood.

Purpose

The spaciousness and openness provided by the empty body allows anything stuck to be naturally unraveled. Similarly, the purification of the subtle body equips us with a powerful tool of visualization that can instantly clear the pathways of the subtle body.

The power of these practices lies in their ability to bypass existing emotional, mental, physical, or energetic blockages, and to immediately allow you to enjoy the experience of perfectly clear channels and energy centers. So, wherever you currently are in your chakra development,

169. Yeshe, *The Bliss of Inner Fire*, 103.

you can evoke the inherent bliss of your subtle body and experience an uninterrupted meditation without any inner struggle.

Feel free to use this effective visualization at any point during your day or whenever you experience an accumulation of stuck energy. Repeat the process again and again until you feel that you have managed to dissipate the stuck-ness.

Note: I strongly recommend combining this technique with another preparatory meditation from the world of Inner Fire, vase breathing, which can be found in chapter 6. Start with this crown chakra technique to form an even more successful practice.

Practice

In the simple yet effective practice of the empty body meditation, you shift from the experience of having a physical body to having a spacelike form, as if all the interior density of your body has been dissolved into space, leaving only its contours, like an empty shell. You remain in this blissful visualization for as long as you wish.

Subtle Body Visualization

Tilopa, the great tenth-century yogi who collected these techniques from different tantric Buddhist sources, described the experience in his *Mahamudra Upadesha*: "Body has no essence, like a plantain tree."[170] The body is hollow, without real substance, like a plantain tree. Plantain trees seem to have a trunk, but once opened, it is revealed that this "trunk" is only rolled leaves. In the same way, the body appears to have a solid essence, but it is made of space.

Think of this spacelike form as your entrance to the world of the subtle body: the channels, the chakras, and the kundalini drops. Thus, in the practice's second stage, you will evoke a vivid vision of your subtle body within the empty space of your body. After stabilizing this vision, you will concentrate on the white kundalini drop within your heart chakra and become one with it. By gazing into the channels and traveling through the subtle pathways as this white heart drop, you effortlessly remove impurities and blockages from your inner being.

Instructions

PREPARATION: This meditation requires between twenty and thirty minutes.

Stage I: Empty Body

1. Sit comfortably, preferably cross-legged on a meditation cushion, with your back straight and your head slightly bent forward. Make sure that your shoulders are not bent forward, but rather are gently bent backward.

2. Close your eyes. First, get in touch with your body in its familiar form, as you normally experience it: made of flesh, bone, and blood. Feel how it is full of dense, physical substance from head to toe. This sense of density is also where your blockages arise from.

3. Now imagine that all the dense and material contents of the body melt into light and dissolve into emptiness. Imagine this happening gradually, one body part after another.

4. If you look at the body using your inner gaze, you find pure space and light—just like how if you looked inside a balloon, you would find only air. The only thing that remains is the outer skin, which now becomes like an empty shell. This empty shell is transparent and glowing, like a rainbow in the sky. Keep sensing your body as utterly clear and empty, without any physical resistance; at the same time, your body's outer skin is transparent and radiant.

5. Perhaps you can feel how, within this openness, the life force begins to flow better and to mend blockages on its way through the subtle channels and chakras.

---

170. Nyenpa, *Tilopa's Mahamudra Upadesha*, 7.

Stage II: Purification of the Subtle Body

1. Take a moment to look at an image of the subtle body to internalize this vision. Now close your eyes.

2. Visualize the three principal channels of your subtle body. They are like a central pillar that holds up a roof. First, focus on the central channel. Visualize a transparent, bluish, and flexible tube, which is extremely thin—as thin as a drinking straw—that starts at the point midway between your eyebrows. This is the upper end of the central channel, and it is the location of what is sometimes called the brow chakra. Picture how this channel continues deep within the brain and then arches up and back; this is where the crown chakra is located. Now, with your attention, follow the channel as it descends from the crown in a perfectly straight line that runs parallel to the front of the spine. The channel pierces through the center of your body, but closer to the front of your spine. Then it ends at a point that is four fingers' width below the navel. This is your solar plexus chakra (sometimes called the navel chakra). Imagine your central channel as shining and completely clear.

3. Now visualize the left and right channels. They start deep within the nostrils, then curve up to the crown, and from there, begin to move downward, parallel to the central channel and quite close to it. However, while they are mostly straight, they loop around the central channel at three meeting points: first, deep within the throat chakra; second, within the heart chakra; and third, inside the solar plexus chakra. Remember, all three chakras reside close to the front part of the spine, within the central channel. You can visualize the side channel that starts on the left as white, and the one that starts on the right as red.

4. For a moment, turn your attention to the meeting point of all three channels below the navel. Perhaps you can notice there, within the solar plexus chakra, a sort of powerhouse of energy or inner heat. Imagine the solar plexus chakra as an upward-facing red triangle and feel how the channels curve upward from it, in the same way that they curve downward from the crown. Move into the very center of the solar plexus chakra and, locating yourself there, intuitively visualize the petals of this chakra.

5. Now visualize the other relevant chakras, starting with the heart. From the point midway between the breasts, move inward to a point just in front of the spine. Imagine the heart chakra exactly in that area, as a white ball. Imagine that inside the white ball there is a tiny drop, and for a moment, place yourself inside

• • • • • • • •

the drop. Visualize yourself turning on the light there, revealing the petals of the heart chakra. Next, move to the throat chakra, directly behind the throat's lump. This chakra is also shaped like a ball. Feel, both through visualization and sensation, this intense energetic confluence. Visualize the petals of the throat chakra. Then move to the crown, the bliss chakra. Find it deep within the brain. Imagine it as a multicolored triangle that is nonetheless white in essence. Place yourself there and visualize the petals of the crown chakra.

6. Having visualized in this way, you can now clear these subtle channels and energy centers quite easily. With your attention, move deep inside the heart chakra and visualize an extremely tiny drop. This is the indestructible drop of the heart. The drop is white with a reddish tint because it contains both lower and upper kundalini energies. It is shining and sparkling. As you concentrate on this drop, you slowly become one with it. Don't look at it from the outside—enter into it and merge your mind with it.

7. As the heart's energy drop, look from this point within the heart chakra down through the central channel and see the solar plexus chakra below. You can even look further and find the secret chakra, which is the lowest end of the central channel. The channel stops either at the end of the cervix, where it opens into the vagina, or deep within the penis, at the inner part of the tip. Just by gazing, you are clearing the lower pathway, all the way into the genitals.

8. Now, as the drop, look up through the central channel and see the throat chakra and the crown chakra. Again, just looking through the upper part of the channel makes the passage clear.

9. As this drop, begin to tour your subtle structure. First, go up through the passage to reach the throat chakra. Look around and feel all the branches of the chakra. Feel how the light of the drop that you are illuminates and corrects all the defects of the chakra. Then move up to the crown. Try to feel how richly branched the crown chakra is; its multiple branches spread, facing downward, in the direction of the throat chakra. Radiate your light as the indestructible drop to purify the entire crown chakra. Now move to the brow chakra, which opens just outside the point midway between your eyebrows. Move through the channel to the opening there. From here you can look at your entire subtle body and see it as a completely radiant form. Again, from the brow chakra, go back into the crown and look down at the throat. Then jump to the throat. From there, go down to the heart and pause inside this point, which is your natural abode.

• • • • • • • •

As the indestructible drop, radiate your light to clear the entire heart chakra. Then continue to the solar plexus chakra. For a while, clear its channels with your light, and finally return to the heart.

10. Now that the passages are clear, continue to travel up and down the central channel, but always return to the heart. By traveling in this way, blocked or crooked channels are opened and straightened. Using the drop from the heart, you can actually regenerate and activate all the channels. The entire web of channels becomes rainbowlike, transparent, soft, and flexible.

11. Try to perceive the entire structure, with one complete glance, like the entirely lit up interior of a building: the central channel, the side channels, the solar plexus chakra, the throat chakra, the brow chakra, the crown chakra, and the drop in the heart chakra. Finally, you can gently and slowly open your eyes.

Kriya Yoga

Swami Satyananda Saraswati (1923–2009) was a prominent twentieth-century Indian yogi. A student of the renowned Swami Sivananda, he was the founder of the Bihar School of Yoga and the author of more than eighty books. One of the hallmarks of his yoga system is a series of twenty kundalini kriya techniques (not to be confused with the other well-known system of kriya yoga propagated by Paramahansa Yogananda).

Historical Background

The term *kriya* means activity or movement, referring to specific movements of consciousness. These practices were drawn from secret teachings described in the yoga and tantra shastras. According to Saraswati, these had been the teachings for the transcendental *sadhana* (spiritual practice) that the Lord Shiva himself gave to his disciple and wife, Parvati.[171]

Prior to Saraswati's time, kriya yoga had been handed down from teacher to disciple by word of mouth in the form of an oral tradition. Although the practices had been described in numerous tantric sources written in Sanskrit, none of the classical scriptures explained the techniques in detail, with the explicit intention of preventing an ordinary practitioner from understanding how to apply them. To this day, only a few of these texts have been translated into other languages. Saraswati, however, chose to open up the "science" of kriya yoga and to present it to the

171. Saraswati, *Kundalini Tantra*, 279.

broader public. To make this ancient system available for the practitioner in the present age, he not only described it in detail but also systematized it in a clear structure, meant to be studied over a period of three years.

The ancient form of kriya yoga evolved over time through practice and experience. The full form of the practice consisted of a total of seventy-six kriyas, out of which only twenty are commonly known. In the following set of meditations, I have chosen to include five techniques out of the twenty as they are presented in Saraswati's book *Kundalini Tantra*.

Purpose

The practice is designed to fully awaken the different layers of the subtle body—including the chakras, the central channel, and the kundalini energy—while its ultimate intention is to lead to the realization of the innermost Self. For this purpose, it makes use of both the frontal (*arohan*) and the back (*awarohan*) pathways of the chakras.

As opposed to other yoga systems and meditation techniques, you are not required to bring your mind under control or to counteract mental disturbances. Your sole focus is to follow specific inner movements that gradually and systematically refine your consciousness and release dormant kundalini energy. As a consequence, all the different faculties of your being may be harmonized and begin to flower into their fullest potential.

Practice

Saraswati divided his set of twenty practices into three sections: *pratyahara*, or preparatory kriyas; *dharana*, or concentration kriyas; and *dhyana*, or meditation kriyas. This enables the meditator to progress safely and gradually through the meditative states of mind and consciousness. Even though I introduce only five meditations here, I have remained faithful to the original progression.

Most of the kriyas consist of a complex combination of asana (body posture), pranayama (breathing techniques), mudra (gestures), bandha (inner locks or contractions), mantra (subtle sounds), chakra (energy center) awareness, psychic passage awareness, and visualization. During the practice, however, all these elements are meant to flow in tandem. Don't worry if this doesn't happen instantly; you may start by learning each component separately and gradually combine them into a fully realized practice. However, I have deliberately selected the least-complex techniques, which mainly consist of visualization.

You don't have to follow the sequence presented here. In any case, Saraswati recommends practicing each kriya for a full week before integrating it into a more complete process. Similarly, you may choose only one of the five kriyas and delve into it independently. Even if you do practice them sequentially, allow a silent meditation in between.

· · · · · · · ·

Saraswati justifiably warns that these kriyas are quite advanced and are too powerful for the average meditator. The traditional recommendation is that if you wish to follow this practice seriously, it is better to study it under the guidance of an experienced teacher, who can ensure that you are fully prepared for it and that obstacles experienced while practicing do not lead to mental or physical imbalances.[172] However, getting to know these practices should not be harmful as long as you avoid pushing yourself too hard, either physically or mentally. If possible, prepare your body and mind by doing some asanas (yoga postures) prior to the practice.

Instructions

PREPARATION: The complete process lasts thirty minutes. Before beginning, take a long look at an image of the subtle body. Try to internalize it as much as possible.

The Discovery of the Chakras (*Chakra anusandhana*)

1. Close the eyes. First, direct your awareness to the root chakra (mooladhara). Then allow your consciousness to slowly ascend the frontal passage of the chakras: from mooladhara to the frontal point of the sacral chakra (swadhisthana) at the pubic bone, the solar plexus (manipura) at the navel, the heart chakra (anahata) at the sternum, the throat chakra (vishuddhi) at the throat, and across to bindu at the top and back of the head. In your head, say the name of each chakra—*Mooladhara, swadhisthana, manipura, anahata, vishuddhi, bindu*—as you pass through these centers.

2. After completing the climb to bindu, let your awareness travel down the spinal passage of the chakras, from bindu all the way down to mooladhara, while mentally repeating *Ajna, vishuddhi, anahata, manipura, swadhisthana, mooladhara*.

3. When you have reached mooladhara, immediately start ascending the frontal passage again while mentally reciting the chakra names.

4. Continue this cyclical flow of awareness throughout the chakras without interruption, swiftly glancing at each chakra along the way. You may visualize your ascending and descending awareness as a thin, silver serpent that moves in an ellipse within your body. Repeat this cycle for nine rounds.

---

172. Saraswati, *Kundalini Tantra*, 279.

Parvati's Lotus *(Shambhavi)*

1. Close your eyes and press your tongue against the upper palate.

2. Visualize a huge lotus flower growing within your spinal passage. Its transparent green roots spread out from your root chakra (mooladhara). Its long and thin green stem extends upward. The lotus flower itself lies in your crown chakra (sahasrara), and it is currently closed like a bud, while the flower's main petals are pink with fine red veins; at the bottom of the bud you find a few light green, immature petals. Try to picture this lotus as clearly as possible. Although you visualize the lotus before your mind's eye, you actually *feel* it in your body.

3. When you exhale, guide your awareness toward the roots of the lotus, and when you inhale, breathe into your throat and allow your awareness to rise slowly throughout the lotus stem, deep within the spinal passage.

4. At the end of the inhalation, reach the closed bud at the top of the stem. Hold your awareness at the crown chakra while holding your breath. Although you can picture the lotus from the outside, be inside it and feel how it begins to open slowly. When the bud opens into a lotus flower, notice the yellow pollen–tipped stamens in its center. Then, let the flower slowly close again and reopen widely immediately after.

5. When the flower has closed again, slowly descend through the stem to the root chakra, following this descent with an in-throat exhalation.

6. Remain at your root chakra for a moment and visualize the roots spreading out in all directions. Then, once again, ascend the stem with an in-throat inhalation. Repeat this process eleven times.

Inner Visualization of the Chakras *(Sushumna darshan)*

1. Close your eyes. Imagine that your mind holds an inner pencil.

2. Direct your awareness to the root chakra (mooladhara) and draw a square in it. Then draw the largest possible inverted equilateral triangle within the square. Add a circle that touches all four corners of the square and prepare four petals, one for each side of the square.

3. Move your awareness to the sacral chakra (swadhisthana). Prepare a circle there with the same radius as the one at your root chakra. Draw six petals around the edge of the circle and a crescent moon inside its bottom.

· · · · · · · ·

4. Now climb to the solar plexus chakra (manipura). Draw a circle in it, and then make the biggest possible inverted triangle to fit this circle. Draw a ball of fire in the center. Finally, add ten petals around the circle.

5. Move on to your heart chakra (anahata). Draw two triangles there, one pointing upward, the other inverted; the triangles are interwoven. Then, surround them with a circle that has twelve petals.

6. Continue to the throat chakra (vishuddhi). Draw a circle there and place a smaller circle within it, like a drop of nectar. Add sixteen petals around that circle.

7. Climb to your third eye (ajna) and make a circle in it. Write a big Sanskrit Om inside it. Add large petals, one on the right and one on the left side of the circle. Moving to bindu, draw a crescent moon with a tiny circle above it.

8. Finally, climb to the crown chakra (sahasrara). Prepare a circle there, and then add the largest possible upward-pointing triangle within that circle. There are one thousand petals around the circle.

9. Now picture all your chakras in their proper places.

Infusing the Divine Prana *(Prana ahuti)*

1. Close your eyes. Visualize and feel a divine hand lying on your head and softly touching it. This divine hand is infusing subtle life force (prana) into your body and mind. As a result, the prana is flowing down from your crown chakra throughout the spinal passage.

2. This may be experienced like a wave of cold, heat, energy, electric current, or a stream of wind or liquid. Allow any inner response to this passage of energy to occur: vibrations, shocks, jerks, or tickling sensations.

3. When the prana has finally reached your root chakra, stop the practice.

The Vision of Your Self *(Swaroopa darshan)*

1. With your eyes closed, become aware of your physical body. Allow it to be completely motionless and steady, like a rock.

2. When you have established your body's steadiness, become aware of the constant flow of your natural breath. Let your body become increasingly stiff: the stiffer it becomes, the more your awareness shifts completely to your breathing.

3. Reach a point at which your body has become as rigid as a stone, to a degree that you couldn't move it even if you tried. At the same time, be fully aware of your breathing and notice that with each inhalation, your body seems to be expanding, while with each exhalation, it appears to be contracting. Realize that since your physical body is as stiff as a statue, it is your subtle body that keeps expanding and contracting. Observe this process of contraction and expansion until it becomes clearly noticeable.

4. At a certain point, you will lose awareness of the physical body and, instead, begin to observe the subtle body directly. However, the contraction will become more pronounced, and eventually you will be able to experience that the subtle body has been reduced to a single point of light.

5. Look closer at that point of light and visualize how it takes the form of a golden egg. Watch this golden egg; it begins to expand and to become increasingly luminous, glowing from the inside.

6. Eventually, let the egg grow until it takes on the same shape as your subtle and physical bodies. This form, which is neither material nor subtle, is glowing light. It is your innermost Self.

Dzogchen

Dzogchen ("great perfection" or "great completeness" in Tibetan), also known as *atiyoga* ("utmost yoga"), is a tradition of highly advanced teachings and meditations in Indo-Tibetan Buddhism.

Historical Background

Throughout the sixth and seventh centuries, Buddhist masters such as Prahevajra (also known as Garab Dorje) and Manjushrimitra taught the nonconceptual practice of Dzogchen in India, while Guru Padmasambhava and Vimalamitra brought the teaching to Tibet in the eighth century. This system was already known then to be powerful enough to bring about sudden spiritual awakening in its practitioners.[173]

The Dzogchen traditions remained quite misunderstood for some time in Tibet. However, in the fourteenth century the great scholar and yogi Longchenpa wrote many texts that elucidated

173. Rinpoche, "Dzogchen."

Dzogchen tantras. During the nineteenth century, Dzogchen became quite widespread among Tibetan Buddhists thanks to the influential teacher Jigme Lingpa (c. 1730–1798), whose lineage of masters taught Dzogchen to many important lamas. Dzogchen was taught in the Nyingma and Bon traditions in Tibet, and it was later incorporated into the various Kagyu schools as well. In the Nyingma classification system of nine vehicles of mind, it is known as the highest of the six tantra vehicles.

Nowadays, Dzogchen-style meditation is frequently taught outside its sutra and tantra contexts—for instance, as a method for achieving a stilled and settled state of mind. Many Tibetan lamas have reservations about teaching Dzogchen formally, mainly because they believe that the practice's immediate approach might be misunderstood by students as a way of bypassing important processes of purification.[174]

Purpose

Dzogchen focuses on the realization of the true essence of the mind. Instead of going through a slow evolution toward Buddhahood, this system invites us to gain insight into the mind that is the cause of both samsara (suffering) and nirvana (liberation). It shows us that in fact, nirvana and samsara are nothing more than states of mind, and you can be awakened at any given moment just by seeing the already enlightened nature of your mind. When you take the time to look into the deepest and subtlest levels of your mind through Dzogchen, you will come to realize that your essential mind has remained untainted and untouched by suffering since the beginning of time.

So, Dzogchen offers us a form of sudden enlightenment by diving directly into the ground of our very being. This ground is beginningless: it is not possible to locate the point in time at which it came into being, since it is the foundation of everything that comes and goes; it gives form to all, but in itself it is formless. And since the ground of our consciousness has no point of beginning, it also has no point of cessation. It is thus perfectly free and unconditional.

It is said that the Buddha himself taught nonconceptual teachings like Dzogchen and Mahamudra—teachings that penetrated directly into the depths of reality and consciousness.[175] On the other hand, to those who couldn't understand these teachings, he gave the more gradual, conceptual, and rule-based spiritual path. You can imagine why it may be difficult for some of us to grasp the idea of having an inherently unpolluted mind while experiencing our mind as packed with difficult memories, past impressions, and inner contradictions. However, Dzogchen meditation advises us to look through the gaps between these thoughts and impressions and to see for ourselves that our mind is mostly made of space. At the level of pure awareness, all the

174. Rinpoche, "Dzogchen."
175. Rinpoche, "Dzogchen."

qualities of Buddhahood are already ours. Nothing needs to be added to this beginningless and endless mind except bringing all these qualities to a state of full functioning.

Because forgetfulness has overshadowed the natural luminosity of our mind, much has been accumulated on the ground of our foundational awareness: memories, karmic tendencies, disturbing emotions, and forms of attachment. So, the aim of Dzogchen meditation is to finally put an end to this forgetfulness and to enable the flowering of all the innate good qualities of our pure awareness.

Practice

Thoughts and emotions appear and disappear constantly. But where do they arise from and disappear to? Your most immediate task in Dzogchen meditation is to reveal the ground of the mind, which gives rise to all your passing states of mind without being affected by any of them. This ground is your awareness. But how can you find this awareness?

In this meditation, you learn to recognize the ground of pure awareness in the spaces between moments of seeing, hearing, imagining, and verbal thinking. Ordinarily, you may not be aware of these gaps between your arising and disappearing thoughts and perceptions, since our habit of focusing only on those thoughts and impressions creates an illusion of continuity. For this reason, Dzogchen meditation first quiets down your mental activity by centering your attention on the space between verbal thoughts and concepts. Each syllable of each thought arises, abides, and ceases. When you are mindful of their tendency to arise, abide, and cease, you realize that you don't need to make any conscious effort: the verbal thought automatically "liberates itself," since it disappears by itself; thus, all that's left for you to do is to settle into the state between thoughts.

To this awareness, you add attention to the microseconds before your sensory experience becomes a concept in your mind. For instance, when you hear a dog barking in the distance, there is a split second in which this is just a pure experience without labeling and words. Resting in these gaps between your sensory experience and your concepts also gets you closer to the ground of your mind.

In the process, you don't analyze anything—you simply notice the place from which your verbal thinking comes and into which it disappears. You also notice that verbal thinking doesn't have a solid existence, since it owes its brief life to the sustaining ground of your awareness. And because thinking happens automatically and dissolves by itself, you don't need to make any effort: you can simply rest on this calm and steady ground, knowing that it doesn't just exist in the gaps. The gaps help you to see that it is always there.

This ground is only the initial revelation of Dzogchen meditation. Under the guidance of Dzogchen masters, we can go deeper and experience and recognize the universal mind that gives rise to all and everything (*essence rigpa*). When you tap into this open-spaced mind and

• • • • • • • •

become immersed in this primordial mindfulness, you don't even need to practice attention. This is called *effortless meditation*, or nonmeditation.

Instructions

Preparation: This meditation requires between thirty to sixty minutes.[176] If possible, meditate in total darkness, or at least in a darker-than-usual environment, to avoid distraction from sensory cognition. During your meditation, observe total silence based on the "three immovables":

- **Immovable Body:** Keep your body straight, with your hands either in the meditation pose on your lap or lightly resting on your knees.

- **Immovable Senses:** Keep your eyes neither closed nor wide open, and gaze forward naturally.

- **Immovable Mind:** Avoid thinking actively about the past or future. When a thought arises, do not follow it out. Refrain from analysis and from being self-conscious of what you are doing. Simply rest in the present moment of fresh and natural awareness.

1. Start by trying to recognize the ground of awareness in between moments of verbal thinking. Find it in between each word or syllable of a verbal thought. Remember, all verbal thoughts arise, abide, and cease. The more you become aware of this fact, the more you can shift your attention to the space in between verbal thoughts. Whenever you allow yourself to "fall" through these spaces, you land on this nonarising and unceasing ground of pure awareness. Note: Don't aim to stop verbal thinking by applying restraint or discipline. After all, the arising, abiding, and ceasing of moments of verbal thinking occur automatically. The only effort you should make is to recognize this automatic occurrence and to remain focused on it with understanding.

2. Meditate on progressively subtler levels. Pay attention not only to clear verbal thoughts but also to elusive mental phenomena, such as mental images; feelings of happiness, unhappiness, or neutral feelings; attitudes like hope, expectation, disappointment, and boredom; and subtle identities. Just like verbal thoughts, these also arise, abide, and cease, so look through the gaps between the disappearance of one and the arising of another.

---

176. The instructions derive from Berzin, "Steps of Dzogchen Meditation."

· · · · · · · ·

3. Add to your attention the recognition of the milliseconds in which you experience something through your senses, just before your thinking has intervened. For example, if you hear anything from the outside world during your meditation, be aware of the milliseconds of "pure hearing" and notice the spaces between your hearing and the thoughts that label and describe.

AFTER THE MEDITATION: To trigger even further the experience of nonconceptual inner space, sit outside, with the sun shining on your back, and gaze into the boundless, clear blue sky in front of you. By looking directly at this outer space, you will arouse the experience of your primordial awareness. You can close your eyes from time to time to contact your innermost space. If you are unable to remain in this space, start again by focusing on the sky.[177]

Mahamudra Meditation

In tantric Buddhist terms, Mahamudra (which translates as "the great seal") is the ultimate, final realization. As a teaching and a meditation, what Mahamudra does is fairly unique: it looks directly into the nature of the mind itself. It simply asks, *What is the mind?* Usually, the object of our concentration is something that our mind looks at. But what happens when we turn our attention to the mind itself?

Historical Background

Tilopa (988–1069) was a tenth-century Indian yogi. Initially a Buddhist monk at the temple of Somapuri in Bengal, he dedicated his young adult life to traveling throughout India in search of teachers and methods of enlightenment. Each of the teachers Tilopa met along the way bestowed on him a teaching and a method that would later be gathered into the path known as the Six Yogas of Naropa. Among other things, Tilopa received initiation into Tummo, the tantric yoga of Inner Fire (see "Vase Breathing" in chapter 6 and "Empty Body" in chapter 10), from Dakini Samantabhadri. It is said that he was given direct a transmission of Mahamudra by the deity-Buddha Vajradhara, after which he retired to intense and profound meditative practice in caves.[178]

Although Tilopa preferred to live his life in remote and inhospitable regions, his fame as a spiritual master attracted excellent students, among them Naropa (1016–1100). Leaving behind

177. Rinpoche, "Dzogchen Meditation," 15.
178. Thrangu, *Tilopa's Wisdom*, 4.

his life as a prince and a married man, Naropa took full ordination as a monk and tantric practitioner, practicing and living at Pullahari Monastery. However, Naropa felt that despite all his knowledge, he knew very little of the direct truth, and he sought Tilopa to receive guidance on Mahamudra. The *Ganges Mahamudra* is the culmination of Tilopa's Mahamudra instructions, which, as the title suggests, took place on the banks of the Ganges.

The *Ganges Mahamudra* was given as a spontaneous song expressing spiritual realization. Later, Naropa passed it on to the Tibetan Marpa Lotsawa, whose appearance in Naropa's life was prophesied by Tilopa. Marpa translated the song and brought it with him to Tibet, where it has been preserved by the masters of the Kagyu, the "Lineage of Transmission."

Tilopa's instructions are a concise and essential presentation of the ultimate outcome of Buddhist meditation: the Mahamudra. Their unique approach lies in their intense focus on the nature of the mind; if you comprehend the unpolluted element of your consciousness—the essential and very subtle mind of clear light—you grasp the nature of all phenomena as well. Tilopa believed that if this mind of clear light could be accessed directly, no other practice was required. The following Mahamudra meditation is an adaptation of Tilopa's instructions: a form of contemplation that makes it easy for us to implement his teachings.[179]

Purpose

While the *Ganges Mahamudra* introduces a highly advanced level of practice, the meditation is astonishingly easy and clear and requires nothing more than an honest gaze into your mind. The goal is to realize for yourself that your mind is not made of confused thoughts, but has a spacelike, clear light nature. Instead of making efforts to transcend your mind, you can use this form of contemplation to reveal its subtle layers. This meditation identifies the mind as a source of inner limitlessness and perfect clarity—and, even more so, as our true resting place.

Relaxing meditations can temporarily halt the mind's frantic movement, but they cannot uproot it. For this reason, it's important to practice insight meditation as well, in which we explore the mind directly and strive to achieve a clear vision of its essence. The mind is the source of our greatest illusions and our greatest illuminations; if you grasp your mind, you instantly understand the nature of all realities. In Buddhist terms, ignorance of the nature of the mind is the source of all samsara (suffering), and understanding the mind paves the way to nirvana (liberation).

Practice

This meditation walks you through a series of analytical investigations of the mind, which appear in six different groups. In each cycle of investigation, you ask yourself a set of questions and use them to look directly into the nature of your mind. You carefully investigate your assumptions

---

179. Barth, *A Meditation Guide for Mahamudra*, 36–42.

• • • • • • • •

about the nature of the mind until all misconceptions and doubts are cleared up. As soon as you decisively and clearly see the essential reality behind these questions, you may continue to the next cycle on the stable basis of your previous recognition.

At first, this practice involves effortful, analytical explorations. With persistence, however, you will be able to start discovering a state of open, mindful lucidity. When this happens, you are welcome to continue meditating silently on this empty, unidentifiable, open awareness.

The key instruction is to look carefully and directly, as guided by the questions. Don't answer the questions intellectually; use them as an immediate reflection of the mind. Do not think about or consider these questions. Listen inwardly, and examine without examining. There is a phrase taken from the world of the Mahamudra tradition: "Moving like a small fish within the lucid waters of the mind."[180] This means that when you inquire into the nature of the mind, you don't try to shake the mind with your examination or bring additional chaos into it—you don't add concepts. Instead, you move ever so lightly and silently, like a tiny fish moving within the water of the mind.

After each cycle, when you feel that you have gained a decisive understanding, rest for a while and resume looking shortly after. Do not attach to flashes of insight. Just relax and continue looking until you experience another simple and quiet understanding. You may experience an undefinable state imbued with mindfulness and a sense of certainty. With time, this is experienced as an indescribable inner vastness and an even stronger confidence. You may come to understand that the mind is like space, in that it remains completely unaffected by any thoughts that arise in it, and you may learn to live with complete confidence in the freedom of your mind just as it is. Like when the sun shines into a room, you are able to see all the "dust" in your mind, but through insight, you can effectively turn this dust into gold.

Instructions

PREPARATION: The meditation usually lasts between twenty and thirty minutes. Either sit with eyes open, but not fixed on any point in space, or close your eyes. Traditionally, the position includes eyes half-open, gazing at no specific objects.

1. With a loose mind, like an open hand, first look into the mind and ask yourself: *Does the mind have any kind of shape? For example, is it round, like a circle? Is it square? Is it the shape of the ground? The shape of a rock? Or the shape of a person? Does the mind have any form to it at all? Does it take the form of the experiences that continually arise—that is, does it have an ever-changing form? Or does it have a fixed form? Or no*

---

180. Yeshe, *Mahamudra*, 74–75.

form at all? If you are certain that the concept of shape or form does not apply to your mind, and that the mind has no form at all, rest in this knowledge.

2. Now look into the mind again. Does it have any color? For example, is it blue? Or green? Red? Black or white? Or does it perhaps have multiple colors? If you realize that the mind has no color at all, and that the concept of color does not apply to your mind, rest in this understanding.

3. Now look again. Does the mind have anything that supports it from the outside? Or from the inside? Does it stem from a material object, or from anyone else? Does it stem from the brain's activity? Does the mind dwell anywhere? Does it rest on a part of the body, or permeate the entire body? Is it inside or outside the form of the body—or both inside and outside the body at the same time? Does it have any location? How can something with no shape or form have a location? If you find any location of the mind, go inside this location and find its boundary. Whenever you find a location that seems to correspond to the mind, go inside this location and open it up.

4. Look again. What is the mind's existential mode? Is it like an open space? If so, is it completely empty? How does it compare to a completely open space? Is it imbued with a lucid, knowing quality? How does it compare to the luminosity of the sun? Is it an inner luminosity? Is there any sense of "inner" or "outer" to it at all? Is it an open lucidity, without form, without color, without location in time and space? If you realize that the nature of the mind is undefinable and beyond imagination or intellectual comprehension, rest in this knowledge.

5. Now look again. Where is the origin or source of the mind? Look with the mind directly at the source of the mind. Where is its abode, or dwelling place, as it is experienced in a calm moment? Where does the mind go? How does it cease? If you realize that the mind itself is completely free from birth, existence, and death, rest in this knowledge.

6. Finally, as you reside in this self-knowing awareness, look into the mind and ask yourself: *Does this awareness ever go away or come back? What makes your experience of it disappear? What makes it return? Is it always there when you consider it?*

AFTER THE MEDITATION: As much as possible, whenever you remember in your day-to-day life, try to look at the mind with the mind.

• • • • • • •

Latihan

Latihan is a common term in Indonesia that refers to any form of exercise or drill, from physical exercise to learning lessons at school to carrying out a military drill. *Kejiwaan* means "spiritual." Thus, this meditation's name simply means "spiritual exercise."

Historical Background

Latihan kejiwaan is the central meditation practice of the spiritual movement Subud, which was founded by the Indonesian Muhammad Subuh Sumohadiwidjojo (1901–1987), more commonly known as Bapak. According to Bapak, the Latihan came to him as a sudden revelation.[181] It is now practiced by thousands of people in eighty-three countries.[182] In later years, the Latihan process influenced the development of some of Osho's dynamic meditations, such as Gourishankar and Devavani.[183]

Purpose

Latihan is about setting the ideal conditions for initiating contact with the divine force of life and learning to receive and be guided by its grace. For this reason, all you have to do in Latihan is still your body and mind until you identify an inner movement that begins to express itself without your volition. Your only task is to respond to it and to follow it. In this way, the practice serves as a perfect metaphor for a life lived in total devotion to the greater reality, driven by the divine source and without the interference of self-will.

Bapak describes this well when he says, "Although the Latihan looks as if it is something without any content if you look at it from the outside, nevertheless, it is this, which all those who are 'searching' are actually looking for…This reality of a human being as a creature of God being able to receive something from beyond his will, is not something new but has occurred ever since the beginning of history."[184] The practice is therefore an open state in which you hope to be filled with life's mysterious spirit, and in this way to find what the seers of the past claimed to have found.

Accordingly, the effects of doing the Latihan vary and are quite unpredictable. The immediate outcome is often described as a pervading sense of well-being and relaxation. However, what a practitioner of Latihan would usually hope for is a gradual strengthening of their sense

---

181. Geels, "Subud," 570.

182. Hunt, *Alternative Religions*, 122.

183. Osho, *Meditation*, 149–50, 164–65.

184. "The Latihan."

of intuition and of the teacher within. Some even claim to receive actual guidance during the practice itself, which inspires them to make important changes in their relationships, family lives, and careers. Aside from being a catalyst for personal development, Latihan is thought of as an initiator of processes of psychic purification and cleansing, ultimately leading to a return to the original "inner feeling" that we possessed when first created.

Practice

Latihan is an unusual meditation technique. In a way that resembles Zen's Zazen (see chapter 4), it involves no instructions or clear stages. It is meant to be a process of receiving—an unforced and uncontrolled process that arises within any person who asks for it, taking place at their own pace and according to their own nature.

The essence of this process is to follow spontaneous movements from within. When the meditator quiets down their being, they become aware of a deeper and subtler life going on inside them, and through these inner movements, they begin to reconnect with something greater than themselves. The movements are comparable to those of a newborn who is unable to understand the movements and sounds they make: they emerge directly from life itself, free from the influence of this world, the psyche, and the will. The conditions for receiving these movements are "patience, acceptance, and submission."[185] Submission, in this context, implies recognizing that one is powerless without the presence of this greater force.

Traditionally, the practice requires an initiation (referred to as "opening") by the Subud movement. Following the initiation, the Latihan is usually performed twice a week with a group, each time for thirty minutes. After sufficient experience has been gained, some people do an additional Latihan by themselves once a week. However, you can certainly practice this meditation by yourself or in the company of other willing meditators.

To practice the Latihan, stand in a relaxed manner and follow whatever spontaneously arises within you. Many people feel a sense of calm and a deepening connection with wisdom, their higher self, or the divine. Some people report an inner vibration or a feeling of electricity running through their bodies. Some feel an impulse to move, utter sounds, laugh, cry, sing, dance, or pray. At other times, the Latihan can be a quiet, inward experience. Prepare yourself for surprising experiences!

Bapak writes, "All we do is we say some very simple words, signifying our surrender…and with no further effort on our part, we are able to receive a movement which comes from the life that is within our life."[186] The movement is likened to the rays of the rising sun that natu-

185. "The Latihan."
186. "The Latihan."

rally dispel the morning dew and mist—in the face of the radiance of this movement that exists within us, any mental and emotional disturbances are swept away.

Instructions

PREPARATION: The meditation usually lasts between forty-five and sixty minutes.[187]

Stage I: Preparing for Latihan (Fifteen Minutes)

1. This stage is compared to getting your house ready for special guests: you freshen up to show respect for your guests, then make your house as clean as possible by gradually letting go of every bit of detritus from your outer life. In this sense, detritus is the thoughts and worries, problems and successes, family and relationship concerns—everything to be let go of.

2. Relax your body, heart, and mind, and put aside your desire for anything of this world, including your desire for happiness, your desire to get closer to the divine, and even your desire for a good Latihan, until you feel like an empty cup that is waiting to be filled. This can be likened to the state just before you doze off, or to a pool of water inside you that becomes increasingly calm until suddenly, it is absolutely still, without even the slightest ripple. Allow yourself to sit quietly until all of a sudden, *you* are quiet without aiding or abetting the process—it just happens.

3. It helps to say some kind of prayer that you will be able to surrender to your full capacity before Latihan begins.

4. You can also visualize a graceful energy descending toward your crown chakra and filling your being while, and at the same time, an energy flows upward from your base. This will help you to get in touch with the vibration within.

Stage II: The Latihan (Thirty Minutes)

1. Stand quietly in this more-or-less empty state and wait until the Latihan or vibration begins in you before you move. If you are really attentive, the first movement you will feel is the power of the divine moving your own breathing. Latihan is your chance to not be a doer of life, but rather a puppet controlled by the puppeteer.

---

187. The instructions derive from Polk, "How to Do the Latihan."

· · · · · · ·

2. Latihan itself is like the arrival of the special guests mentioned above. Each guest brings a gift, and your job is simply to receive each gift as it was given, with no thinking, judging, or trying to understand it—just accept or receive each gift as it has come to you.

3. Body movement is important, although it should not be forced. The progress in the Latihan starts with the physical body. Impurities are thrown off as we move. These movements are the early manifestations of the gifts; they contain the purification that our bodies and souls need.

4. Do not judge your own Latihan or try to make it "spiritual." Sometimes, what comes to the surface from deep inside can be disturbing. Don't stop Latihan when something difficult or hard is surfacing. Keep it authentic and have the courage to follow whatever you are receiving, be it coarse or fine.

5. You will feel the vibration of the Latihan, or at least a movement that starts up on its own, quite independently from your thinking or wishing. Then you just have to trust—since you are open, and you have quieted down as best you can— that this little skipping or waving of your hand, or this song that has suddenly started up without your thinking about it, *is* your Latihan!

6. Unlike in a willed meditation, don't force your mind into quietude. Instead, allow the thinking processes to take place. After a while, you will find yourself thinking, but also watching yourself thinking, as you move around. Pay attention to the movements rather than the thinking. Feel the soles of your feet touching the floor to help you pay attention to your body; you can pay attention to the different vibrations you feel in each part of the body and the feelings that accompany those vibrations. In Latihan, understanding is the last element to be purified, so our thinking may not be very productive early on.

7. Don't think that after all the movement has stopped, your Latihan has ended. There is the "second Latihan," the part that arises after the flurry of purification movements has quieted down. Ask yourself, *Is there anything more that the divine would have me receive in my Latihan?* In this second part, indications or receivings tend to arise. Those indications may be related to your life's journey, an unknown talent, a deep insight about your true self, or a moment of ineffable peace and praise. And sometimes, there is nothing—it is not up to us.

8. After the Latihan, sit quietly for a while. It is important to "come down." The state of Latihan is powerful, even when it is quiet; your body may still be vibrat-

ing. In this post-Latihan quietude, we unwrap the gifts that we were given in the Latihan itself. We are quiet and peaceful, and therefore, clear messages often come. This can be a precious time of receiving guidance for your daily life.

Meditate on This: Meditation and Bliss

Bliss is the emotion or feeling of the crown chakra. It is also so much more than that. It is a multilayered experience that is physical and energetic, as well as mental, emotional, and spiritual. Bliss doesn't await you only at the heart of your crown chakra practices. In fact, it is one of the most important feelings you can encounter throughout your meditative journey.

In Hinduism, it is said that the direct revelation of brahman—the expanded reality without limit or edge—includes three facets. These facets, which arise together, are combined into the term *sat-cit-ananda*. *Sat* is absolute reality, or absolute being; it is the component of reality itself. *Cit* is undifferentiated consciousness, the element of absolute or pure consciousness. Last, there is *ananda*. *Ananda* means bliss or the purest form of joy, a joy that is completely beyond the duality of pleasure and pain.[188]

This is different from the sacral chakra's joy, which derives from the senses—the celebration of the here and now of the visible world. Bliss is a joy not of this world. It is the joy of the release from the senses.

As you get in touch with absolute reality and pure consciousness, sooner or later your meditation will carry the fragrance of bliss. Bliss must be one of the components of your experience of the greater reality, since this trio appears together: pure being, pure consciousness, and pure joy.

Bliss Shows You the Way

Some meditators report experiencing states of neutrality, emptiness, nonattachment, and silence. However, if all these states are devoid of bliss, this is a sterile form of meditation. Peace and serenity are usually strongly emphasized in meditative teachings, but this can sometimes be at the risk of forgetting that neutrality doesn't mean feeling nothing. Even your neutrality is supposed to be blissful! At a certain point, your meditation must be filled with profound, uncontainable, and independent happiness. Being neutral and feeling nothing actually reflects a limited experience, an inability to reach the ecstatic union of the higher chakras.

Tantric traditions, some of whose preliminary techniques were introduced in this chapter, put a strong emphasis on great bliss as the basis for entering reality. In fact, tantric teachings are bliss-oriented paths, and they clearly differentiate bliss from what they call "ordinary samadhi."[189] Ordinary samadhi is a state of neutrality, peace of mind, and deep concentration. But

188. Easwaran, *The Upanishads*, 338–39, 342.
189. Yeshe, *The Bliss of Inner Fire*, 132.

• • • • • • •

this again reflects an awakening of the lower chakras rather than a crown chakra awakening, which is the supreme realization—or, as tantric Buddhist teacher Lama Yeshe used to call it, the "real chocolate."[190]

There are several reasons why bliss has been greatly emphasized by these traditions. One is that bliss is the way the divine signifies its presence. In the absence of bliss, your experience is only about what is *not:* no attachment, no disturbance, no thoughts, no identification with emotions, and no connection to the world. But what *is* there? Remember the *sat-cit-ananda* principle: as soon as the divine becomes conscious of itself through you, it expresses itself through bliss. This is the bliss of self-recognition, of the inner declaration: "Finally, I have found myself!" Thus, bliss is your signal that reality is here.

A second reason is that bliss is the best indication we are on the right path. It is the emotion with which the source attracts us, like sweets and candies that are spread along a trail to let us know we should follow. In the depths of meditation, then, we find bliss, but also through bliss—through the delicious intensification of joy—we progress to a greater depth in our meditation. Bliss is the bright star that shines in the dark sky of our being.

A third reason that bliss has been a prominent tantric principle is that it is an all-purifier. It literally consumes and absorbs the personality, which is incapable of containing too much happiness.

Of course, the experience of bliss has different levels, depending on the depth of our meditation. In the early stages, it may be experienced as profound serenity or sweetness. You may feel softness and calm joy. These are like the distant echoes of bliss, but not the bliss itself. The closer you get to the crown chakra, the more you become consumed by this radiating sun of bliss that sends rays throughout your being.

Interestingly, in Vedantic Hinduism, bliss is the subtlest, innermost veil that surrounds the supreme Self. Bliss is synonymous with the causal body, and accordingly the causal body is called *anandamaya kosha. Kosha* is a layer or sheath, and together with *ananda*, pure joy, it means "a sheath of bliss." So when you approach the supreme Self, you first go through this bliss body, and when you get in touch with bliss, you know that you have entered the last body. Naturally, when you reach the supreme Self and merge with it, you go beyond even bliss and shed this last covering. This doesn't imply that you will never be blissful again, but only that you have understood the function of bliss: it was your divine signal, reality's perfume, indicating that you were on the right path.

The bliss of meditation is an experience consisting of four levels:

---

190. Yeshe, *The Bliss of Inner Fire*, 154.

1. Bliss as an energetic phenomenon

2. Bliss as an emotional phenomenon

3. Bliss as a mental phenomenon

4. Bliss as a spiritual phenomenon

We need to understand all four, since only together do they compose the experience of bliss with totality. After all, in itself, bliss is an indescribable state.

Bliss as Energetic Phenomenon

Before anything else, bliss is energetic, not emotional. It is the jump of kundalini Shakti through the central channel, toward and into the crown. In the same way, bliss can be the downward flow of cosmic kundalini, or the drop of kundalini, bindu, that melts and streams downward through the central channel.

Notice that in all three of these phenomena, there is one common element: the central channel. This is because the central channel is the conduit of bliss. When it is open and active, it is the source of bliss itself. If you remember the vase breathing practice (chapter 6), as long as the energy flows throughout the side channels, it is as if we are split within ourselves; our inner world is a world of two. And a subtle world of two reflects a psychological split as well: contradictory and opposing forces, and consequently, a lack of harmony, totality, and unity within us.

The sushumna, the central channel, is the line of unity. When it becomes active, it swallows the two side channels, and with them, it swallows our inner fight. Thus, all contradictions are resolved in the sushumna. When the energy flows through the sushumna, our various energies become unified, and this sense of one energy, of perfect unity within us, is bliss.

Then, as the unified energy finally flows into the crown chakra, it transforms into an orgasmic sensation that spreads in the brain. Sometimes we feel this sensation in the form of either chilling energy or fiery, burning-hot energy. There are reasons for the different forms that this energy takes, but this doesn't matter in the context of understanding bliss. Whether hot or cold, bliss is the transformation of sexual energy into brain energy.

Remember, the kundalini makes its leap through the sushumna from the sacral chakra, which is also our sex chakra. So when it jumps, it also gathers sexual energy with it. This is the reason we experience such an orgasmic feeling, although it is quite different from the orgasmic feeling that takes place in the sexual organs, because it is in a highly refined form.

If you progress in this way and begin to experience this kind of crown chakra orgasm, sexual orgasm becomes relatively unimpressive. First of all, it is quite limited and not as total. Second, it involves a loss of energy. For this reason, when you begin to experience the blissful orgasm of the crown chakra, you no longer recognize sexual orgasm as a lasting enhancement. This doesn't mean you will never engage in sex again, only that you will have a different sense of proportion.

So, energetically speaking, supreme happiness is the result of flow through the sushumna, the opening of the crown chakra, the melting of the kundalini drop at the back and top of the head, and the transformation of sexual energy into brain energy. In this sense, bliss must be physical. It must also be orgasmic and permeate our subtle nervous system. It goes deeper than sexual orgasm can. It is far from neutral, since union can never be neutral—can you imagine reuniting with your lover after a long time, and just feeling "okay" about it?

Bliss as an Emotional Phenomenon

Emotionally, one of the problems that many of us have is that we don't allow ourselves to be fully and totally happy. So the very concept of bliss—and later, the appearance of bliss in our meditation—confronts us with these psychological blockages.

By nature, we believe happiness should come in small quantities, in moderation. It is like a bank account we draw from minimally and cautiously, a little bit at a time. You smile a little bit, you love a little, and your meditation is a little blissful. You may enjoy your meditation practice, but only in a limited sense. Your encounter with reality through meditation, however, is destined to go so much deeper.

Of course, sometimes our meditative experience is not deep and intense enough. You may be thinking, *But I haven't had the experience of bliss yet!* There is a real possibility that you aren't having a blissful experience because of this underlying blockage; you may enter your meditation while unconsciously not allowing yourself to feel too much happiness. Therefore, we need to learn to dare to be deeply, unashamedly, intoxicatedly happy.

One reason for the existence of this psychological blockage is a conditioning of our brain. For the brain, bliss is considered nothing less than dangerous. Being immersed in bliss implies being inattentive, overlooking danger. If you feel bliss, a total joy that makes the world around you disappear, your primitive brain signals, *There may be a predator around, or something terrible just around the corner! You cannot allow yourself not to be on guard.* A second brain alarm informs you that soon enough, this joy is going to be replaced with sorrow, so there is no point in being too happy. You are going to get hit by life anyway, so why be blissful now? And yet a third reason is that being overjoyed is considered antisocial. This is a deep social taboo: you need to appear respectable, serious, and self-possessed, and you certainly must not lose your ground; being too smiley is undignified. As a result, you may be afraid of being criticized or even mocked.

Your brain's alarms are not only inefficient, but also destructive. If you listen to the warnings, you will never be able to realize for yourself that bliss has nothing to do with ordinary happiness, and that therefore it is not the opposite of sorrow. Your bliss will not be replaced by sorrow because bliss is beyond sorrow and happiness. Bliss is supreme. It is untouched. It is unrelated to this tireless pendulum of happiness and sorrow. Even more, bliss is your freedom from dependency on this external pendulum. And if it is the social taboo that hinders your bliss, remember that social limitations are a part of the world we strive to let go of in meditation. If you are worried about what others think, then what kind of freedom from the world can your practice offer you?

When I observe people meditating without a glow on their faces or eyes saturated in the joy of knowing, I know that something is missing. Sometimes people look even more gloomy and disconnected when they meditate. Again, they may lack the necessary depth of understanding and experience. But unfortunately, more often than not it is because they either suppress their bliss for social reasons, or they do not understand their own experience and filter out certain aspects of it due to conditioning. The brain, after all, is sophisticated: it can block bliss even before it arises. That's why it is so important to be aware of what is available for us in the depths of meditation and the ways that we might limit this revelation.

Now, why is bliss so essential on the emotional level? It is because this type of happiness dissolves and absorbs the self. Remember, the self cannot be this happy! It is simply unable to contain this amount of happiness. This is a part of its predicament. It must always stop before the joy becomes too overwhelming, which is, of course, ironic, since at the same time we strive to achieve happiness. But when bliss comes, it wipes away the inherent suffering of the separate self—and from the perspective of the crown chakra, being a separate self is the cause of suffering. Since bliss is the one feeling that cannot be contained by the I-thought, you literally drown yourself in happiness.

Bliss as a Mental Phenomenon

Bliss is not just a feeling—it also involves the joy of wisdom, knowing, and understanding. When you are immersed in *sat-cit-ananda*, your bliss intermingles with the wise knowledge of reality. In tantric Buddhism, there is a prayer associated with the Inner Fire meditation, which has been referred to several times in this book. The prayer repeats the sentence: "I implore you to bestow upon me the wisdom of bliss and emptiness."[191] Thus, wisdom, bliss, and emptiness (absolute reality) are interlinked.

The experience of bliss is not some sentimental pleasure. It is a profound experience, and when it arises, it is unified with the wisdom that understands the nature of reality. If it were merely a strong feeling, it could evaporate without leaving any deep impression. Even worse, this type of bliss could also give rise to desire, because it is so orgasmic that you replace sexual pleasure with

191. Yeshe, *The Bliss of Inner Fire*, 14.

• • • • • • •

bliss and want to endlessly repeat it. But real bliss is closely associated with wisdom. The two are truly inseparable; they nourish and sustain each other.

This means that bliss leads to wisdom, and wisdom leads to bliss. On the one hand, bliss is so powerful that it can actually dissolve the entire world and take you directly to knowledge of reality. On the other hand, if you understand and gain insight, bliss appears as a natural result. Wisdom also makes it possible for you to understand why you are in bliss and what the meaning of that bliss is.

So, if you understand, you immediately become blissful. Your true self recognizes itself, and with every recognition you become filled with bliss, which indicates that this is true and real. And you know that your insight is correct because it is followed by this extraordinary feeling, a feeling that doesn't fall within the range of feelings the separate self can contain.

Bliss as a Spiritual Phenomenon

In blissful meditation, we shift from ordinary happiness to bliss. However, the term *happiness* may be deceiving because we can never be perfectly happy, and certainly not continuously happy, as long as our happiness relies on changing circumstances. It is more accurate to say that we shift from the search for happiness, or from waiting for a future happiness, to bliss. Since lasting ordinary happiness is practically nonexistent, searching for it is, by nature, a false search. For this reason, we can only move from a hopeless search for happiness to bliss. Thus, your meditative journey does not require letting go of happiness, but only a realization that there is no lasting happiness in the world.

Spiritual bliss is the shattering of the illusion of ordinary happiness. You come to realize that the world is not the source of happiness—happiness is letting go of the world. This is the simple trick: letting go of the hope for happiness in the world *is* lasting happiness, or bliss.

Many people say that they no longer believe in the project of happiness. They will immediately agree that happiness is unattainable and unrealistic to yearn for. But if someone really didn't believe in the search for happiness, they would instantly become liberated, and as a result, they would also instantly become immersed in bliss. If this hasn't happened to them, it means that secretly, they are still waiting.

So, the happiness of the crown chakra is the direct outcome of freedom from unreliable ordinary happiness. This feeling of transcendent joy arises directly from your release from the dual relationship with the world. In other words, it is achieved when you no longer wait because you have come to realize that there is no world to wait *for*. Thus, your need for constant negotiation with the world comes to an end in the crown chakra.

Your bliss derives from knowing that you have found a form of happiness that cannot be taken away from you. This is, after all, happiness as a state, not an experience—happiness as a component of reality, an integral part of *sat-cit-ananda*. It is the immediate feeling that follows the very sense of union with reality.

The message of this section is to just let it happen. Don't inhibit your meditative joy. Now that you know about the possibility, open your being to it. Of course, don't start getting worried about not attaining bliss—if you start thinking about this in that way, you will hinder it from a different direction. Simply use this understanding to expose the false boundaries that the thinking machine has set for you and to gain a deeper understanding of your natural meditative experience.

CONCLUSION

If you have followed this book's journey step by step, you have completed two processes. First, you have enkindled each of your seven main energy centers by discovering their associated meditation techniques. Second, you have gained a complete view of the world of meditation, with its seven potential experiences, based on the seven-chakra principle. These two processes are, essentially, one and the same, and in this summary I will explain why.

Having reached the crown chakra's mountaintop, we can enjoy not only a spectacular view of the planet of meditation, but also our increased meditative capacity. This enhanced capacity would not have been possible if we had immediately begun our journey with the crown chakra techniques. From one chapter to another, we have generated momentum within our energy system. What is this momentum, exactly?

The very principle of summarizing the journey of the chakras and their related meditations is an essential dimension of the crown chakra: the crown signifies the summation of the chakra system. Sometimes, the crown chakra may seem so "up there," superior, and abstract, as if it has nothing to do with the others "down here." But in so many ways, the crown chakra includes the other six chakras within it. The crown chakra is the totality of the chakra system. So it can only open by unifying all the others in its awakening. This is an extraordinary thing. The crown chakra makes all seven into one. It is the energy center that unites all the chakras into one perfect column: the central channel. In this sense, the crown chakra and the central channel are inseparable.

When all seven chakras unite into this one column, they no longer function as separate dimensions. For this reason, whenever you focus on all seven of your chakras, from the bottom up or from the top down, you also collect all their different energies into one immense energy line. And when this line has been established, the crown chakra inevitably awakens. You may understand this based on your direct experience of the kriya yoga set of practices: as soon as you enkindle each of the chakras in the right order, they begin to spin and rotate intensely, one

· · · · · · ·

after another, until they eventually melt into one continuum. Losing their distinct boundaries, they combine into one column of light. Therefore, the ultimate purpose of the chakras is not to function forever as separate entities, but to become one inseparable being: your inner body.

When all of your energy centers form this unified line, they instantly awaken the central channel and, in this way, lead you to the original state of your being, your true nature. In the deepest sense, moving from the root chakra all the way back to the crown implies moving backward in time: you move back from the most material and condensed plane of the root chakra, all the way to the formlessness and pure light of the crown chakra, and then beyond that. So your meditative journey, if followed all the way, takes you to the original state of oneness and formlessness.

At the same time, your accomplished meditative journey creates a new you: a unified being, with all the possible dimensions of your inner experience awake and functioning. This being is governed by the crown chakra's supreme consciousness, so everything takes place under its light.

Remember that the seven chakras are the breaking of white light through a prism into seven different colors. While the crown has its own distinct color, it is, at its deepest core, pure white light, and so it contains all the other chakras. Imagine this as the way that the divine reality gave rise to the world: the white light is broken through a prism of creation and as a result, seven dimensions come into being. Finally, these seven dimensions pour into the human form as seven different perspectives and experiences.

But this means that moving in the other direction is a possibility—combine the seven colors, pass them through the prism in the opposite direction, and together they will reform a pure white light. Of course, we all need these different colors of creation as they manifest in us and outside us. Creation without color would be one indistinguishable mass of energy. How boring! Each of these colors enables us to experience one highly meaningful dimension of the human experience. So these colors, in the form of our seven chakras, are a key to creation, each covering a different facet of our reality.

But there comes a point at which we want to return home, to the original and unified state of our being. Although the play of colors is magnificent, we miss reality in its complete sense: the reality before the breaking of the white light.

Ultimately, this is what the meditative journey is all about: reversing the order of creation and returning to the state of white light, the one colorless color of our true and complete being. If our meditation is persistent, we move back from the colors, through the prism, into a blissful, pure light existence. Another way to phrase it is we move back from the diverse experiences of reality to an ultimate and transcendent state.

This is the role of the central channel, which appears both in the seventh group of meditations, but also as the unifying principle of all the possible groups and techniques. Your medita-

* * * * * * *

tive journey is fundamentally all about moving to a life within the central channel—settling in this channel as your true home and innermost body. The more you meditate, the more you experience everything *from* this channel. You look at the world and communicate with it *from* this channel. In the deepest sense, when we speak of the true or innermost self, or of our "core," these are all just different names trying to metaphorically capture the reality of our central channel.

Energetically speaking, this is where our meditation leads us. Meditation both creates and returns to existence in this channel: we realize this inborn unity in us, but we also strive to establish it and to finally become one. After all, we begin our journey of meditation by finding so many different voices inside our mind and heart, and the process is all about taming these voices, just as it is about identifying the already-silent mind from which they appear and into which they naturally disappear.

Living in the central channel, you will find something extraordinary: all the distinct roles and purposes of the seven groups become synonyms of one another. Compassion and heart-opening become synonymous with wisdom and clarity, and wisdom and clarity become synonymous with light and bliss. Instead of many available experiences, you will finally have discovered one state of existence. You may have felt during this book's journey that some of the meditations and their associated dimensions were in conflict with other groups and aspects, or that by devoting your entire attention to one of the groups, you must ignore and suppress all the others. But in the world of meditation, love, pure awareness, independence, and joy are just words that strive to capture the magnitude of meditation steeped in reality and the here and now. In the union of the seven chakras, white light can be nothing but white light, and ultimately, when there is only one state, there is absolutely no state.

One powerful and highly satisfying way to fulfill this path of unifying the seven chakras into a continuum is by dividing the week into seven consecutive chakra days. Since, fortunately, there are seven days for seven chakras, you can meditate each day based on one of the seven groups. On Monday, choose one or two of the five meditations from the root chakra group; on Tuesday, one or two of the techniques from the sacral chakra meditations, and so forth. In this way, your week becomes the ultimate path of meditation: the way of the central channel. The natural order of the seven days makes it possible for you to focus on each group of meditations separately and to come into contact with their unique fragrances and the specific experiences of life that they facilitate, but at the same time you move persistently and repeatedly through the column and ignite its immense meditative powers. As a result, the chakras begin to align, and by the time you have reached Sunday, you will be steeped in a vibrating, Buddha-like state of self-realization and a perfectly awakened central channel. And since the week is not only a linear process, but an ongoing cycle as well, you will have stimulated the microcosmic orbit: a seven-day circle leading you to an ever-deepening revelation of inner wholeness and completeness.

· · · · · · ·

BIBLIOGRAPHY

Chapters 1–3

Batchelor, Stephen. "When to Let Go of the Dharma, Too." *Tricycle*, September 24, 2019. https://tricycle.org/trikedaily/buddhist-parable-of-the-raft/.

Dass, Ram. *Be Here Now*. New York: Harmony, 1978.

Easwaran, Eknath, trans. *The Upanishads*. Tomales, CA: Nilgiri, 2007.

Jayakar, Pupul. *J. Krishnamurti: A Biography*. Haryana: Penguin Books India, 1986.

Kelly, Liz. *The Rosary: A Path into Prayer*. Chicago: Loyola Press, 2004.

Osho. *Meditation: The First and Last Freedom*. New York: St. Martin's Griffin, 2004.

Ross, Ashley. "How Meditation Went Mainstream." *Time*, March 9, 2016. https://time.com/4246928/meditation-history-buddhism/.

Thorpe, Matthew, and Rachael Link. "12 Science-Based Benefits of Meditation." *Healthline*. Last modified October 27, 2020. https://www.healthline.com/nutrition/12-benefits-of-meditation.

Tolle, Eckhart. *The Power of Now: A Guide to Spiritual Enlightenment*. Novato, CA: New World Library, 2004.

Tzu, Lao. "Tao Te Ching." Translated by Gia-fu Feng and Jane English. Wussu. Accessed January 8, 2022. https://www.wussu.com/laotzu/laotzu49.html.

Chapter 4

Anālayo, Bhikkhu. "Buddhist Antecedents to the Body Scan Meditation." *Mindfulness* 11 (2020): 194–202. https://doi.org/10.1007/s12671-019-01259-8.

Bibliography

Dienstmann, Giovanni. "Walking Meditation—The Ultimate Guide." Live & Dare. Accessed June 15, 2022. https://liveanddare.com/walking-meditation/.

Dudeja, Jai. "Benefits of Tadasana, Zhan Zhuang, and Other Standing Meditation Techniques." *International Journal of Research and Analytical Reviews (IJRAR)* 6, no. 2 (June 2019): 607–18. https://www.academia.edu/39926090/Benefits_of_Tadasana_Zhan_Zhuang_and_Other _Standing_Meditation_Techniques.

Fujita, Issho. "Zazen Is Not the Same as Meditation." Barre Center for Buddhist Studies, spring 2002. https://www.buddhistinquiry.org/article/zazen-is-not-the-same-as-meditation/.

Goodheart, Steven. "Mindfulness of Breathing—A Short Teaching by Thich Nhat Hanh." *Metta Refuge* (blog), February 8, 2010. https://mettarefuge.wordpress.com/2010/02/08 /mindfulness-of-breathing-a-short-teaching-by-thich-nhat-hanh/.

Hanh, Thich Nhat. "Walk Like a Buddha." *Tricycle*. Accessed June 24, 2022. https://tricycle .org/magazine/walk-buddha/.

———. *Breathe, You Are Alive!: Sutra on the Full Awareness of Breathing.* Berkeley, CA: Parallax Press, 1988.

———, trans. "Sutras: Discourse on the Full Awareness of Breathing." Plum Village. Accessed February 14, 2022. https://plumvillage.org/library/sutras/discourse-on-the-full-awareness -of-breathing/.

Kabat-Zinn, Jon. "About the Author." Guided Mindfulness Meditation. Accessed April 23, 2022. https://www.mindfulnesscds.com/pages/about-the-author.

———. "The Body Scan Meditation." Palouse Mindfulness. Accessed February 14, 2022. https://palousemindfulness.com/docs/bodyscan.pdf.

———. "Jon Kabat Zinn Body Scan Meditation Guided Meditation." People in Pain Network. Uploaded July 18, 2016. YouTube video, 45:27. https://www.youtube.com /watch?v=u4gZgnCy5ew.

Micunovic, Igor. "Zhan Zhuang: First Part." *Meer*, May 24, 2020. https://www.meer.com /en/62294-zhan-zhuang-first-part.

Yen, Sheng. *Attaining the Way: A Guide to the Practice of Chan Buddhism.* Boston: Shambhala, 2006.

"Zazen Instructions." Zen Mountain Monastery. Accessed April 24, 2022. https://zmm.org /teachings-and-training/meditation-instructions/.

• • • • • • •

Zenji, Eihei Dogen. "The Principles of Zazen." *Tricycle*, spring 1994. https://tricycle.org/magazine/principles-zazen/.

Chapter 5

Celestine, Nicole. "Broaden-and-Build Theory of Positive Emotions." *Positive Psychology*. Last modified March 29, 2022. https://positivepsychology.com/broaden-build-theory/.

Chia, Mantak. *Healing Love through the Tao: Cultivating Female Sexual Energy*. Rochester, VT: Destiny Books, 2005.

———. *The Inner Smile: Increasing Chi through the Cultivation of Joy*. Rochester, VT: Destiny Books, 2008.

Chia, Mantak, and Michael Winn. *Taoist Secrets of Love: Cultivating Male Sexual Energy*. Santa Fe, NM: Aurora Press, 1984.

Clifford, M. Amos. *Your Guide to Forest Bathing: Experience the Healing Power of Nature*. Newburyport, MA: Conari Press, 2018.

Easwaran, Eknath, trans. *The Upanishads*. Tomales, CA: Nilgiri, 2007.

Eisler, Melissa. "Laughter Meditation: 5 Healing Benefits and a 10-Minute Practice." Chopra, March 10, 2017. https://chopra.com/articles/laughter-meditation-5-healing-benefits-and-a-10-minute-practice.

Farkic, Jelena, Gorana Isailovic, and Steve Taylor. "Forest Bathing as a Mindful Tourism Practice." *Annals of Tourism Research Empirical Insights* 2, no. 2 (Nov. 2021): 1–9. https://doi.org/10.1016/j.annale.2021.100028.

Harper, Donald. "The Sexual Arts of Ancient China as Described in a Manuscript of the Second Century B.C." *Harvard Journal of Asiatic Studies* 47, no. 2 (Dec. 1987): 539–93. https://doi.org/10.2307/2719191.

Ortner, Jessica. *The Tapping Solution for Weight Loss & Body Confidence: A Woman's Guide to Stressing Less, Weighing Less, and Loving More*. Carlsbad, CA: Hay House, 2015.

Osho. *Meditation: The First and Last Freedom*. New York: St. Martin's Griffin, 2004.

Riggio, Ronald E. "There's Magic in Your Smile." *Psychology Today*, June 25, 2012. https://www.psychologytoday.com/intl/blog/cutting-edge-leadership/201206/there-s-magic-in-your-smile.

• • • • • • •

Wile, Douglas. *Art of the Bedchamber: The Chinese Sexual Yoga Classics Including Women's Solo Meditation Texts*. Albany, NY: SUNY Press, 1992.

Winn, Michael. *Way of the Inner Smile: Self Acceptance—Tao Path to Inner Peace*. Inner Alchemy Series, Chi Kung Fundamentals 1. Accessed February 14, 2022. https://healingtaousa.com/wp-content/uploads/pdf/innersmile_ch01.pdf.

Yogananda, Paramahansa. "Self-Realization: Knowing Your Infinite Nature." Paramahansa Yogananda. Accessed April 24, 2022. http://yogananda.com.au/py_talks/self-realization1_infinite_nature.html.

Chapter 6

Erzen, Jale. "The Dervishes Dance—The Sacred Ritual of Love." *Contemporary Aesthetics*. Accessed February 16, 2022. https://contempaesthetics.org/newvolume/pages/article.php?articleID=514.

Gurdjieff, G. I. *Life Is Real Only Then, When "I Am": All and Everything, Third Series*. London: Penguin, 1999.

Harel, Keren, Johanna Czamanski-Cohen, and Nataly Turjeman. "The Spiritual Experience of Sufi Whirling Dervishes: Rising Above the Separation and Duality of This World." *The Arts in Psychotherapy* 75 (Sept. 2021). https://doi.org/10.1016/j.aip.2021.101831.

Henrike. "Meditation in Motion—Sufi Whirling for Beginners." The Auroville Adventure, February 15, 2021. https://adventure.auroville.com/index.php/2021/02/15/meditation-in-motion-sufi-whirling-for-beginners/.

Kabat-Zinn, Jon. "Jon Kabat Zinn - Mountain Meditation." Antonio Sega. Uploaded November 21, 2016. YouTube video, 10:02. https://www.youtube.com/watch?v=Yx2iOYusYeE.

———. "Mountain Meditation Script." Palouse Mindfulness. Accessed February 15, 2022. https://palousemindfulness.com/docs/mountain%20meditation.pdf.

Katie, Byron (@ByronKatie). "Reality is always kinder than the story we tell about it." Twitter, January 5, 2011. https://twitter.com/ByronKatie/status/22695817823391744.

Malinowski, Peter. "Advanced Tibetan Buddhist Meditation Practice Raises Body Temperature." *Meditation Research* (blog), July 19, 2013. https://meditation-research.org.uk/neuroscience/advanced-tibetan-buddhist-meditation-practice-raises-body-temperature/.

Mullin, Glenn H. *The Six Yogas of Naropa*. Boulder, CO: Snow Lion, 2005.

· · · · · · ·

"Osho No-Dimensions Meditation." Osho Active Meditations. Accessed April 24, 2022. https://www.oshoactivemeditations.co.in/osho-no-dimensions-meditation/.

Ouspensky, P. D. *In Search of the Miraculous*. San Diego: Harcourt Brace Jovanovich, 1977.

"Part V: The Fourth Way." BePeriod. Accessed June 17, 2022. https://ggurdjieff.com/fourth-way/.

"Possible Foundations of Inner Exercises." The DuVersity. Accessed April 28, 2022. https://www.duversity.org/foundationexercises.htm.

Saraswati, Swami Niranjanananda. *Prana and Pranayama*. Munger, Bihar, India: Yoga Publications Trust, 2009.

Sivananda, Sri Swami. *The Science of Pranayama*. Rishikesh, Uttarakhand, India: Divine Life Society, 1997.

Venkatesananda, Swami. *Vasistha's Yoga*. Albany, NY: SUNY Press, 1993.

Yeshe, Lama. *The Bliss of Inner Fire: Heart Practice of the Six Yogas of Naropa*. Somerville, MA: Wisdom Publications, 1998.

Chapter 7

Bashir, Shahzad. "Movement and Stillness: The Practice of Sufi Dhikr in Fourteenth-Century Central Asia." In *Meditation in Judaism, Christianity, and Islam: Cultural Histories*, ed. Halvor Eifring, 201–212. London: Bloomsbury Academic, 2013. https://doi.org/10.5040/9781472552532.CH-014.

Bourgeault, Cynthia. "Prayer of the Heart." Wisdom Waypoints. Accessed April 27, 2022. https://wisdomwaypoints.org/resources/prayer-of-the-heart/.

Bramble, Matt. "The Six Stages of Metta-Bhavana (Loving Kindness)." *Embodied Philosophy*, May 17, 2016. https://www.embodiedphilosophy.com/the-six-stages-of-metta-bhavana-loving-kindness/.

Chödrön, Pema. "How to Practice Tonglen." Lion's Roar, August 26, 2020. https://www.lionsroar.com/how-to-practice-tonglen/.

———. *Welcoming the Unwelcome: Wholehearted Living in a Brokenhearted World*. Boulder, CO: Shambhala, 2020.

Dienstmann, Giovanni. "Sufi Meditation and Breathing Practices." Live & Dare. Accessed February 14, 2022. https://liveanddare.com/sufi-meditation.

· · · · · · ·

Bibliography

Easwaran, Eknath, trans. *The Upanishads*. Tomales, CA: Nilgiri, 2007.

Geels, Antoon. "A Note on the Psychology of Dhikr: The Halveti-Jerrahi Order of Dervishes in Istanbul." *The International Journal for the Psychology of Religion* 6, no. 4 (1996): 229–51. https://doi.org/10.1207/s15327582ijpr0604_1.

Gunaratana, Bhante Henepola. "11 Benefits of Loving-Friendliness Meditation." *Tricycle*, March 30, 2019. https://tricycle.org/trikedaily/benefits-loving-friendliness-meditation/.

Gupta, Amrit. *Two Great Masters: Living a Happy and Joyous Life*. Delhi, India: Motilal Banarsidass, 2020.

Hisamatsu, Eiji, and Ramesh Pattni. "Yoga and the Jesus Prayer—A Comparison between Aṣṭāṅga Yoga in the Yoga Sūtras of Patañjali and the Psycho-Physical Method of Hesychasm." *Journal of Hindu-Christian Studies* 28 (2015): 7. https://doi.org/10.7825/2164-6279.1606.

Kearney, David J., Carol A. Malte, Carolyn McManus, Michelle E. Martinez, Ben Felleman, and Tracy L. Simpson. "Loving-Kindness Meditation for Posttraumatic Stress Disorder: A Pilot Study." *Journal of Traumatic Stress* 26, no. 4 (Aug. 2013): 426–34. https://doi.org/10.1002/jts.21832.

Little, Tias. "Awakening the Power of the Heart: Two Sacred Yogic Meditations for Activating and Opening the Heart Chakra." *ConsciousLifestyle*. Accessed February 15, 2022. https://www.consciouslifestylemag.com/heart-chakra-opening-meditation/.

Louchakova, Olga. "The Essence of the Prayer of the Heart." ResearchGate. Accessed February 14, 2022. https://www.researchgate.net/publication/265154766_The_Essence_of_the_Prayer_of_the_Heart.

McKnight, Daphna. "Tonglen Meditation's Effect on Levels of Compassion and Self-Compassion: A Pilot Study and Instructional Guide." Thesis, Upaya Buddhist Chaplaincy Training Program, 2010–2012. https://upaya.org/uploads/pdfs/McKnightTonglenThesis.pdf.

Nakamura, Kojiro. "A Structural Analysis of *Dhikr* and *Nembutsu*." *Orient* 7 (1971): 75–96. https://doi.org/10.5356/orient1960.7.75.

Osho. *Meditation: The First and Last Freedom*. New York: St. Martin's Griffin, 2004.

Prafullananda, Brother. "Paramahansa Yogananda 100 Years of Yoga in the West." *The Eden Magazine*. Accessed February 14, 2022. https://theedenmagazine.com/paramanhansa-yogananda-100-years-of-yoga-in-the-west-2/.

Saraswati, Swami Satyananda. *Kundalini Tantra*. Munger, Bihar, India: Yoga Publications Trust, 2012.

Tolle, Eckhart. *The Power of Now: A Guide to Spiritual Enlightenment*. Novato, CA: New World Library, 2004.

Vaughan-Lee, Llewellyn. "Dhikr as an Archetype of Transformation." The Golden Sufi Center, August 2010. https://goldensufi.org/dhikr-as-an-archetype-of-transformation/.

Chapter 8

Berg, Richard E. "Sound." *Encyclopaedia Britannica*. Last modified November 5, 2020. https://www.britannica.com/science/sound-physics.

Burger, Ariel. "On Hitbodedut." Ariel Burger. Accessed February 14, 2022. https://arielburger.com/wp-content/uploads/Ariel-Burger-On-Hitbodedut.pdf.

Deslippe, Philip. "From Maharaj to Mahan Tantric." *Sikh Formations* 8, no. 3 (2012): 369–87. https://doi.org/10.1080/17448727.2012.745303.

Easwaran, Eknath, trans. *The Upanishads*. Tomales, CA: Nilgiri, 2007.

"Full Text of Siva Samhita." Internet Archive, January 7, 2000. https://archive.org/stream/SivaSamhita/SivaSamhita_djvu.txt.

Gard, Tim, Britta K. Hölzel, and Sara W. Lazar. "The Potential Effects of Meditation on Age-Related Cognitive Decline: A Systematic Review." *Annals of the New York Academy of Sciences* 1307, no. 1 (Jan. 2014): 89–103. https://doi.org/10.1111/nyas.12348.

Hersey, Baird. *The Practice of Nada Yoga: Meditation on the Inner Sacred Sound*. Rochester, VT: Inner Traditions, 2013.

Hunt, Tam. "The Hippies Were Right: It's All about Vibrations, Man!" *Scientific American*, December 5, 2018. https://blogs.scientificamerican.com/observations/the-hippies-were-right-its-all-about-vibrations-man/.

Kramer, Chaim. "Hitbodedut & Jewish Meditation: How To." Breslov, January 24, 2014. https://breslov.org/hitbodedut-jewish-meditation-how-to/.

Monaghan, Patricia, and Eleanor G. Viereck. *Meditation: The Complete Guide*. San Francisco: New World Library, 2011.

Muktibodhananda, Swami, ed. *Hatha Yoga Pradipika: Light on Hatha Yoga*. Munger, Bihar, India: Yoga Publications Trust, 1998.

• • • • • • •

Osho. *Meditation: The First and Last Freedom.* New York: St. Martin's Griffin, 2004.

"Practice the 12-Minute Yoga Meditation Exercise." Alzheimer's Research & Prevention Foundation. Accessed April 28, 2022. https://alzheimersprevention.org/research/kirtan-kriya-yoga-exercise/.

Rattana, Guru. "Lesson 15—Kirtan Kriya for Evolutionary Change." Kundalini Yoga. Accessed February 15, 2022. https://www.kundaliniyoga.org/lesson_15.

Shannahoff-Khalsa, David S. "An Introduction to Kundalini Yoga Meditation Techniques That Are Specific for the Treatment of Psychiatric Disorders." *The Journal of Alternative and Complementary Medicine* 10, no. 1 (June 2004): 91–101. https://www.doi.org/10.1089/107555304322849011.

Shulman, Yaacov Dovid. "Awake at Night." *Breslev Magazine,* September 13, 2008. https://breslev.com/312613/.

Chapter 9

Blacker, Melissa Myozen. "The Wonder and Mystery of Zen Koan Practice." *Lion's Roar,* November 16, 2020. Accessed April 28, 2022. https://www.lionsroar.com/the-wonder-mystery-of-zen-koan-practice/.

Chia, Mantak. *Darkness Technology: Darkness Techniques for Enlightenment.* Chiang Mai, Thailand: Universal Healing Tao, 2002. https://archive.org/details/darknesstechnologybymantakchia2002/mode/2up.

"Darkness Retreat – Ancient Technology for Spiritual Alchemy." *Tibetan Buddhist Encyclopedia.* Last modified October 15, 2013. http://tibetanbuddhistencyclopedia.com/en/index.php/Darkness_Retreat_%E2%80%93_Ancient_Technology_for_Spiritual_Alchemy.

Dokras, Uday. *How to Build a Sri Yantra Temple.* San Francisco: California Institute of Integral Studies, 2022. https://www.academia.edu/74276769/How_to_build_a_Sri_Yantra_Temple.

Glattfelder, James B. *Information—Consciousness—Reality: How a New Understanding of the Universe Can Help Answer Age-Old Questions of Existence.* The Frontiers Collection. Cham, Zug, Switzerland: Springer, 2019.

Godman, David, ed. *Be As You Are: The Teachings of Sri Ramana Maharshi.* London: Penguin, 1988.

• • • • • • •

Hake, Stephanie E. "How and Why to Analogize Socratic Questioning to Zen Buddhist Koan Practice." *SOCRATES* 2, no. 3 (Sept. 2014), 27–45. https://www.socratesjournal.com/index.php/SOCRATES/article/view/16.

Hooper, Carl. "Koan Zen and Wittgenstein's Only Correct Method in Philosophy." *Asian Philosophy* 17, no. 3 (Nov. 2007): 283–92. https://doi.org/10.1080/09552360701708753.

Huet, Gérard. "Śrī Yantra Geometry." *Theoretical Computer Science* 281, no. 1–2 (June 2002): 609–28. https://dl.acm.org/doi/10.5555/570606.570631.

Maharshi, Ramana. "Ramana Maharshi Enlightenment Story." Awaken, June 6, 2017. https://awaken.com/2017/06/ramana-maharshi-enlightenment-story/.

Marion. "Osho Speaks on Darkness." *Darkness Retreats* (blog), June 3, 2016. https://darknessretreats.wordpress.com/2016/06/03/osho-on-darkness/.

Melina, Remy. "Are We Really All Made of Stars?" *Live Science*, October 13, 2010. https://www.livescience.com/32828-humans-really-made-stars.html.

Meyer, Marvin, trans. *The Gospel of Thomas: The Hidden Sayings of Jesus*. New York: Harper San Francisco, 1992.

Osho. *Meditation: The First and Last Freedom*. New York: St. Martin's Griffin, 2004.

Saraswati, Swami Satyananda. *Kundalini Tantra*. Munger, Bihar, India: Yoga Publications Trust, 2012.

Schlütter, Morten. *How Zen Became Zen: The Dispute Over Enlightenment and the Formation of Chan Buddhism in Song-Dynasty China*. Honolulu: University of Hawai'i Press, 2008.

Strand, Clark. "Green Koans Case 12: The Original Face." *Tricycle*, September 16, 2010. https://tricycle.org/trikedaily/green-koans-case-12-the-original-face/.

Suzuki, Daisetz Teitaro. *The Zen Koan as a Means of Attaining Enlightenment*. Tokyo: Charles E. Tuttle Co., 1994.

Tarrant, John. "How to Practice Zen Koans." *Lion's Roar*, June 22, 2021. https://www.lionsroar.com/how-to-practice-zen-koans/.

"The Brain Science Behind Dark Room Therapy." *Amaya*, January 20, 2018. https://www.amaya.org/articles-home/2018/1/20/the-brain-science-behind-dark-room-therapy.

"The Golden Ratio Triangles." Sri Yantra Research Center. Accessed June 20, 2022. https://sriyantraresearch.com/Article/GoldenRatio/golden%20ratio%20triangles.html.

• • • • • • •

"The Tradition." *Darkness Retreats* (blog). Accessed April 29, 2022. https://darkretreats.com /dark-retreat-tradition/.

Yedor, Konchok. "So What's Deity-Yoga?" *Tibetan Spirit* (blog), June 14, 2018. https://tibetan spirit.com/blogs/news/so-whats-deity-yoga.

Yeshe, Lama. *The Bliss of Inner Fire: Heart Practice of the Six Yogas of Naropa*. Somerville, MA: Wisdom Publications, 1998.

———. *Introduction to Tantra: The Transformation of Desire*. Edited by Jonathan Landaw. Boston: Wisdom Publications, 2001.

"Zen Koan." Newcastle Tai Chi. Last modified March 24, 2022. http://www.newcastletaichi .co.uk/zen_koan.htm.

Chapter 10

Barth, Peter. *A Meditation Guide for Mahamudra*. Petaluma, CA: Mahamudra Meditation Center, 1998. https://documents.pub/document/a-meditation-guide-for-mahamudra -a-meditation-guide-for-mahamudra-peter-barth.html.

Berzin, Alexander. "Steps of Dzogchen Meditation." *Study Buddhism*. Accessed February 15, 2022. https://studybuddhism.com/en/advanced-studies/vajrayana/dzogchen-advanced /how-to-meditate-on-dzogchen/steps-of-dzogchen-meditation.

———. "What Is Dzogchen?" *Study Buddhism*. Accessed February 15, 2022. https://study buddhism.com/en/tibetan-buddhism/tantra/mahamudra-dzogchen/what-is-dzogchen.

Easwaran, Eknath, trans. *The Upanishads*. Tomales, CA: Nilgiri, 2007.

Geels, Antoon. "Subud: An Indonesian Interpretation of Sufism." In *Handbook of Islamic Sects and Movements*, edited by Muhammad Afzal Upal and Carole M. Cusack, 568–88. Leiden, Netherlands: Brill, 2021.

Hunt, Stephen J. *Alternative Religions: A Sociological Introduction*. London: Routledge, 2003.

Lao-Tzu. "Tao Te Ching." Translated by J. H. McDonald. Accessed February 16, 2022. https:// www.unl.edu/prodmgr/NRT/Tao%20Te%20Ching%20-%20trans.%20by%20J.H..%20 McDonald.pdf.

Nyenpa, Sangyes. *Tilopa's Mahamudra Upadesha: The Gangama Instructions with Commentary*. Translated by David Molk. Boulder, CO: Snow Lion, 2014.

• • • • • • •

Polk, Halimah. "How to Do the Latihan." Subud Voice. Accessed April 30, 2022. https://www
.subudvoice.net/subud-voice-english/notes-on-how-to-do-the-latihan/

Rinpoche, Anam Thubten. "Dzogchen: The Non-Conceptual Path to Liberation." Buddhist-
door Global, December 10, 2020. https://www.buddhistdoor.net/features
/dzogchen-the-non-conceptual-path-to-liberation/.

Rinpoche, Khenpo Sangpo. "Dzogchen Meditation." Translated by Lama Changchub. March
19, 2008. http://www.sangye.org/english/Dzogchen_Meditation.pdf.

Saraswati, Swami Satyananda. *Kundalini Tantra*. Munger, Bihar, India: Yoga Publications Trust,
2012.

"The Latihan." What Is Subud? Accessed April 30, 2022. http://www.whatissubud.net/what
issubud/about_latihan.html.

Thrangu, Khenchen. *Tilopa's Wisdom: His Life and Teachings on the Ganges Mahamudra*. Boulder,
CO: Snow Lion, 2019.

Yeshe, Lama. *The Bliss of Inner Fire: Heart Practice of the Six Yogas of Naropa*. Somerville, MA:
Wisdom Publications, 1998.

———. *Mahamudra: How to Discover Our True Nature*. Edited by Robina Courtin. Somerville,
MA: Wisdom Publications, 2018.

"Dzogchen Meditation." *Tibetan Buddhist Encyclopedia*. Last modified January 30, 2016. http://
tibetanbuddhistencyclopedia.com/en/index.php/Dzogchen_Meditation.

To Write to the Author

If you wish to contact the author or would like more information about this book, please write to the author in care of Llewellyn Worldwide Ltd. and we will forward your request. Both the author and publisher appreciate hearing from you and learning of your enjoyment of this book and how it has helped you. Llewellyn Worldwide Ltd. cannot guarantee that every letter written to the author can be answered, but all will be forwarded. Please write to:

Shai Tubali
℅ Llewellyn Worldwide
2143 Wooddale Drive
Woodbury, MN 55125-2989

Please enclose a self-addressed stamped envelope for reply,
or $1.00 to cover costs. If outside the U.S.A., enclose
an international postal reply coupon.

Many of Llewellyn's authors have websites with additional information and resources.

For more information, please visit our website at http://www.llewellyn.com.